Our current political era is filled with mourning and loss. This powerful, intimate, beautiful book offers a transformative path toward healing and resurgence.

—JORDAN FLAHERTY, author of *No More Heroes:*
Grassroots Challenges to the Savior Mentality

Rebellious Mourning offers thoughtful, artful essays by resisters on the meanings and uses of grief and mourning. This collection encourages us as people and organizers to understand the Phoenix-like power of these emotions. A primary message here is that from tears comes the resolve for the struggle ahead.

—RON JACOBS, author of *Daydream Sunset:*
'60s Counterculture in the '70s

In our imperfect world, grief is distributed as unequally as wealth. Certain losses and lives are mourned while others are cruelly disregarded; a minority pays attention to suffering while the majority turns away. This intimate, moving, and timely collection of essays points the way to a world in which the burden of grief is shared, and pain is reconfigured into a powerful force for social change and collective healing.

—ASTRA TAYLOR, author of *The People's Platform:*
Taking Back Power and Culture in the Digital Age

The great Wobbly agitator, Joe Hill, famously told us, "Don't mourn, organize!" But he was talking about the loss of hope and confidence that we can contribute to the struggles for justice, that it is a way of life, a culture of resistance. These essays by some of the most dedicated organizers among us today show that honoring and remembering—yes, mourning—actually strengthens our solidarity and vision. Cindy Milstein has created an essential and dynamic work.

—ROXANNE DUNBAR-ORTIZ, author of
An Indigenous Peoples' History of the United States

Grief is often regarded as one of those "negative emotions" we simply have to "get through." But can it also be a process of sharing and learning, motivating us to make the world a better place? This book's answer is a resounding yes!

—GABRIEL KUHN, author of *Playing as If the World Mattered: An Illustrated History of Activism in Sports*

Political organizers, whose lives are devoted to ending the injustice that causes inordinate grief in others, too often dismiss our own grief as shameful or self-indulgent. But this beautiful collection of essays is a clarion call to turn and face the truth of our own sorrow—and its power, as editor Cindy Milstein writes, to "open up cracks in the wall of the system." Here, thinkers, organizers, and artists, from Ferguson to Appalachia to Fukushima to Oaxaca to maximum-security prisons, share their lives, their work, and the various ways in which acknowledging grief—that unavoidable leveler of souls—can allow despairing, isolated peoples to rise together as one.

—SUSIE DAY, author of *Snidelines: Talking Trash to Power*

Rebellious Mourning gathers together a motley assortment of grief narratives—voices of authentic mourning usually segregated and silenced by design. This groundbreaking anthology offers access to diverse experiences of what it feels like to grieve for those we've lost, within the context of all-too-often-deadly systems of global hegemonic control. Milstein and contributors explore the challenge of making contact with the pain of mourning not as a liability but rather a necessary step toward the reclamation of collective power. As such, *Rebellious Mourning* represents an indispensable road map by which those of us grieving many kinds of losses might find our way back to generative struggle, during a time when the Left so urgently needs new sites for building connection.

—KATHLEEN MCINTYRE, editor of *The Worst*

Like songs of sorrow sung together, or laughing in pain and survival around a campfire, this book leaves us whole, grounded, ready for movement, as grief shared in connection should.

—CINDY CRABB, author of *Learning Good Consent: On Healthy Relationships and Survivor Support*

REBEL

lious

MoUR

NING

EDITED BY
CINDY
MILSTEIN

AK PRESS

REBELLIOUS

MOURNING

/

THE

COLLECTIVE

WORK

OF

GRIEF

Rebellious Mourning: The Collective Work of Grief
Edited by Cindy Milstein

All essays © 2017 by their respective authors
This edition © 2017 AK Press (Chico, Edinburgh, Baltimore)

ISBN: 978-1-84935-284-0
EBOOK ISBN: 978-1-84935-285-7
Library of Congress Control Number: 2017936241

AK Press	AK Press UK
370 Ryan Ave. #100	33 Tower St.
Chico, CA 95973	Edinburgh EH6 7BN
USA	Scotland
akpress@akpress.org	ak@akdin.demon.co.uk

The above addresses would be delighted to provide you with the latest
AK Press distribution catalog, which features several thousand books,
pamphlets, zines, audio and video recordings, and gear, all published or
distributed by AK Press. Alternately, visit our websites to browse the
catalog and find out the latest news from the world of anarchist publishing:
www.akpress.org | www.akuk.com | revolutionbythebook.akpress.org

Designed by Quemadura
Printed in Michigan on acid-free, recycled paper
Cover illustration: street portrait of David Ware, who was killed
January 23, 2007 by law enforcement agents in Ypsilanti, Michigan

TO

CHIKANOBU MICHIBA

(1967–2016)

ALL THOSE LOST LIVES
NAMED IN THIS BOOK

ALL THE LOSS HELD BY
THOSE STILL LIVING

AND MY THREE
NOW-DEAD PARENTS,
BARB AND DAVE MILSTEIN,
AND MARY BURKS

REBELLIOUS
MOURNING

PROLOGUE
/
CRACKS IN
THE WALL

CINDY MILSTEIN

Your struggle is a crack in the wall of the system. Don't allow Ayotzinapa to close up. Your children breathe through that crack, but so do the thousands of others who have disappeared across the world.

So that the crack does not close up, so that the crack can deepen and expand, you will have in us Zapatistas a common struggle: one that transforms pain into rage, rage into rebellion, and rebellion into tomorrow.

—SUBCOMANDANTE GALEANO, "The Crack in the Wall: First Note on the Zapatista Method," on the 43 disappeared Ayotzinapa students

We are, at present, swimming in a sea of grief. That sea includes death, but it is also so much larger, encircling all sorts of sorrows. In a better world, many of these disappearances would be avoidable, even unimaginable. For now, given the loss-filled waters we inhabit, how to better navigate through them, and without drowning? How to shift course, veering closer to a more humane self and society?

Such loss is not new by any means. But it feels all the more imperative in a time marked globally by rising fascism and authoritarianism, the largest displacement of people in human history, and the greatest structural devastation of the very basis of life, the ecosystem as a whole.

I come to this anthology through my own pain, yet it is inseparable from the pain of this world. I have traversed "the worst," sometimes deftly, oftentimes not; sometimes with others, too frequently alone. This pain laid bare much cruelty, some of it systemic, some of it due to socialization. One of the cruelest affronts, though, was the expectation that pain should be hidden away, buried, privatized—a lie manufactured so as to mask and uphold the social order that produces our many, unnecessary losses. When we instead open ourselves to the bonds of loss and pain, we lessen what debilitates us; we reassert life and its beauty. We open ourselves to the bonds of love, expansively understood. Crucially, we have a way, together, to at once grieve more qualitatively and struggle to undo the deadening and deadly structures intent on destroying us.

Cracks appear in the wall.

Rebellious Mourning gathers firsthand, frontline stories— works of artful wordsmithing and agile thinking—speaking to what it looks like when people collectively yet personally disquiet centuries of loss. It asks its contributors and readers to journey without answers, with curiosity, by walking directly into our grief. It sees the work of grief, and spaces for it, as something that similar to water and libraries, should be freely, healthily, and publicly available to all. In this way, precisely be-

CINDY MILSTEIN

/

4

cause we can more openly experiment with sharing the fullness of life, we can begin to rehumanize the world and ourselves. For if we can't inhabit the essentials of what it means to be a compassionate human being, we surely can't be the people capable of inhabiting communities of trust, reciprocity, and care.

Indeed, by walking headlong into my own pain and that of others, I've stumbled onto more intimacy and sensitivity, honesty and insight, than ever before—something that would not have happened without the hurt. At the hospice that honored my parents' wishes to die, as one example, I learned that it's possible to cultivate a counterhegemonic culture, in which our behaviors are guided by the intertwined ethics of alleviating suffering and accentuating quality of life.

That walking has also revealed much evidence of hearts taking hold of their own brokenness, generously aided by and mutually aiding others. In the class-war-torn social fabric of San Francisco's Mission District, which I called home until the eviction epidemic got the best of me, I discovered that organizing "solidarity not charity" direct actions does more than facilitate greater resistance and even victories against rampant displacement. For those being forcibly relocated, it can lift them out of their suicidal despair, and into the understanding embrace of others facing similar loss of home and place. Eviction defense becomes, concurrently, emotional defense.

I've witnessed pain transformed into weapon, wielded by caring communities in the fierce battle for a slightly less painful world. On the streets of the Bay Area, along with many others, I've accompanied families whose loved ones have been murdered by police. My neighborhood engaged in public rituals that were equal parts making and defending do-it-ourselves shrines, marching side by side in processions of remembrance and protests of rage, spray painting and wheat pasting a culture of defiance, angrily disrupting police fictions, and joyously creating community celebrations to honor our dead. Such collective works of grief help invent grassroots forms of justice in the face of a police state that grants itself exemption from any culpability.

There are innumerable other illustrations, of course, like those drawing from the courage forced on people by unasked-for circumstances, turning a place-name—such as Ferguson or Ayotzinapa, Gaza or Greece—into a flash point. There are proper names, like Oscar Grant or Freddie Gray, or single words, such as deportation, refugee, or HIV, that voice an unwavering resolve, made visible and poignant. But all the collective works of grief that emerge from these deceptively simple words interweave mourning with the fight for truth and freedom. There is no separation, just as loss should never be alienated from life.

And as we strive to make our social relations less alienated, almost anything becomes far more bearable. Or as this anthology contends, we can better bear our manifold unnecessary losses when they are worked through in common, on commons:

CINDY MILSTEIN

/

6

spaces that we create and sustain to use, share, and find comfort in, but also spaces that are ours to self-determine.

"In common" is not equivalent to "the same." *Rebellious Mourning* is a sampler of varied sorrows, and varied manners of working through grief, in varied collective ways. It offers no prescriptions for how best to mourn, nor does it touch on every possible form of what's been stolen from us, because there is far too much theft for one book. It tries not to homogenize or universalize the myriad of losses, individual and social. Their gamut and magnitude—from colonialism to incarceration, climate catastrophe to poverty, rape to chronic illness, one's culture to one's dignity—play out on different bodies in differentially brutal ways.

But the stories within are all shining light on what those in power try to make invisible. They reply to Judith Butler's query in *Precarious Life*: "What counts as a livable life and a grievable death?" Neither the diversity of our losses, nor their enormity, then, should tear us apart. *Rebellious Mourning* maintains that there is something uniquely connective in the sharing of personal tribulations. And so this collection sits with the heaviness we feel in a world that, we're told, has no future. The volume gathers narratives that don't shy from rawness and authenticity, humility and hurt. It brings into dialogue works that exude compassion and humanity. It seeks to do the public work of grappling out loud with conundrums and tensions and yet also promise.

It is an inevitable part of the human condition: we mortals will experience countless losses. For much of our time on earth, loss was perceived as an organic part of the life cycle, human and nonhuman. Grief was processed in close-up, communal ways, integrated into daily beliefs and practices. People made sense of loss together, acknowledging the physical and emotional aches it provokes as organic, too.

Over human history, loss also became the impetus for rebellions and revolutions, including those that challenged—and still do—the instrumental logic of capitalism, which inherently turns us into mere things, commodities, thereby privatizing and wholly debasing our lives.

The power of what became known as the Ayotzinapa 43—named after the 43 students from a largely indigenous teachers' college who were pulled over by police on their way to a protest in Mexico City and have not been seen since—is, at heart, its demand for the intrinsic value of life, meaning a demand for freedom: "They were taken alive, and alive we want them back."

As the Zapatistas and Ayotzinapa families make clear, to borrow from the poetry of Subcomandante Galeano again: "*You think we're trying to take down the whole wall? It's enough to make a crack* . . . [in] order to imagine everything that could be done tomorrow."

Our grief—our feelings, as words or actions, images or practices—can open up cracks in the wall of the system. It can also pry open spaces of contestation and reconstruction, intervul-

CINDY MILSTEIN

/

nerability and strength, empathy and solidarity. It can discomfort the stories told from above that would have us believe we aren't human or deserving of life-affirming lives—or for that matter, life-affirming deaths.

Little did I know when I began this project—or more precisely, felt drawn to put the dialectic of loss, grief, and resistance into some sort of word-image book—that it would be all that much more relevant and needed by the time it was published. My hope in curating this anthology is that its poetics supply abundant material for a world that might have a future, part dress rehearsal, part experiment. I hope, too, that the narratives here do not craft safe spaces but rather brave ones, without neatly packaged or happy endings, yet still illuminating what it means to bring care and grief into our collective aspiration to repair the world as well as ourselves. I see this work as gift economy, as labor of love, as what it means to be simply, complexly, human, damage and all, in all our messy bittersweetness.

*

When I invited people to contribute to *Rebellious Mourning*, I didn't fully realize what I was asking of them—or myself for that matter. It was an invitation, in essence, not merely to open oneself up to old wounds but also to pick incessantly at the scar tissue. Writing about grief is remembering it, and dismembering it too, thereby discovering all sorts of aches and pains that one hadn't seen at the original time of loss and mourning. Or hadn't felt. Writing for *Rebellious Mourning* became prismatic, refracting the array of new and inherited hurts that can stretch across one's life.

The contributors had to choose a single story to tell in this book, but between the lines, between all the reworking and editing, they were forced to grieve old losses all over again and frequently unearth new ones. And potentially sustain more battle wounds. Many of them also experienced further losses during the course of their writing—often far worse and numerous ones.

So my profoundest respect goes out to everyone who contributed to these pages. I know it meant risking anew being "undone," to borrow again from Butler's *Precarious Life*, without knowing where that would end or how it might transform you. It took fortitude to rip bandages off, making yourself vulnerable —to your own pain, to me, and now to your readers. My heart and gratitude are handed to you all.

The book you, dear reader, now hold in your hand was long in gestating. Innumerable people, conversations, and even chance encounters shook up its form, time and again. It's an altogether different yet far better work for those challenges. Indeed, that this anthology went through various starts and fumbles, dérives and detours, only made for a more generative process and, as I trust should be abundantly and sometimes-tearfully clear, powerful read.

To all those who generously gifted me their suggestions, insights, mutual aid, and/or love in myriad ways toward what has now been birthed as *Rebellious Mourning*, I return the gift with big thanks and/or much love, in alphabetical order, to Mia Amir, Mike Avila, Harmony Chapman, Stefan Christoff, Zoë Dodd, Finn Finneran, Mary Foster, Kris Galbraith, Molly Goldberg, Evelyn Gutierrez, Natasha Hargovan, Lish Zalk Hilgers, Helen Hudson, Margaret Killjoy, Marilyn Koschik, David Langstaff, Elaine Levine, Kate Levy, Laura and Bruce MacDonald, Todd May, Kathleen McIntyre, Karen Milstein, Ona and Gemma Mirkinson, Marko Muir, Lilian Radovac, Clarissa Rogers, Oscar Salinas, Andréa Schmidt, A'isha Shariffa, Jen Soriano, Pavlos Stavropolous, Lorna Vetters, Ra Washington, and Susanne Zago, among others I've likely forgotten to name directly.

Indirectly, I want to acknowledge the wisdom and support of a psychoanalyst in Manhattan, the Mutual Aid Self-Care project at the Base in Brooklyn, two therapists at the Liberation Institute in San Francisco, a grief counseling workshop in Madison, and Hospice of Lansing and Stoneleigh Residence, along with various grief groups and death cafés in various cities; people who engaged with such open hearts when I tested out ideas related to this book at the Montreal Anarchist Bookfair and Solidarity Houston; and people I met at random who opened up to me about their losses and mourning, whether we conversed in YMCA locker rooms or assisted living communities, on an airplane or public plaza.

I also want to acknowledge all those who gave so much of

themselves to make this book possible. Thank you to all the authors and editors who wrote blurbs, and with such exuberance. I can't thank Wren Awry enough for skillfully drafting a concise description of the book to fit on the back cover and elsewhere. I'm beyond-words grateful to Jeff Clark for so aptly honoring the contents of *Rebellious Mourning* with his graphic design brilliance; he became, in essence, collaborator on what we both view as a dream project, and always with loving encouragement and a sharp eye for detail. And there aren't enough words, either, to express my gratitude to AK Press. This is my third book on AK, alongside other projects we've done together, and I feel humbled to be a part of this self-managed anarchist press, which feels like my anarchist home and family as well. The entire AK crew was unanimously thrilled about this book and its aspirations, and has supported it nonstop along the way. But Zach Blue and Charles Weigl, in particular, have been remarkable accomplices, lending me their savvy and intelligence, nudging me when needed to rethink aspects of this collection, and offering loving compassion during the hard parts especially. I couldn't have done this without them.

CINDY MILSTEIN

/

FEELING IS NOT WEAKNESS

/

ON MOURNING AND MOVEMENT

BENJI HART

Many of the movements currently taking place on a global scale —particularly the ones here in the United States—represent political shifts I've been dreaming of for as long as I can remember. The materializing of militant struggles for racial, economic, and environmental justice, heralded by black and brown women, queers and youths, is to me miraculous, and more than I've ever dared to hope for. Given all this, it's hard to explain why the emergence of these movements has made me so sad.

A piece of my sadness is mourning. Each day there are new names of trans women, teenagers, queer people, fathers, mothers, and babies who have been murdered, assaulted by police, or swallowed up by prisons. I am hearing their stories, witnessing the revolting details in videos, filled with their relentlessly violent themes. I am mourning the loss of their wisdom, their light. I am grieving for their families, our family. I am mourning for the lives of young oppressed people, the violence they face or will be facing soon.

But another part of the sadness comes from a different place. It is derived from the confrontation of a political and economic reality that, in truth, is easier to avoid. It is the realization that up to this moment of upheaval, much of my ability to transcend

/

violence has not been my ability to confront or interrupt it but rather to ignore it.

As the direct recipients of state violence in all its forms—police killings, mass incarceration, school closings, and budget cuts—many of us are able to get up in the morning, endure our daily lives, because we don't examine our oppression head-on—at least not consistently. We understand—and have even been taught—that we cannot allow ourselves to feel the constant rage and pain we deserve to feel. It's unsustainable, and much of our community's conventional wisdom tells us it is not effective.

Yet the emergence of a movement means, precisely, confrontation. Marches, blockades, rallies, and die-ins all place us squarely in the path of the state's violent tendencies, but also create numerous outlets for the expression of our rage and pain. We are on constant guard for the violence we know we should expect, but we are also living at its heart, in the midst of the catharsis of our own anger, trauma, and hurt. This, in turn, means we commit to inhabiting our own violent reality in ways we might otherwise intentionally avoid.

Conversely, as a person of color who has long existed in white, middle-class spaces, I'm used to having to explain my perspectives as an oppressed person ad nauseam, and used to having them dismissed. I'm used to being condescended to by people who have never experienced my hardships, told that I am too young to speak to the historical realities of my own people, or that my worldview as a queer, black person is too insular, too limited.

Yet even as current organizing blows the lid off white complacency, proving the tired claims of black and brown communities, and even as members of my own community awaken to the true state and purpose of the police system, a small and strange part of myself has emerged. It is a small, strange, and sad part of me that wishes they were right, wishes I was exaggerating, wishes I had made everything up. The vindication of years of my own imploring has left me feeling not justified but sad. I am sad to be right, sad that my reality is as horrific as I have often sensed it to be. Ironically, the vision I have long urged others to see is suddenly one from which I wish I had the privilege to turn away.

In fall 2015, I marshaled a "musical march" in honor of Rekia Boyd, a twenty-two-year-old black woman who was killed by an off-duty police officer at Douglas Park in Chicago. The demonstration, called They Don't Care about Us, was envisioned, organized, and led entirely by black and brown elementary and high school students. For many of them, it was their first time organizing or protesting.

The march began in the park where Rekia was murdered, then took to major Chicago streets, blocking traffic and occupying whole intersections. The youths sang, danced, drummed, and recited chants they had written to honor those they'd lost to state violence.

As the march progressed, energy and joy swelled, but so did conflicts with drivers and the police. Some got out of their cars to yell at marchers, threatening the marshals as we protected the youths, and even drove their cars directly into the crowd of celebrating young people. The longer the demonstration went on, the more impacted by fear the young organizers became, this being the first time many of them had witnessed such confrontations.

At one point in the march, as police cars with lights and sirens blazing closed in around the procession, an eight-year-old girl in a purple coat and micro braids who I did not know and had not met before ran up behind me, grabbing my arm.

"Are the police gonna get us?" she asked earnestly. Tears were coursing down her cheeks, but her eyes were wide and serious.

"No," I replied, "nothing is going to happen to the young people. The grown folks are here to protect you all, and if anyone gets arrested it will be us. I promise."

I squeezed her gloved hand, and she walked along with me for a while before running to catch up with some of her friends in another part of the procession. Yet the moment stayed with me long after the march was over.

I wanted so much to cry with her, though I didn't. I wanted

to cry for the fear in her eyes, a fear that no one should have to feel, but that young black women must learn to feel as a means of self-protection. I wanted to cry because watching young black people learn the harsh truths their elders have already learned—and many have come to accept—is heartbreaking. Yet I had to stay vigilant, and the march pressed onward, denying us what, at the time, it felt like we needed: a longer moment to acknowledge each other, hold each other, mourn together.

Indeed, yet another layer of my sadness is a true reckoning of just what the social, political, and economic reality of black and brown people in this country is. While the uprisings from Ferguson to Baltimore have initiated some into conversations around state violence and modern apartheid, for those of us who live it on a daily basis, current movements for justice have revealed to us that our violent experiences are not localized or isolated. Instead of knowing simply the stories of our families, our friends, our own run-ins with the law, there is suddenly (inter)national documentation of just how often we are harassed and assaulted, imprisoned and killed, and how consistently the state is getting away with it. Our anecdotal evidence, while compelling for our own lives, is abruptly and jarringly being placed in a global context, and the sheer numbers of lost lives paints a picture that in some ways is grimmer than the one that only encompasses our block, our neighborhood, or our city.

It is sad to realize that it's not one officer, one department.

FEELING IS NOT WEAKNESS

/

It's depressing to realize there is an entire network designed to harm us, and shield those who do harm. It is demoralizing to comprehend how formidable the giant of empire is.

And then my sadness is compounded with guilt. I am guilty for being sad. Sadness feels weak. I know in my head that the point of talking heads' propaganda, the point of state murder, police acquittals, harassment, and imprisonment, is demoralization. I feel guilty for being demoralized.

I should be angry. I should be fiery with unquenchable passion. I should be as relentless as the state. If I am sad, the state has won. If I am sad, the fight is over.

Yet I think back to the girl bundled in a purple coat who grabbed my arm. I think about why that moment wounded me so deeply, and why it stands out from all the other similar moments. It was a window in time where two strangers allowed themselves to be real and vulnerable together. It was a moment where, instead of turning our shared hurt, fear, and frustration on one another in the form of anger or violence, we expressed it through tears, through holding, through care. Protest—not repression—created that fraction of a second in which we were allowed to be scared, be hurt, and be strong—together.

This is what, most recently, I am reminding myself: feeling is not weakness. It is not a new realization but rather one I have been giving myself new permission to inhabit. Feeling, though it may make me vulnerable, does not make me weak. Mourning is what I should do when people I love are taken from me. Experiencing hurt around the realities my people and I face is more than understandable; it shows that I have not given in, not accepted the current, violent reality as inevitable, not forfeited belief in my own right to life.

The same qualities that make the state overwhelming are the ones that make it weak. An unfeeling devotion to profit, to the grotesque amassing of resources, at the expense of community, people, and planet, is not strength. There is, in fact, nothing sadder than investing in the sacrifice of life and love for material gain, for control, for power. The state's lack of feeling, inability to care, indicates the gross miscalculations on which it is founded. It is proof of the inherent imbalance at its core—one maintained only through brutal force. It is evidence of the inevitable downfall encoded in its cold mechanisms.

The most intense violence—which we are seeing ramp up—the intentional erasure of history, the use of militaristic force and solitary confinement, the reneging of basic rights, and multifold acts of assault and abuse, will never stop our communities from feeling. It will never end our love for our own lives, for the lives of our ancestors, and our children. It will never dissuade us from fighting back.

My sadness is proof of my love, and my love proves that I am driven by profound spiritual bonds to my people—past, present, and yet to come. And just as it is unsustainable for us to ignore violence, ignore the political reality of our oppression, it is equally unsustainable to pretend it has not affected us, and that it is not affecting us every day.

Being affected does not imply weakness. Rather, it implies the presence of all the qualities the state does not possess, the tenets that make struggle worthwhile, make it sustainable, and the realization of a justice that is more sweepingly beautiful.

Pretending I am not sad, hiding my pain, will not make me stronger. In fact, suppressing my true self, ignoring the fear and rage that surround loss, is exactly what in the long run will weaken me. When we talk of self-care, self-defense, and self-preservation, we need to talk not about overcoming our feelings of grief but allowing them, making room for them. We need to talk about movement building that allows us to feel—in all the different ways that may come—and does not expect us to erase or bottle up our sadness in the name of organizing, leadership, or action.

This is not to dismiss the conventional wisdom of some of our elders and community members. The mourning process is a demanding and painful one. It can leave us feeling broken, as in many ways mourning is the struggle to acknowledge loss. The challenge of learning how to mourn is also the challenge of striking balance, of figuring how to take space, make room, and step back from the labor of movement building when we need to pause and allow for our own sadness. We often avoid mourning because we believe we do not have the luxury to breakdown, to stop and really feel. I suggest we need to recognize both when sadness is keeping us from moving and when the urgency of movement is blocking our need to feel grief.

Let us not push forward so decidedly that we do not stop to mourn. It is not merely OK to grieve. It is wholly necessary if we are to remain connected to our collective power, truly invested in our liberation, and whole enough to sustain ourselves in struggle. We need to grieve for those we have lost, for ourselves, for our bodies, for the land, for our families and our ancestors. For movement building is emotional labor, and it rises and swells and crashes in unison with our hearts.

Let grief be part of the movement-building process for which we allow hallowed space, and let it build within us the compassion, wisdom, and rage that propel us into new battles.

*

Benji Hart is an artist, activist, and writer currently living in Chicago. Much of his work focuses on using the dance form vogue as a tool for teaching black and brown queer history, and planning direct actions. More of his writing can be found at his blog, Radical Faggot, at radfag.com. He would most like to thank the youths of Village Leadership Academy, Assata's Daughters, and all the fierce, black, femme organizers and survivors in Chicago for inspiring this piece.

FEELING IS NOT WEAKNESS

/

THE CONDITION
OF BLACK LIFE
IS ONE OF
MOURNING

CLAUDIA RANKINE

A friend recently told me that when she gave birth to her son, before naming him, before even nursing him, her first thought was, I have to get him out of this country. We both laughed. Perhaps our black humor had to do with understanding that getting out was neither an option nor the real desire. This is it, our life. Here we work, hold citizenship, pensions, health insurance, family, friends, and on and on. She couldn't, she didn't leave. Years after his birth, whenever her son steps out of their home, her status as the mother of a living human being remains as precarious as ever. Added to the natural fears of every parent facing the randomness of life is this other knowledge of the ways in which institutional racism works in our country. Ours was the laughter of vulnerability, fear, recognition, and an absurd stuckness.

I asked another friend what it's like being the mother of a black son. "The condition of black life is one of mourning," she said bluntly. For her, mourning lived in real time inside her and her son's reality: At any moment she might lose her reason for living. Though the white liberal imagination likes to feel temporarily bad about black suffering, there really is no mode of empathy that can replicate the daily strain of knowing that as a black person you can be killed for simply being black: no hands in your pockets, no playing music, no sudden movements, no

/

driving your car, no walking at night, no walking in the day, no turning onto this street, no entering this building, no standing your ground, no standing here, no standing there, no talking back, no playing with toy guns, no living while black.

Eleven days after I was born, on September 15, 1963, four black girls were killed in the bombing of the 16th Street Baptist Church in Birmingham, Alabama. Now, fifty-two years later, six black women and three black men have been shot to death while at a Bible-study meeting at the historic Emanuel African Methodist Episcopal Church in Charleston, South Carolina. They were killed by a homegrown terrorist, self-identified as a white supremacist, who might also be a "disturbed young man" (as various news outlets have described him). It has been reported that a black woman and her five-year-old granddaughter survived the shooting by playing dead. They are two of the three survivors of the attack. The white family of the suspect says that for them this is a difficult time. This is indisputable. But for African American families, this living in a state of mourning and fear remains commonplace.

The spectacle of the shooting suggests an event out of time, as if the killing of black people with white-supremacist justification interrupts anything other than regular television programming. But Dylann Storm Roof did not create himself from nothing. He has grown up with the rhetoric and orientation of racism. He has seen white men like Benjamin F. Haskell, Thomas Gleason, and Michael Jacques plead guilty to, or be convicted of, burning Macedonia Church of God in Christ in Springfield, Massachusetts, just hours after President Obama was elected. Every racist statement he has made he could have heard all his life. He, along with the rest of us, has been living with slain black bodies.

We live in a country where Americans assimilate corpses in their daily comings and goings. Dead blacks are a part of normal life here. Dying in ship hulls, tossed into the Atlantic, hanging from trees, beaten, shot in churches, gunned down by the police, or warehoused in prisons: Historically, there is no quotidian without the enslaved, chained, or dead black body to gaze upon or to hear about or to position a self against. When blacks become overwhelmed by our culture's disorder and protest (ultimately to our own detriment, because protest gives the police justification to militarize, as they did in Ferguson), the wrongheaded question that is asked is, What kind of savages are we? Rather than, What kind of country do we live in?

In 1955, when Emmett Till's mutilated and bloated body was recovered from the Tallahatchie River and placed for burial in a nailed-shut pine box, his mother, Mamie Till Mobley, demanded his body be transported from Mississippi, where Till had been visiting relatives, to his home in Chicago. Once the Chicago funeral home received the body, she made a decision that would create a new pathway for how to think about a lynched body. She requested an open coffin and allowed photographs to be taken and published of her dead son's disfigured body.

THE CONDITION OF BLACK LIFE

/

Mobley's refusal to keep private grief private allowed a body that meant nothing to the criminal-justice system to stand as evidence. By placing both herself and her son's corpse in positions of refusal relative to the etiquette of grief, she "disidentified" with the tradition of the lynched figure left out in public view as a warning to the black community, thereby using the lynching tradition against itself. The spectacle of the black body, in her hands, publicized the injustice mapped onto her son's corpse. "Let the people see what I see," she said, adding, "I believe that the whole United States is mourning with me."

It's very unlikely that her belief in a national mourning was fully realized, but her desire to make mourning enter our day-to-day world was a new kind of logic. In refusing to look away from the flesh of our domestic murders, by insisting we look with her upon the dead, she reframed mourning as a method of acknowledgment that helped energize the civil rights movement in the 1950s and '60s.

The decision not to release photos of the crime scene in Charleston, perhaps out of deference to the families of the dead, doesn't forestall our mourning. But in doing so, the bodies that demonstrate all too tragically that "black skin is not a weapon" (as one protest poster read last year) are turned into an abstraction. It's one thing to imagine nine black bodies bleeding out on a church floor, and another thing to see it. The lack of visual evidence remains in contrast to what we saw in Ferguson, where

CLAUDIA RANKINE

/

30

the police, in their refusal to move Michael Brown's body, perhaps unknowingly continued where Till's mother left off.

After Brown was shot six times, twice in the head, his body was left facedown in the street by the police officers. Whatever their reasoning, by not moving Brown's corpse for four hours after his shooting, the police made mourning his death part of what it meant to take in the details of his story. No one could consider the facts of Michael Brown's interaction with the Ferguson police officer Darren Wilson without also thinking of the bullet-riddled body bleeding on the asphalt. It would be a mistake to presume that everyone who saw the image mourned Brown, but once exposed to it, a person had to decide whether his dead black body mattered enough to be mourned. (Another option, of course, is that it becomes a spectacle for white pornography: the dead body as an object that satisfies an illicit desire. Perhaps this is where Dylann Storm Roof stepped in.)

Black Lives Matter, the movement founded by the activists Alicia Garza, Patrisse Cullors, and Opal Tometi, began with the premise that the incommensurable experience of systemic racism creates an unequal playing field. The American imagination has never been able to fully recover from its white-supremacist beginnings. Consequently, our laws and attitudes have been straining against the devaluation of the black body. Despite good intentions, the associations of blackness with inarticulate, bestial criminality persist beneath the appearance of white civility. This assumption both frames and determines our individual interactions and experiences as citizens.

The American tendency to normalize situations by centralizing whiteness was consciously or unconsciously demonstrated again when certain whites, like the president of Smith College, sought to alter the language of "Black Lives Matter" to "All Lives Matter." What on its surface was intended to be interpreted as a humanist move—"aren't we all just people here?"—didn't take into account a system inured to black corpses in our public spaces. When the judge in the Charleston bond hearing for Dylann Storm Roof called for support of Roof's family, it was also a subtle shift away from valuing the black body in our time of deep despair.

Anti-black racism is in the culture. It's in our laws, in our advertisements, in our friendships, in our segregated cities, in our schools, in our Congress, in our scientific experiments, in our language, on the Internet, in our bodies no matter our race, in our communities, and, perhaps most devastatingly, in our justice system. The unarmed, slain black bodies in public spaces turn grief into our everyday feeling that something is wrong everywhere and all the time, even if locally things appear normal. Having coffee, walking the dog, reading the paper, taking the elevator to the office, dropping the kids off at school: All of this good life is surrounded by the ambient feeling that at any given moment, a black person is being killed in the street or in his home by the armed hatred of a fellow American.

CLAUDIA RANKINE

/

The Black Lives Matter movement can be read as an attempt to keep mourning an open dynamic in our culture because black lives exist in a state of precariousness. Mourning then bears both the vulnerability inherent in black lives and the instability regarding a future for those lives. Unlike earlier black-power movements that tried to fight or segregate for self-preservation, Black Lives Matter aligns with the dead, continues the mourning, and refuses the forgetting in front of all of us. If the Rev. Martin Luther King, Jr.'s civil rights movement made demands that altered the course of American lives and backed up those demands with the willingness to give up your life in service of your civil rights, with Black Lives Matter, a more internalized change is being asked for: recognition.

The truth, as I see it, is that if black men and women, black boys and girls, mattered, if we were seen as living, we would not be dying simply because whites don't like us. Our deaths inside a system of racism existed before we were born. The legacy of black bodies as property and subsequently three-fifths human continues to pollute the white imagination. To inhabit our citizenry fully, we have to not only understand this, but also grasp it. In the words of the playwright Lorraine Hansberry, "The problem is we have to find some way with these dialogues to show and to encourage the white liberal to stop being a liberal and become an American radical." And, as my friend the critic and poet Fred Moten has written: "I believe in the world and want to be in it. I want to be in it all the way to the end of it be-

THE CONDITION OF BLACK LIFE

/

cause I believe in another world and I want to be in that." This other world, that world, would presumably be one where black living matters. But we can't get there without fully recognizing what is here.

Dylann Storm Roof's unmediated hatred of black people; Black Lives Matter; citizens' videotaping the killings of blacks; the Ferguson Police Department leaving Brown's body in the street—all these actions support Mamie Till Mobley's belief that we need to see or hear the truth. We need the truth of how the bodies died to interrupt the course of normal life. But if keeping the dead at the forefront of our consciousness is crucial for our body politic, what of the families of the dead? How must it feel to a family member for the deceased to be more important as evidence than as an individual to be buried and laid to rest?

Michael Brown's mother, Lesley McSpadden, was kept away from her son's body because it was evidence. She was denied the rights of a mother, a sad fact reminiscent of pre–Civil War times, when as a slave she would have had no legal claim to her offspring. McSpadden learned of her new identity as a mother of a dead son from bystanders: "There were some girls down there had recorded the whole thing," she told reporters. One girl, she said, "showed me a picture on her phone. She said, 'Isn't that your son?' I just bawled even harder. Just to see that, my son lying there lifeless, for no apparent reason." Circling the perimeter around her son's body, McSpadden tried to disperse the crowd: "All I want them to do is pick up my baby."

McSpadden, unlike Mamie Till Mobley, seemed to have little desire to expose her son's corpse to the media. Her son was not an orphan body for everyone to look upon. She wanted him covered and removed from sight. He belonged to her, her baby. After Brown's corpse was finally taken away, two weeks passed before his family was able to see him. This loss of control and authority might explain why after Brown's death, McSpadden was supposedly in the precarious position of accosting vendors selling T-shirts that demanded justice for Michael Brown that used her son's name. Not only were the procedures around her son's corpse out of her hands; his name had been commoditized and assimilated into our modes of capitalism.

Some of McSpadden's neighbors in Ferguson also wanted to create distance between themselves and the public life of Brown's death. They did not need a constant reminder of the ways black bodies don't matter to law enforcement officers in their neighborhood. By the request of the community, the original makeshift memorial—with flowers, pictures, notes, and teddy bears—was finally removed by Brown's father on what would have been his birthday and replaced by an official plaque installed on the sidewalk next to where Brown died. The permanent reminder can be engaged or stepped over, depending on the pedestrian's desires.

In order to be away from the site of the murder of her son, Tamir Rice, Samaria moved out of her Cleveland home and into a homeless shelter. (Her family eventually relocated her.) "The whole world has seen the same video like I've seen," she said about Tamir's being shot by a police officer. The video, which was played and replayed in the media, documented the two seconds it took the police to arrive and shoot; the two seconds that marked the end of her son's life and that became a document to be examined by everyone. It's possible this shared scrutiny explains why the police held his twelve-year-old body for six months after his death. Everyone could see what the police would have to explain away. The justice system wasn't able to do it, and a judge found probable cause to charge the officer who shot Rice with murder, while a grand jury declined to indict any of the officers involved. Meanwhile, for Samaria Rice, her unburied son's memory made her neighborhood unbearable.

Regardless of the wishes of these mothers—mothers of men like Brown, John Crawford III, or Eric Garner, and also mothers of women and girls like Rekia Boyd and Aiyana Stanley-Jones, each of whom was killed by the police—their children's deaths will remain within the public discourse. For those who believe the same behavior that got them killed if exhibited by a white man or boy would not have ended his life, the subsequent failure to indict or convict the police officers involved in these various cases requires that public mourning continue and remain present indefinitely. "I want to see a cop shoot a white unarmed teenager in the back," Toni Morrison said in April. She went on to say: "I want to see a white man convicted for raping a black woman. Then when you ask me, 'Is it over?' I will say yes." Morrison is right to suggest that this action would signal change, but the real change needs to be a rerouting of interior belief. It's an individual challenge that needs to happen before any action by a political justice system would signify true societal change.

The Charleston murders alerted us to the reality that a system so steeped in anti-black racism means that on any given day it can be open season on any black person—old or young, man, woman, or child. There exists no equivalent reality for white Americans. We can distance ourselves from this fact until the next horrific killing, but we won't be able to outrun it. History's authority over us is not broken by maintaining a silence about its continued effects.

A sustained state of national mourning for black lives is called for in order to point to the undeniability of their devaluation. The hope is that recognition will break a momentum that laws haven't altered. Susie Jackson; Sharonda Coleman-Singleton; DePayne Middleton-Doctor; Ethel Lee Lance; the Rev. Daniel Lee Simmons, Sr.; the Rev. Clementa C. Pinckney; Cynthia Hurd; Tywanza Sanders; and Myra Thompson were murdered because they were black. It's extraordinary how ordinary our grief sits inside this fact. One friend said, "I am so afraid, every day." Her son's childhood feels impossible, because he will have to be—has to be—so much more careful. Our mourning, this mourning, is in time with our lives. There is no life outside of our reality here. Is this something that can be seen and known by parents of white children? This is the question that nags me. National mourning, as advocated by Black Lives Matter, is a mode of intervention and interruption that might itself be assimilated into the category of public annoyance. This is altogether possible; but also possible is the recognition that it's a lack of feeling for another that is our problem. Grief, then, for these deceased others might align some of us, for the first time, with the living.

*

Claudia Rankine is the author of five collections of poetry, including Citizen: An American Lyric *and* Don't Let Me Be Lonely; *two plays, including* Provenance of Beauty: A South Bronx Travelogue; *and numerous video collaborations; and is the editor of several anthologies, including* The Racial Imaginary: Writers on Race in the Life of the Mind. *For* Citizen, *Rankine won the Forward Prize for Poetry, the National Book Critics Circle Award for Poetry (*Citizen *was also nominated in the criticism category, making it the first book in the award's history to be a double nominee), the Los Angeles Times Book Award, the PEN Open Book Award, and the NAACP Image Award. A finalist for the National Book Award,* Citizen *also holds the distinction of being the only poetry book to be a* New York Times *best seller in the nonfiction category. Among her numerous awards and honors, Rankine is the recipient of the Poets & Writers' Jackson Poetry Prize and fellowships from the Lannan Foundation, the MacArthur Foundation, United States Artists, and the National Endowment of the Arts. She lives in New York City and teaches at Yale University as the Frederick Iseman Professor of Poetry.*

CLAUDIA RANKINE

/

DUST OF
THE DESERT

LEE SANDUSKY

There are three shrines in a mountain saddle in the Altar Valley. The saddle looks like a half-moon, as if someone from above took a bite out of the middle of the gargantuan peak. In this crux, there is the shade of Mexican blue oaks and spindly, stunted-looking junipers, full of fragrant, inedible berries. Shade in this desert is sparse. Under these trees are piles of trash, sun-bleached plastic water gallons degrading into splinters along with cans, once full of beans or tuna, now empty, turning to rust. There are backpacks, torn sweaters, and handmade shoe covers that leave no footprint in the sandy washes—the dry stream and riverbeds of the Sonoran Desert. There are toothbrushes, makeup kits, and other personal items discarded off the main trail. The trail winds up the mountainside from the south, from south of the border between Nogales and Sasabe, and heads north to a network of other paths carved into the desert, which if followed correctly, lead past Border Patrol checkpoints into the interior of the United States.

One shrine is for La Virgen de Guadalupe, another is dedicated to the Patron Saint of Migrant Santo Toribio, and the third to Santisima Muerte—the Saint of Death. In little crevices around these shrines are prayers written on scraps of paper; there are crucifixes, rosaries, and broken glass candles. All the

/

components of these shrines came from Mexico and were important enough items for someone to carry as they walked for days through the inhospitable terrain.

Next to these shrines there is water. Some of it is a little green tinted, dredged up out of a cattle tank, put in thick black plastic jugs, carried here by migrants, and left as an offering to the saints or small gift for other travelers who were not lucky enough to have passed the tank. The water is murky and teeming with bacteria, but it's lifesaving all the same.

We too leave water. But we walked from the north heading south, and this shrine is our destination, not a stopping point. The water we leave is in clear plastic jugs with blue lids, and is pure and bacteria free. I scribble with a Sharpie *aqua pura para migrantes* and *suerte* on the sides of a gallon. The desert landscape is littered with thousands of black jugs carried from the south and clear gallons graffitied with well wishes brought from the north.

*

People walk between three days and several weeks in order to pass through the borderlands—that land north of Border Patrol checkpoints considered the interior of the United States. The place we call Triple Shrine, in the saddle of Bartolo Mountain, lies at the heart of this journey. Triple Shrine is half a day's walk south of our camp, an off-the-grid first aid clinic tucked away

LEE SANDUSKY

/

on a dirt road outside Arivaca, Arizona. The camp sits about twelve miles as the crow flies from the US-Mexican border.

Over the years at this camp and in the surrounding desert, I have gotten to know hundreds of people from Mexico, Guatemala, El Salvador, Honduras, Belize, and Ecuador as well as people who grew up in the United States and consider it home yet have birth certificates from the nations to which they were deported. As we provide care for those lost and injured in the desert, they often share their complex stories of where they come from and why they are walking through the Sonoran Desert. The camp has served as a place of respite for a myriad of people over the past decade, and despite some similarities in the stories of those coming to seek asylum or as economic refugees, there is no archetypal migrant found here.

My head is full of stories shared with me in the desert. I try to recall details, but so often the faces of the people whose stories have forever changed me seem to have faded from my mind. In my time at the clinic I've met children, mothers, and fathers as well as people five years younger than me yet aged decades beyond their years. Walking through the desert is the cheapest and most dangerous way to cross into the United States without papers, and so frequently the people we meet are poor, but sometimes they are middle class. There are urbanites, and people who have never left their mountain village before this journey; people who are distrustful of me; and people who I now call friends. I've met indigenous Guatemalans whose Spanish is as shaky as mine, and people whose first language is English.

One of the first people I ever met in the desert turned out to be a US citizen. He spoke fractured English, although said he was from Nogales—a city split in two by a border wall. He had been visiting some friends in Sasabe when cartel members kidnapped and tortured him, and then forced him to carry supplies for a group of smugglers transporting burlap sacks of drugs on their backs. The group abandoned him in the desert after another cartel member picked up the smugglers and contraband. We let him use our phone so he could call his mother, who hadn't heard from him for weeks. The Border Patrol agents and sheriffs were highly skeptical of his story, and treated him harshly, but ultimately he proved his status and filed a police report, and they dropped him back off at his home in the city.

At the clinic I met a man nicknamed Bigotes (in English, moustaches) who was deported from his home in the United States after he got entangled in a messy love affair, was shot by a jealous man, and went to a hospital to be treated for gunshot wounds. The hospital staff called immigration when he failed to produce legal documents. He told raucous stories while he healed from severe dehydration and a twisted knee.

Right before another man arrived at our clinic, bandits had captured him in the desert and told him they were going to torture him as they extorted his family. He narrowly escaped with his life; he ran away with shots ringing out behind him. This man, the father and grandfather of US citizens, was ripped from his life in Utah after a routine traffic stop and was fighting like hell to make it back to his family. Last I heard of him, he never made it home.

I also recall the Jamaican Guatemalan who hit on me while I was checking his blood pressure. He told me *tus ojos son bonitos como los de mi abuelita* (your eyes are beautiful like those of my little grandmother). I laughed it off, and later he told me that if he didn't make it to his destination and if I ever visited Lago Atitlán in Guatemala, he would love to have me as a guest at his home near the lake. The idea that I could just hop a plane and land in his country as a tourist while he was walking through hell to enter mine was not lost on either of us.

I provided care for a developmentally disabled man of fifty who was fleeing cartel violence in Sinaloa, Mexico. His sister had made it to the interior of the United States, and he was coming to live with her. I left the clinic the same day he did, and the next day I attended the court proceedings that mass prosecute seventy individuals a day in Tucson with charges of illegal entry. The man was shackled in chains at the wrists and ankles. He didn't see me sitting in the back until he pleaded guilty. He waved to me as he was led out of the courtroom by US marshals. I followed up with him during his six-month sentence in a for-profit prison that lies an hour north of my home in Tucson.

One of the strongest people I've ever met was a tiny fifteen-year-old girl journeying alone from El Salvador; she recounted how she rode *La Bestia*—the infamous and deadly freight train used by Central American migrants through Mexico. After months of traveling, she found herself abandoned by the cartel guide paid to get her into the United States, only to have a gun pointed at her head by a Border Patrol agent, who then left her in the midst of the desert without taking her into custody. The worst part, she told me as she taught me to make pupusas one night at the clinic, of the several days she spent alone in the vast desert was the howls of coyotes in the night; she thought they were wolves coming to eat her.

I think often of another woman, an upper-middle-class business owner from Mexico City who was crossing to reunite with her lover. She didn't have family members or friends who had crossed, and didn't know the state of affairs on the border. She didn't know she would have to pay tenfold the initial cost of the journey to extortionists over the course of a torturous month or about the preposterously high rates of sexual assault of female travelers. She kept telling me, *I'm like you. I volunteer to help people. I can't believe this has happened to me. People need to know about this.*

*

All over the nation, televised and in print, there are news articles describing the backstory of each of the five recreational hikers or mountain bikers who perished from the heat wave that struck Arizona in June 2016. Two of the dead were not citizens;

they were tourists from Germany. The news describes the tragedy of lost life, of how easily one dies of dehydration or heatstroke even just a few miles from civilization. It reports on the search-and-rescue initiatives for these people who passed away in the mountains outside Tucson and Phoenix.

There is public grief, discussion in the city about how terrible this needless loss of life is, and sympathy for the family members of the five dead. I feel it too. I have hiked these trails that these people died on. I have had heatstroke, felt dizzy and nauseous; I have feared my body's ability to withstand. As I read the reports, I ache for their families and think to myself, *I could have been one of them; that could've been one of my friends.*

But these headlines are inaccurate; the death toll is certainly far more than five. There are dozens, hundreds possibly, who perished in the borderlands during this heat wave. The majority of those who died are not US citizens, nor tourists with visas and German bank accounts.

I used to think the lack of news coverage of the death of people of color was negligence on the part of the media, but it's bigger than that; perhaps it's cultural, systemic. Some death and injustice is expected, not shocking or newsworthy, because it's been in the backdrop of our culture since the inception of the United States.

In November 2014, mass graves of undocumented immigrants were uncovered outside Falfurrias, Texas. Border Patrol agents had been finding corpses and skeletons of undocumented people in the brush of South Texas, and turning them over to a private funeral home. Rather than recording DNA and potentially providing closure to the families of the dead, or allowing for proper burial, the funeral home placed most of the bodies in trash bags and piled them into mass graves. These sites received some national media attention, but quickly and decisively a court in Texas ruled there was "no evidence" of wrongdoing in the case, although the funeral home collected tens of thousands of taxpayer dollars to gather DNA and properly bury the bodies. No one was charged, and there was no change of policy for how the remains of undocumented people are handled. There were never any numbers released concerning the amount of people dead in the mass grave, let alone names or stories about those who perished.

In the United States, there are communities whose deaths and murders are justified because of the color of their skin, because of their criminalized existence. One of those communities is the population crossing the border, the millions of undocumented people living "illegally" in the interior of the United States along with the tens of thousands of Mexican and Central American citizens locked up in detention centers and for-profit prisons. Their legal status in this country translates into easily justified deaths because they are committing the crime of crossing the border; death is justified as the penalty for this crime.

The undocumented community that loses so many of its people to murder by border enforcement and policy in general cannot easily speak up; it is not given the same platform as citizens to publicly grieve its people or demand the attention of the outside world. According to official estimates, only half of those who die in the borderlands are ever recovered. The millions of undocumented people living in the United States are often silenced by their lack of rights, the fear of raids and deportation, the reality of the borderlands where people die and go unsearched for, where mass graves are considered legal even as the bodies within them are marked as illegal.

It's not just the media or state policy that is to blame for this disparity in the value of life of a citizen versus that of a noncitizen, or a white person versus that of a black or brown person. Rampant xenophobia and racism in this country have crafted a culture where the death of migrants in the desert, or murder of people of color by police or the state, is inconsequential. I recall the words of the forest ranger who issued my permit at the Cabeza Prieta Wildlife Refuge when I was on a search and recovery for three dead humans. She said, *You know you're helping criminals, right? Scum of the earth. These aren't mom-and-pop types coming to work anymore. No, scum of the earth, get what they deserve.*

State and corporate powers have conspired to funnel undocumented people into the deadliest parts of the borderlands, and the people who have traveled through these places or lost family to the desert and brush know what is happening in the borderlands regardless of the lack of media. In a world that frequently invalidates the humanity of those who perish in the border-

DUST OF THE DESERT

/

lands, communities that have lost loved ones as well as communities in solidarity know that these people did not "get what they deserve" when they died from exposure, dehydration, and deadly Border Patrol tactics. There is grief and mourning, even if it is hidden from public view.

How many people died that week this past June on the border and will never be searched for? How many bodies will never be recovered? In two weeks in this climate, corpses become skeletons, and over time the skeletons become the dust of the desert. There may never be closure for the families of those who died. There are few newspaper reports that make readers feel the pain of loss, or think to themselves, *That could've been me or someone I love*. Because the truth of the matter is that for those of us who can pass through interior checkpoints, that couldn't have been us: dead in the desert, unsearched for, never laid to rest by loved ones.

*

The border between the United States and Mexico has been the hardest thing I've ever tried to write about. It is more than a boundary on maps, more than a line drawn in the sand that separates nation-states. It is a two-thousand-mile stretch that means countless things to millions of people, all with different backgrounds and different reasons for living, working, or migrating through. The border is a physical expanse that has consumed the lives of thousands over centuries; it is a modern-day

LEE SANDUSKY

/

glimpse of the bloody history of colonization and blatant racial division that the United States is founded on; it is a boundary that lives in the memories of those who have crossed it, those who have lived in it, even those who have simply heard about it in the news. There have been hundreds of books, histories, and poems written in attempts to make sense of this intangible realm where physical space, macroeconomics, and personal histories intertwine into crisis. The border is oceans and brush and desert. The border is Border Patrol checkpoints and drug-cartel territory and stolen native land. The border is a low-intensity war zone as well as home to many.

Ultimately the border is a land of polarity, a land of illegal and legal, a land of can-pass-through and cannot-pass-through checkpoints. There are people here, Border Patrol agents and militia, slashing full water gallons, but also there are people leaving the water they cannot spare so that others who need it just a little more than they do can survive. There are people hanging effigies of migrants in trees to serve as a warning, and there are others who risk the freedoms and privileges they were born into so as to help those in need. There are too many complicated players to truly make sense of this place, to make sense of all the death. Stories of death and hope inundate the community here—the community of locals in the borderlands, those of us from the city, and the hundreds of volunteers who come from all over to organize and provide mutual aid.

So often the work we do has no easy conclusion; we search

DUST OF THE DESERT

/

51

for those we never find, and no matter how many thousands of gallons of water we put in the desert, still the rates of death due to exposure and dehydration steadily climb. Resistance in the borderlands can feel like an endless battle against the border militarization complex—a mechanized, murderous, and intangible enemy—and burnout isn't a foreign concept. Frequently it feels as though the state, corporations, and media have successfully stripped the thousands of people crossing the border of their humanity.

Despite the border apparatus and xenophobic rhetoric designed to dehumanize, imprison, and kill, though, there are many communities comprised of hundreds of individuals working in solidarity with those crossing through the borderlands, listening to stories, providing aid, and organizing in a myriad of ways to rise up against the militarization of the borderlands. Seeing how the state strips people of their dignity and drives them into the deadliest parts of the desert brought my community together in the first place. Border work is predicated on ending the deaths of those crossing—currently an insurmountable task—and much of the action we take is in response to grief, but also anger and hope; the three are inseparable motivations that sustain organizing and action within our community.

When I leave the clinic and go back to the city, I try to spend a day or two self-isolating. I light candles for those I have met who are still traveling through the desert, and my heart feels heavy with worry for the future that awaits them. I try to sit

LEE SANDUSKY

/

with the chaos of never again seeing these people whose stories will perhaps forever haunt me, and I cannot fathom the grieving of the undocumented communities that have lost family members in the borderlands. I attempt to understand my place, my comfortable place, as a US citizen, floating between worlds, between the no-man's-land south of interior checkpoints and mundane urban existence.

Yet I do not hold this grief alone. When I need to rant or cry or scream, I seek out my friends—fellow solidarity workers who know exactly what it means to walk between these two worlds, to go from a world of drones and human hunting and scattered human remains into the city where none of the suffering from the hills just outside the city is heard. When there is seemingly no end to the sea of grief and death in the borderlands, it is the stories of survival that pull us together and keep us going. It is the moments when I hike deep into the desert wilderness with some of my closest friends and see green water carried by migrants left for others that help me make sense of this ugly world, that allow me a glimpse of a world where not everyone is out to destroy others.

The work we do is in solidarity with those crossing the border and living without papers in the United States, but our grief is not necessarily in solidarity; our grief is our own. I grieve for the loss I feel when I part ways with someone in the desert, and the pain I feel because murderous policies permit mass graves and deport people I know. I grieve when I come across bones in

DUST OF THE DESERT

/

53

the desert that turn out to be human, although my sorrow is inherently different than that of the family of the person I've found. I am just one in a community that walks between two disparate worlds, and frequently our only solace is in one another, in talking about the small victories, in speaking of the bizarre and hilarious colliding of cultures at our camp clinic. When things feel bleakest, we often collectively recall and share with others the stories of the people we have met who have survived despite a multibillion-dollar budget to track them down. Together we all mourn what the media and mainstream society refuse to acknowledge: the importance and complexity of the lives of those who travel through the borderlands. When the pain of interfacing with so much near-invisible suffering becomes too much, the only thing left to do is to walk south on the trails together, carrying as much water as we can to leave for those walking north.

Although we leave water in a thousand crevices throughout the Sonoran Desert, it is within the crux where there are shrines honoring La Virgen de Guadalupe, Santo Toribio, and Santisima Muerte where collective grieving and collective action visibly merge. Migrants themselves have crafted these shrines and carried with them symbols of hope to leave as a mark in the desert. No matter how hard the state attempts to dehumanize the untold numbers of people coming through this desert, it has failed at eradicating all their hope. No matter how hard the state attempts to criminalize aid for others in need, it has failed at destroying solidarity. In this land where water is life and the lack of it is death, a water bottle has become a symbol of resistance to the murderous policy of the state. Water, brought from both the north and south, is offered to those in need; it is also offered to the saints, so they'll watch over the living and dead in this perilous desert.

We leave water by the three shrines, as our scrap of a message for safe journeys and, too often, plastic memorial stones for those who don't make it.

*

Lee Sandusky has spent the past four years living in Tucson and organizing on the ground with a grassroots, consensus-based organization called No More Deaths / No Mas Muertes—an umbrella organization for several separate working groups that each interface with migration differently; she has worked primarily with the search-and-rescue team and Desert Aid. Lee is currently working with a collective to compile and edit an anthology of creative pieces about how borders impact life in the Sonoran Desert. She'd like to thank all the people who are working visibly or invisibly to dismantle the systems of control that keep people from moving freely and apart from their communities, and in particular her fellow Desert Rats, who have poured innumerable drops of blood, sweat, and tears into the borderland.

HER BROTHER

SYED HUSSAN

I have no faith in this government, Hussan.

We are sitting in a chain coffee shop above a subway station at the end of the line. The seats are beige and red. Beside us, a man and woman are loudly urging a stranger they have just met to buy into their pyramid scheme.

This passport that I took from them is tainted. I just want to burn it. I want to go back and die on my motherland. She hurt me less.

She massages her neck; hypertension she says.

They killed my brother. They beat him to death in a prison. And they got away with it.

Today is almost one year since her brother died in a maximum-security prison where he was jailed without charges or trial on behalf of federal immigration.

He was the only uncle my children knew and now he's dead. And it's worse; my son was in prison for three years, charged with a murder that took place when he was in class. Then they let him go, and all they said was sorry. They put my little boy in a cage, for no reason, for no reason. And then they said they were sorry. My son, he came out sick. He lives on pills. He was getting better, and then he heard about his uncle's death and now he's sick again.

She adjusts her pink scarf. Her elderly sister slowly strokes her cheek.

/

They thank me every so often. These two Somali women who have lived through the civil war in Mogadaishu and have the warmest of smiles. They tell me to be strong. They tell me that I am doing important work. As I wipe away my tears, they nod knowingly.

Though the tragedy is entirely theirs, in their grace, they are caring for me.

Look, they told us to come here as refugees. So we did. Then they jailed us and killed us. They will do it to the Syrians too.

We talk about Syrian refugees. Twenty-five thousand Syrian refugees have been flown here. It is the Great Canadian Project, the immigration minister says every time he sees a news camera.

Eighteen hours after Alan Kurdi's four-year-old body washed ashore the consciousness of the world, I helped organize a demonstration in Toronto.

Over a thousand people gathered. We chanted. We sang. We held on to each other. We cried. We screamed. We clutched hands, and sobbed tears.

We carried pictures of Alan, his brother, Galib, his mother, Rehana. His family wanted to apply to bring him and themselves to Canada but didn't have the money to do so. Over and over again we said Alan should be here.

We marched. We sat. We ran. And finally we arrived at the immigration offices where just a few weeks ago some of us had organized a vigil the day after her brother's death.

SYED HUSSAN

/

Her brother—the black Somali man, with a history of mental health issues and convictions for petty crime. Her brother—the man jailed for three years without cause, without an end. His vigil had twenty-five people. Her brother—the refugee who should be here.

Standing before a thousand people joined in sadness and grief, I said inspiring things about the power of people's movements. With one voice, the crowd thundered in chants.

In my heart I wondered, who cries for her brother? Will you cry the next time someone dies in immigration detention? What stories can you write on a faceless child's light-skinned body that you cannot see in a black adult's face?

Over the next month, in thirty cities, forty-five demonstrations took place. Tens of thousands of people across these lands marched, all of them holding the same placards: Alan, Ghalib, and Rehanna should be here. News footage showed people from Thunder Bay to the Arctic, from coastal cities on the Atlantic and Pacific, chanting "no hate, no fear, refugees are welcome here."

We willed little Alan's body to hold all of our meanings. We turned his silenced laughter into the cacophony of our political desires.

As we insisted that Alan should be here, I wondered what would happen if he did make it here? Would he grow up to be shot nine times in the chest by a police officer from seven feet away, as happened to Syrian Sammy Yatim? Would he grow up to be denied mental health support and die like her brother, pinned down and struggling on a hospital bed?

It was election season in Canada. As we marched, the electioneering stopped. The sitting immigration minister never started up his campaign again; he eventually lost his seat. All the political parties made promises, swearing to protect refugees.

They said nothing about the thousands who languish in prisons, the hundreds of thousands who are undocumented, the many more who have been deported.

Wherever you are, you've probably heard some of the rest of this story. Justin Trudeau, handsome, well meaning, slick, won the elections.

He urged people to open up their homes to refugees, and hundreds of groups of five amassed $30,000 each to sponsor refugee families.

With great fanfare, Canada flew in 25,000 Syrian refugees. That's 0.2 percent of the 12.1 million displaced Syrians. That's 0.04 percent of the total number of displaced people in the world.

A drop of safety in an ocean of grief.

The mass demonstrations stopped. Our pain, in this place called Canada, at the drownings in the Mediterranean was assuaged by images of airlifted arrivals at airports and promises of sunnier ways. Many of us who took to the streets now congratulated ourselves on a job well done, and moved on.

SYED HUSSAN

/

The deaths, they continue. Today, June 30, 2016, 2,866 people have drowned in the Mediterranean since the start of the year.

Say it with me: two thousand, eight hundred, and sixty-six. Does spelling it out make it more real?

How many friends do you have on Facebook? The average number is 338. Imagine them all dying. Now imagine all their parents dying. Now imagine all their grandparents dying—in a span of six months—by drowning.

Drowning. When your head goes underwater, your trachea seals. Your body tries to save you from water entering into your lungs and ends up shutting out the oxygen. Self-asphyxiation. You don't shriek when you drown, or wave your arms or struggle. You go limp. Your eyes roll into the back of your head, and your mouth opens up. Only when you have died does the water flood in.

It's not the water that kills you; it's your body protecting you from the water. Like the refugees and migrants, who, in their attempts to save themselves, die. Killed by the ocean blue where murders can be written off as tragedy. The dead do not scream; they wash up on shores in the hundreds and thousands.

Unlike the Palestinian mothers crying for their children, the Argentinean Mothers of the Plaza de Mayo, the families of the drowned rarely march for them in public. There are no daily vigils by the families of those drowning in the Mediterranean or perishing crossing the Rio Grande. We, those who live with

HER BROTHER

/

the murderers, we do. And as we see some lives saved, we forget those who aren't.

What makes certain deaths worthy of grieving? How do some names turn into calls for action, and why are others swiftly forgotten? What do we do when those in power subsume our cries of rage for their own ends? Should we amass in pain in the streets when that pain may be turned into apologies, monuments, claims of righteousness? Why do we cry in public and weep in private?

I know not for certain. But perhaps we do it to write our own histories. We form bonds that outlast the few moments of media spectacle. We welcome those who join us briefly in these moments, and we hold them close. And then as the noise fades, we look around and see who is still here with us. Here not in passing rage but rather a deep grief that arises from a place of love, a collective, universal yearning: never again, never again, never again.

She never sheds a tear. Often she laughs.

I keep it all on the inside. This country, it tells me to harden up. I don't show my pain, ever, ever. But inside I am grieving.

I want change. For me, for us, for all the other sisters and mothers. We must live.

*

Syed Hussan is a migrant justice organizer based in Toronto. The name of the man who died in detention has been left out at the family's request for privacy.

SYED HUSSAN

/

IT TAKES AN OCEAN
NOT TO BREAK

LEANNE BETASAMOSAKE SIMPSON

i knew you were going to try and kill yourself before you did it. i knew because before all this happened you were the only person my seven-year-old nephew with asperger's ever let hug him. you were eighteen and you were just shining, your even brown perfect skin competing with the bright blue sky for my attention. god, you were perfect. i was in love with the idea that finally we had given birth to a generation that didn't have to spend their adult lives recovering from their child-hoods. you weren't going to drown yourself in anything, you were just going to smile and fight in some mythological honorable way we'd all only imagined. then i found out your mama was about to die and every time you looked me in the eye i wanted to cry, because i knew there was a diagnosed train wreck coming your way and i didn't know how someone so perfect could survive.

after the accident we had the same three-line conversation for a month. therapy-lady suggested that it was insane for me to keep doing this with you, but fuck. i wasn't in therapy to take therapy-lady's advice. at least not all of it. i was there because i didn't want to fuck up my kids. That's not true. i was there so i didn't commit suicide.

    it was too much to ask of a white lady.

/

after we stopped having the same three-line conversation over and over again you started to apologize to everyone for putting us through your accident. then you'd forget you apologized, and so a few hours later, you would do it all over again. it wasn't you talking, it was your team of therapists as they tried to get you to accept responsibility for your "bad choices" and the completely hellish reality those "choices" delivered you to.

therapy-lady was helping me "knit positive experiences into the fabric of my life." that sounded like unattainable crazy talk to me, but i liked that she said fabric. Everyone else i knew said material.

bringing up trauma from my life made therapy-lady cry, especially if it was "aboriginal" themed. she said "aboriginal" a lot, and i knew she was trying to be respectful so i planned on letting it slide until the breaking point and then i was going to let her have it in one spiraling long manifesto. therapy-lady liked to compare my life to refugees from war-torn countries who hid their kids in closets when airplanes flew over their houses. this was her limit of understanding on colonized intimacy. she wasn't completely wrong, and while she tried to convince me none of us had to hide our kids anymore, we both knew that wasn't exactly true. i knew what every ndn knows: that vulnerability, forgiveness, and acceptance were privileges. She made the assumption of a white person: they were readily available to all like the fresh produce at the grocery store.

LEANNE BETASAMOSAKE SIMPSON

/

lucy says that i made a critical mistake on my first day of therapy. "you have to lay all of your indian shit out on the first day, drug abuse, suicide attempts, all the times you got beat up, all of that shit. then you sit back and watch how they react. then you'll know if they can deal or not." lucy had a social work degree but she didn't buy it, which is always useful.

i wondered if these people had ever even thought of driving their car off a bridge? had they ever felt an overwhelming need for release? had they ever experienced the kind of pain that makes bad choices utterly rational? suicide's not something you do to other people, it's something you do for yourself.

i told you to stop apologizing. i told you it wasn't your fault. fuck sakes. i told you that you were in an enormous amount of pain. i told you that you were the fucking strongest person i'd ever known. i told you i knew why you did it.

lucy was right. but now i was two years invested in therapy-lady and plus i liked to interview therapy-lady about happy people like i was an anthropologist. apparently happy people celebrate their birthdays. apparently happy people express their emotions as a way of processing experiences. apparently the ability to throw yourself in front of a bus and not get that hurt isn't something happy people strive for.

if you're nish and you can't survive being dragged under the bus, you're not going to survive. period.

IT TAKES AN OCEAN NOT TO BREAK

/

i want to suck the shame out of all forty-three of your broken bones.

i worried therapy-lady was trying to assimilate me into a plasticy christian that can stand in the middle of a car wreck and thank the heavenly father for the band-aid they found in their purse. So while therapy-lady was crocheting my life of happy moments into a big fucking smothering scarf, i was imagining the release of ending it all. i was imagining floating away from the weight.

you apologized to me every day for another thirty days.

therapy-lady wanted me to tell her what i was getting out of these thirty-day conversations.
     "intimacy."
     "that's intensity, not intimacy. do you know the difference?"
     "probably not."
     i try again.
     i decide she can't possibly ever get it.

when it first happened, everyone was praying for you to live. i wanted
to trust you. you saw what was laid out before you and you made a
choice.
     shit. that's not what I'm supposed to say. i'm supposed to say i'm glad
you're alive. i'm glad it didn't work. i'm supposed to look you in the eye
and tell you that it's all going to be better, and when you don't believe

LEANNE BETASAMOSAKE SIMPSON

/

70

me, i'm supposed to tell you to trust me. the mother in me has to be the beacon of your future ok self that tells you unequivocally not to trust your feelings because they will pass. what's that crap that therapy-lady says? "the feelings are real, but they are not reality." yeah. that's it. your feelings are real, but they are not your reality. don't get tricked.

the mother in me has to believe i can heal you by loving you, because no one actually believes that, except for mothers.

fuck. why was the universe trying to destroy you? why didn't you get some say? sometimes people's lives are just shit through no fault of their own and not even fucking oprah's cash and her toolbox of privileged platitudes can fix it. sometimes people just drown in their own heads for no particular reason. sometimes people are just sad. you know, if it had worked, i would still have respected you. i would have respected your decision, and i would have missed you and loved you the same as i do now.

but it didn't work and now you're in this mess, with all the shit that got you to this point in the first place and all the new shit of being shattered pieces of skin arced over the pavement. i'm scared for the point where you heal enough to see how monumentally bad this is.

she asks me again, "what's in it for you?"

i think about stealing her desk.

i give another incorrect answer.

"again, what is in it for you?"

"love."

"love?"

IT TAKES AN OCEAN NOT TO BREAK

/

"love. and that is all."

i change the subject to anxiety. therapy-lady loves talking about anxiety. me the poor depressed indian. her the white fucking pathologizing savior. i tell her my anxiety and i are codependent, but in a lovely way. she tries to convince me the world is a safe place, and that i'm not a little kid anymore and that it's possible that no one will ever hit me again. sometimes when she says things like that, it's like i've never heard them before and so i ask if i can borrow her pen, so i write them down on my hand. and then i go back to worrying that my jeans are too dirty for her white ikea couch, and that maybe i'll leave a big gray stain of me on it.

i'm getting in the car right now, and i'm driving north to you. it'll take me a couple of days to get there. i want to pick you up, and i'm going to stitch every one of your broken bones back together with kisses, and then i'm going to drive us to the coast. i'm not sure which one. but i like the feeling of listening to music and driving and driving for days to get to somewhere different.

i think you're going to like that feeling too.

*

Leanne Betasamosake Simpson is the author of This Accident of Being Lost, Dancing on Our Turtle's Back, The Gift Is in the Making, *and* Islands of Decolonial Love, *and the editor of* Lighting the Eighth Fire, This Is an Honour Song *(with Kiera Ladner), and* The Winter We

LEANNE BETASAMOSAKE SIMPSON

/

Danced: Voice from the Past, the Future, and the Idle No More Movement (*Kino-nda-niimi collective*). *She holds a PhD from the University of Manitoba and has lectured at universities across Canada. Leanne is a Michi Saagiig Nishnaabeg and member of Alderville First Nation.*

IT TAKES AN OCEAN NOT TO BREAK

/

YOUR GRIEF
IS MY GRAVE

KAI CHENG THOM

WHO IS WORTH MY LOVE,
MY STRENGTH, AND MY RAGE?

—MARK AGUHAR AKA CALLOUTQUEEN

On March 12, 2012, Mark Aguhar, fat trans femme of color icon, revolutionary artist, and self-proclaimed Tumblr calloutqueen, died of suicide in Chicago. She was twenty-four years old. On the same day, I turned twenty-one in Montreal and attempted my own suicide. We had never known each other, Mark and I. In fact, I only became familiar with her incredibly beautiful, unrelentingly snarky body of work after her passing. But still, I feel an admittedly presumptuous sense of connection to her, a strain of magical thinking that leads me to believe that there must be something more that we share than just the day that she died and the day that I didn't.

The year 2012, it seemed to me, was one of public grief—of death and giddy despair and upheaval and rebirth. A pseudohistorical, pseudoscientific (though from a certain perspective, perhaps not entirely untrue) "ancient Mayan prophecy" that the world was going to end in that year caught fire in the consciousness of global pop culture. In Quebec, where I live, a massive student movement—including my entire social circle of so-

/

called activist kids in our early twenties—clashed with riot squad police in the streets over the government's proposed tuition hikes in a massive outpouring of rage and loss over Quebec's decaying "socialist" roots.

In fact, it was through public expressions of grief that I first became acquainted with who Mark was. In the days after Mark's death, a certain queer corner of the Internet flared with eulogies and memorials celebrating her fierce, scathingly honest critiques of racism, transmisogyny, and fatphobia within the mainstream gay community; her gorgeously ugly, undeniably sexy aesthetic; and the complex, raw intelligence of the thoughts that she posted daily on her blog. If I remember correctly, it was while randomly scrolling online as I lay in bed, muscles still shaking from the drugs I'd tried halfheartedly to overdose on, that I stumbled across her obituary.

It seemed so unfair, so *ironic*, to me that this powerful, visionary person—this Asian trans femme who seemed so much braver and stronger than me—was gone from the world while I, closeted, gender confused, full of self-loathing and cowardice, was still here. In Mark's work, in the scalding heat of her language and intensely erotic resonance of her imagery, I saw someone whom I looked up to, was scared of, and wanted to be. I saw someone freer and more powerful than I could ever become.

I didn't grieve Mark in that moment that we crossed paths between life and death. I was jealous of her.

KAI CHENG THOM

/

I HATE UR WHITE DICK.

—MARK AGUHAR AKA CALLOUTQUEEN

From the moment we begin to identify or be identified as trans women of color, we are haunted by the public spectacle of death. Up until recently, the vast majority of trans women of color to come into the public eye were dead trans women of color—a trend that has shifted only slightly with the appearance of celebrities such as Laverne Cox and Janet Mock. Death is the dominant, the ultimate, narrative that colonial Western society has to offer us: death by suicide and murder and sexually transmitted infections. And in death, trans women have become intrinsically associated with grief, yet with the kind of grief that objectifies and exploits us publicly while silencing our voices.

Who benefits from a story about poor, downtrodden, murdered, and suicidal trans women? Who benefits from the dozens of articles shared online each year about yet another one of us dead under tragic circumstances? Media outlets perhaps? Or journalists and documentary makers looking to cover a beat? Or maybe liberal "activists" looking to soothe their consciences with a bit of hand-wringing, with "raising awareness" and no action, as though we were an endangered species of animal (not that awareness-raising campaigns are saving too many endangered species these days)?

But it does trans women ourselves no good to become associated with, to internalize, this understanding of ourselves as

YOUR GRIEF IS MY GRAVE

/

walking funerals waiting to happen, as hapless victims waiting for salvation. That Mark was no meek victim becomes immediately obvious to anyone who takes even the briefest moment to examine the body of work she left behind.

"I don't need to be strong, I need for the world to stop being so fucking weak, that my sisters are being swallowed up before my eyes," she wrote in a post dated November 11, 2011.

Trans women are warriors. Our very existence demands it.

I'D RATHER BE BEAUTIFUL THAN MALE.

—MARK AGUHAR AKA CALLOUTQUEEN

Relationships between trans women of color are complicated. There are many reasons for this, most of which have to do with the intensity of the social and psychological violence that is directed at us on a constant basis. Most of us spend so much time learning to survive in isolation that the presence of "another one" can be destabilizing. White, cisgendered heteropatriarchy pits us against each other, forcing us to fight for the few positions of prosperity available to us as well-paid entertainers and tokens of the white gay and lesbian movement. We are taught so intensely, for so long, to hate ourselves that it becomes a reflex to dislike anyone in whom we see ourselves reflected too closely.

So I don't know if Mark and I would have been friends exactly had we known each other in life. Even now, I wonder what she would think of me writing this essay, if she is watching me from somewhere and throwing shade at this assumed intimacy and my audacity in trying to weave her legacy into my words. Maybe she would have thought that I was a sellout or derivative bitch.

But god, I like to imagine that we would have been friends, femme sister warriors in arms and long, black hair extensions. I like to fantasize that she'd come over on weeknights, and I'd make us coconut curry chicken for dinner, and we would watch makeup tutorials on YouTube and make snarky comments about the thin little white girls doing them. We would paint each other's nails. And she would tell me her stories, and I would tell her my fears, and I would offer her my tenderness, and she would teach me her strength.

You see, I didn't know many trans women back in 2012 (although I would later discover that a couple good friends had been closeted, like me). Like Mark, I was a young Asian trans femme coming of age in a queer community that worshiped white, cisgendered male beauty and pretended to be having revolutionary sex (as if there were such a thing) while ignoring—and perpetuating—racism, misogyny, and class war. Like so many young people in the massive student strike movement, I was looking for a reflection of my rage and anguish and desire, and found myself nowhere. My femininity felt like something horrible growing inside me, something freakish and disgusting and ludicrous, something that got me attacked in the street and raped by older men, instead of something sacred.

So one night in Montreal, as people chanted in the streets and police helicopters snarled in the skies, I tried to kill myself. I took the rage and rebellion in my heart that I didn't know what to do with and tried to destroy my body. It strikes me as I write this that perhaps all trans women's suicides are, in a way, political suicides. Rather than the act of utter self-debasement and self-pity that it is so often understood as, suicide—the refusal to submit to living in a world that degrades and exploits and rapes us without relent—might be seen as collective struggle, revolutionary violence, turned inward. I wonder what Mark would say to that.

These are the axes:

1

Bodies are inherently valid

2

Remember death

3

Be ugly

4

Know beauty

5

It is complicated

KAI CHENG THOM

/

6

Empathy

7

Choice

8

Reconstruct, reify

9

Respect, negotiate.

—MARK AGUHAR AKA CALLOUTQUEEN

Grief will make you think strange things. I can't say I truly grieve Mark. At the end of the day, I never knew her, and never will, no matter how much I wanted to. I won't tell that lie. I do grieve a world in which she and I could have met, could have spoken, could have known sisterhood and communion, could have felt the strength of each other's arms. I grieve the trans femme family I did not have. The love we couldn't give each other, and the anger we could not share. Someone stole that chance from us. This is what I grieve.

Mark was vociferous in her defense of suicide as a legitimate choice for queer femmes of color living in a society that hates us. I second this, even as I am thankful for my own life. It is too easy to fall down the trap of either glamorizing or repudiating suicide, of overestimating or denying the agency involved in the act of death. The truth lies somewhere in the complicated place where body and belief collide.

YOUR GRIEF IS MY GRAVE

I

I can't stop thinking about Mark. On my birthdays especially, I am haunted by her words and images, the soul she shared so fearlessly with the world. I have no right to claim any special bond to her except for my longing for sister, for mother, for the goddess that she has come to represent—the goddess who died on my birthday. In the wildest moments of my magical thinking, I find myself imagining her as practically a Christlike figure, a trans femme of color Jesus in flawless makeup, dying to give life to girls like me.

How ridiculous. How wrongheaded. But then, don't all trans women die and grieve, and live, for each other, in a kind of way? Don't our bodies carve out room for the next generation by the very fact of our existence, even as we pass from this world to the next?

At the very least, I know that I am not alone in these thoughts. When I look to my trans sisters, especially those of my generation—the Internet generation, connected as we are by images and the written word—I see Mark everywhere. Her words and artworks, posted and reblogged and tweeted over and over again by trans girls like me, searching for meaning in our own bodies, our own selves. And if I cannot really "know" Mark, if her true personhood remains out of reach behind the twin veils of suicide and public narrative around it, then I may take some comfort in knowing that her work creates a bridge between me and other trans femmes of color. In the echo chamber of our questions, our grief, there is connection, and in our connection, there is life.

Around the threads of truth that Mark has given us, we wind our own stories, and from those threads, we wind ourselves possibility, relationships, a future in which we can live.

I grieve and honor that. I honor Mark. I honor all trans femmes. I honor all women, and all those who live and die as warriors, unseen. I honor life and death, and the strength it takes to do both.

BLESSED ARE THE SISSIES
BLESSED ARE THE BOI DYKES
BLESSED ARE THE PEOPLE OF COLOR
MY BELOVED KITH AND KIN
BLESSED ARE THE TRANS
BLESSED ARE THE HIGH FEMMES
BLESSED ARE THE SEX WORKERS
BLESSED ARE THE AUTHENTIC
BLESSED ARE THE DIS-IDENTIFIERS
BLESSED ARE THE GENDER ILLUSIONISTS
BLESSED ARE THE NON-NORMATIVE
BLESSED ARE THE GENDERQUEERS
BLESSED ARE THE KINKSTERS
BLESSED ARE THE DISABLED
BLESSED ARE THE HOT FAT GIRLS

YOUR GRIEF IS MY GRAVE

/

BLESSED ARE THE WEIRDO-QUEERS
BLESSED IS THE SPECTRUM
BLESSED IS CONSENT
BLESSED IS RESPECT
BLESSED ARE THE BELOVED WHO I DIDN'T
DESCRIBE, I COULDN'T DESCRIBE, WILL
LEARN TO DESCRIBE AND RESPECT AND LOVE
AMEN.

—MARK AGUHAR AKA CALLOUTQUEEN,
"Litanies to My Heavenly Brown Body"

*

Kai Cheng Thom is a writer and performer based in Montreal and Toronto, Canada, unceded indigenous territories. Her work has been published widely online and in print. She is author of the novel Fierce Femmes and Notorious Liars: A Dangerous Trans Girl's Confabulous Memoir *(Metonymy Press) and the poetry collection* a place called No Homeland *(Arsenal Pulp Press).*

Mark Aguhar was a multimedia artist and blogger. Her work is known among trans and queer communities for its critical interrogation of white supremacy and transmisogyny as well as its provocative and unapologetic exploration of queer femme of color sexuality.

KAI CHENG THOM

/

FRAGMENTS
TOWARD
A WHOLE

KEVIN YUEN KIT LO

The small, abandoned schoolhouse held a library in the back with books piled upon books, about plants and birds, philosophy and math, ancient Greek tragedies, poetry, and the history of North America. In the front, there was a freezer that stored frozen meat, chicken, and boxes of popsicles, Freezies. An old rotary telephone sat on a small desk next to a surprisingly slim and weathered regional directory of phone numbers. It was the last trace of civilization before the long, swooping climb up the mountain to the octagonal log cabin. As rumor had it, the schoolhouse was burned to the ground by a mob of angry locals, and the cabin overgrown.

If those trees could talk, what would they say? Because I wasn't the only one, the first, or the last, as special as I may have felt then—being from the big city, having friends who were girls. I was even "cool" compared to the other boys. But in those woods, I felt like I was special, the only one. He made sure of it.

One evening after dinner, over a decade and a half later, my dad casually mentioned his reason for sending me to Cape Breton, for sending me to Don's school. My brother, a teenager at the time, an immigrant's first son, was having a hard time at school, thrashing about for his identity among his peers. My grades were good; head buried in books, and I seemed well adjusted enough. My parents thought it might be OK to send me

/

away for the year, to focus their energies on my brother and his rebellion. I had loved the summer camp. It was fun, and I wanted to go. A year in the woods might do my frail young body some good.

*

Hi Cindy,

So nice to hear from you, and thanks for inviting me to collaborate on this anthology.

I don't think I ever told you, it's something I've held pretty close over the years, but I was sexually abused as a kid from the ages of around ten to fourteen at a summer camp and alternative school in rural Nova Scotia. As a teenager, I did my best to block out the experience, but obviously it did fuck me up, and comes back to haunt me even today.

At a talk I gave recently about my graphic design practice and activist work, at the end of a lengthy Q&A, I was asked a pretty typical question about my sources of inspiration, what drives me to do the work I do, and so on, and I responded, almost unconsciously, that it was born out of trauma, out of necessity. I wasn't trying to be dramatic or deep. It just kinda came out. I was quite tired by that point, and I don't really know what I meant by that answer, but I'd like to explore it, and explore it publicly. It feels like it's about damn time.

Love and Solidarity,

Kevin

KEVIN YUEN KIT LO

/

The veracity of my memories is questionable. It was a long time ago, and I was just a kid. I can't recall or describe any of the specific pain I may have felt then. Or any desires. The word I used most often was *betrayal*, and the phrase "he was like a father to me." But I mostly repeated these words only to myself, until I actually believed them. No one else knew anything. We were all just trying to get by, black-clad teenage smokers; we were all hurting, runaways and cast-offs, self-harming in the most creative ways.

I was playing arcade games downtown, Street Fighter II. How old was I? The man kept feeding me quarters as he watched me play. Enthralled by the free games, I didn't even notice him standing behind me, slowly touching me, rubbing me, until I nearly came in my pants. I pulled away and hurriedly stumbled out of the arcade, bitterly ashamed. I didn't look back, though; it was only a ghost, an echo from those woods.

Adolescence in essence is all about trust. This obscure lyrical fragment, as self-evident as it seems, has always hit home. The broken trust—of others, adults, white men, teachers, cops, of authority of any kind, of those you hold dear, those you let in close, but especially of your own mind and body, which were now clearly two separate, irreconcilable things.

Or are these merely the clichés I've learned since then? Notions such as the "loss of childhood," the inability to maintain healthy relationships, fear of intimacy, low self-confidence, and the dislike of gym class and team sports.... Didn't we all feel these things? Isn't such fragmentation and alienation simply what late capitalism sows in us? The "sensitive ones" at least. Isn't it why we all ended up here, hanging out in the margins, trying to rebuild that trust by scheming together, creating the relationships that we simply couldn't "out there"? How do you disentangle these things?

In truth, I never really understood my experience as *the* most terrible thing. I wasn't physically harmed, and I never lacked for much during my childhood. My abuse was simply part of the fabric of who I was, an invisible prop that gave me an excuse for my weaknesses and insecurities, a straw man for my undirected anger. Almost thirty years on, it's still not *the* most terrible thing, but it is still *a* thing. In my relationships, in my fragmented memory and sense of self. How does one move on from this, how does one heal, especially when no one else knows? A secret that is allowed to fester.

We were awarded points for spotting and naming animals, and the rarer the animal, the more points we got. Deer, red-tailed hawks, bald eagles, moose, foxes, coyotes, and bears. No one ever saw a bear, though. The points were then tallied up and converted into dollars we could spend at the gift shop in the national park. I loved that gift shop, and camping in that park. One summer I made enough points to buy an illustrated hardcover book listing the traditional indigenous healing plants and methods of the region. It was the best.

On a small mattress set in the corner of the second floor of the cabin, carefully walled off by books, Don changes the script. I was used to him jacking me off by then, anticipating it with ' confused excitement and fear. It's amazing how he could find the time and space to do these things, with the gaggle of kids running around, hanging on his every word, his every gesture. Often, Lorna, his wife the academic, wasn't too far off either, reading and writing in silence. She held her wisdom in silences.

This time he presses up behind me under the thin summer sheets. The mattress is thin, too, and the floorboards are set wide enough apart to drop quarters through, so we have to be quiet. This much I know. As he strokes me, I start to feel the insistent push of his cock between my ass, but it takes me a moment to figure out what's happening. The girth and rigidity and heat are foreign to me. I still don't understand how there are all these parts that make up a body, and that they can grow and change. It's just a body. It's just me.

The rhythmic pushing lasts for what seems like an eternity. I'm not sure what he's looking for. But my body doesn't let him in; my body is too small, too tight. Finally, frustrated, Don flips himself over and places his mouth around my tiny, sprung-up cock.

That wall of books held a small treasure, a book of photos of

FRAGMENTS TOWARD A WHOLE

/

Brooke Shields from *The Blue Lagoon*. In quiet times, when the other boys were outside playing, I would go upstairs and hide in the corner to flip through it with one hand, while touching myself with the other. I memorized those images; she became a goddess to me, her imagined smooth skin a surrogate for his rough fingers and lips.

In 2010, I was rediscovering my activism after a long and difficult relationship had failed. At a boycott, divestment, and sanctions panel, Areej Ja'fari, a young Palestinian activist from the Palestine Freedom Project, recounted her story. I have little recollection of what she said, but the feeling her words evoked, the visceral anger and sadness, straddling the line between hope and hopelessness, is easy to identify. Her words brought me to the edge of tears. As I left the conference, I dutifully picked up all the flyers and pamphlets for all the events and projects I planned to soon engage in. But walking home that night, I didn't think of Palestine at all. I was busy asking myself, "What connection do I have to this faraway land and its people, its suffering?" It's the kind of question that critics ask of young activists all the time. "Why do I care? Do I even care?" Or was I just desperately trying to get at that feeling, the sadness that might pierce the numbness, the validated anger, the promise of catharsis? Palestine, a Godspeed song, or crushing cigarettes out on my arm—did they all serve the same selfish end? An addict, hoping that someone else's tears might loose my own.

That moment when we lay in the park, staring at the stars, and I finally told you. It was a cool summer night. You held me close and told me all the things I needed to hear, asked all the right questions, led me to answers that made sense of things. I forgot the loneliness and started to form a vision of our future together. You gently kissed me, told me it was OK, and it was. I felt calm, collected, and complete.

Except that moment never happened.

Instead, it was winter, I was half drunk and on the edge again, and we were walking through the snow to the bus stop. "Yeah, I was abused as a child." You didn't look away. "But I'm OK now. I've dealt with it. I didn't get it that bad compared to the others. It's just kinda fucked up." At least you didn't look away.

I was fucked for years before I was ever kissed.

I've told most of my lovers since then. Moments before or right after sex, and they were all to a tee perfectly kind with me. They carried the weight, reacted quietly and calmly, silently even, for what was there to really say? The sex was good? I'd like to believe there was wisdom in these silences too, but sometimes I feel I'd be better served by being buried in noise.

*

FRAGMENTS TOWARD A WHOLE

/

I need to get off. I don't know why. I need to dive into the nearest strip club, and pound back a gin and tonic, or five. I need something, cocaine, although where the hell am I gonna score right now? Fuck, I just want to pay a beautiful woman to dance for me, grind on me—to bad hip-hop. I want to feel her weight, smell her scent. I can afford three, maybe four songs, right?

I want to smashy-smash-smash. We've been marching "peacefully" for weeks. I want to spill out into the streets with a thousand of my closest friends screaming "no justice, no peace, fuck the police!" Surround myself in bodies and righteous noise. Piss off the bourgeois pricks sipping their cocktails on the terraces. Shake up this fucking city.

But the streets are too full tonight. I walk by the club twice more, a nervous ball wreaking havoc in my stomach. I want . . . I'm frustrated. Isn't there a back door, some way to get in without being seen? Maybe I should walk by one more time for good measure. What the hell am I thinking? Fuck this, I walk the long way back home, anxious and ashamed at myself, slowly weaving through the lingering crowds.

*

In those woods, we played at being Indians. I learned how to track and hunt and trap, how to build a compound bow, lean-to, or basic dugout. The boys wore buckskin loincloths and necklaces made from bone. Often, nothing more. At night, we read the Iliad—all of it—by the light of a gas lamp. And after that, we read the Odyssey. The water from the stream was the coldest and clearest I have ever tasted. For a while, I did believe those trees could talk.

In 1992, I'm fourteen. I'm sitting in front of the television at my brother's friend's house party. I feel so cool because it's late at night and he invited me, but far too awkward to interact with anyone there. Sinead O'Connor is on *Saturday Night Live*, singing a cappella in a white dress, with shaved head, framed in darkness. People are laughing and smoking and drinking and flirting behind me. The camera slowly zooms in to her face, "and everywhere is war," the intensity in her voice, her eyes, her breath, and then the words delivered. "Child abuse, yeah . . ." And repeated, "child abuse, yeah . . ." My world freezes. I'm sure I'd heard the words before, but never on television, never spoken, sung to me. "Children . . ." She pulls out a picture of the pope and tears it to shreds. She stares straight ahead, unwavering, staring straight into me. "Fight the real enemy." The televised crowd is stunned silent; it does not applaud. The screen cuts to a commercial. My world shatters. It is the first time I connect those words with what happened to me, and the distance between the lush woods of Cape Breton and the teenage streets of Toronto collapses. Everywhere is war.

In Montreal in 2012, the city is engulfed in the longest student strike in history. That night, the first after a new law is put in place that basically makes any protest illegal, the cops are out in full force. So are we. I feel the true depth of my fear during a po-

FRAGMENTS TOWARD A WHOLE

/

lice kettle, and the ball in the pit in my stomach expands out-ward, making the tip of my fingers tingle. Frantically glancing around me at all the pressed-up faces and bodies, I realize we're gearing up to rush the police line. The riot cops are all around us, banging their shields, closing in on us one step at a time. Was there any other choice? I can't do this; I'm not fast enough, not strong enough. This is fucked. In an instant, we're all running and screaming, straight into a wall of batons and body armor. I don't get through, but others do. It all happens so fast. I'm on the ground in an armlock, but I tried. I finally fucking tried.

Later, during the arrest, a cop refers to me as a girl as he pulls me out of the crowd. "*Ey, la fille, viens-ici.*" Another makes racist remarks as he puts my hands into zip ties, referring to me as Kim Jong-un, telling me to go home to daddy, making weird "Asian" noises at me. I am trying to act tough, but I am crying. I under-stand that they are not just bigots; they are trained for this, to identify and exploit their subject's weaknesses.

We're sitting under a large tree in the vast, rural yard of one of the campers' parents' home. It is the end of summer, and we're dropping the kids off at their homes, one at a time. I am a counselor now. I know I am leaving soon, and that I'm too old to come back. I'm too old not to know that this is wrong. He knows this, too. He unbuttons my jeans and goes down on me. His beard scratches up against my stomach, but he's taking his time, going extra slow. I try my hardest to think of the girls back home in Toronto, the girls who are my friends, all the Brooke

Shields. It doesn't work. So this time, I look down to see what he's actually doing, watching the top of his balding head bobbing up and down, side to side. I feel his quickening breath, verging on desperation. He's getting older as well.

*

In 2000, Donald Charles Knight, a former teacher in Cape Breton, was sentenced to six years in prison after pleading guilty to five charges of sexually abusing young boys. The judge reduced the sentence to three years because of time already served. Six students between the ages of 10 and 15 were abused at Knight's Alternative School in Forest Glen, N.S., between 1984 and 1993.

The news clipping above is all I've managed to find online about Don and his camp, the only "proof," tagged onto an appendix of abuses in an article about a Catholic boarding school in Ontario. I didn't testify during the trial, though I was asked to, by both sides. "Because he loved you," Lorna had pleaded. She stayed true until the end. I can't remember what the other side had asked of me, or how it was presented, only that it seemed equally ridiculous by then, that there could be some connection between the sanctioned laws executed in some faraway courthouse and what I experienced in those woods, between halted breaths. There are no laws, no justice, for ghosts, and it seemed that the only way through, was forward.

*

FRAGMENTS TOWARD A WHOLE

/

Dear J., I'm sorry. I can't imagine what it was like to be the only girl at camp. Thank you for choosing to hold my hand, for lying next to me in the cabin, on the picnic table, on the dry grasses near Meat Cove. It couldn't have been easy to pick my hand to hold. And then years later, in the small town on the East Coast, when I came to visit you and your brother, for Christmas, you saved me again, this time in a more literal fashion. It was my own fault for calling those frat boys out, on New Year's Eve no less, and high on mushrooms. But I knew what he was going through there, as a long-haired poet who leaned toward the gay (as we might say then), and in a town like that. I couldn't let their taunting go unanswered. I'm pretty sure they would have thrown us off the bridge if you hadn't intervened.

Your brother told me later that he rallied some skate punk friends to get revenge for our beatdown. An epic showdown between the jocks and queers. I never really believed him. Our lies always sounded so similar, and I understood his desperate need to belong to something.

I imagine those frat boys as cops now. It's a stretch, but the cliché seems to hold. As a designer, I'm trying to draw a pattern here, trying to form some sort of meaning. To create something concrete and useful, for myself now, and for others. At the very least to shine a light on something too often cast in shadows, even among our friends and allies. But it's elusive, the knowledge is embodied, and the flesh and blood of it doesn't translate well. It was a long time ago. We didn't have the language then

KEVIN YUEN KIT LO

/

that we have now, the language that we are slowly, collectively building to speak of these things, about interpersonal power, its abuses and vectors, nor about care, and its necessity within our communities.

More years passed, and we met again in your small studio in Montreal. What did we say to each other? How long did we talk for? Did we speak openly about what Don did to me, to us, to your family? Or was it all nuance and drawn-out silences? All I remember is the cigarettes we smoked, the emotion trapped in our throats, and the wetness of our eyes.

*

Dear Cindy,

I'm sorry it's taken me so long to get back to you. I'm trying to push through this last draft on a night bus moving between Toronto and Montreal. Ironically, we're running an hour late. This has been a difficult text to write, and I had lost my momentum for a while. But the darkness and movement seems to be coaxing me toward some sort of ending, if not any sort of real conclusion. I've thought for a while about how this text could fit better into your anthology, trying to tease something more out of it. And it occurs to me that the collective work of grief is happening right now, on this bus between Toronto and Montreal, to your new home in Michigan. In the history of how we met in struggle, and my decision to write about this with you. Beyond anything else, that when you asked me for something, this is what I decided to give, in full trust, and in turn to make public within our communities. It feels good that I, that we've, simply gotten this far.

In thanks,

Kevin

*

Kevin Yuen Kit Lo is a graphic designer, educator, and community organizer based in Montreal.

LUNGFUL OF MOUNTAIN

WREN AWRY

It was just past dawn when four of us walked out of the verdant forest that blankets Coal River Mountain and onto the gray, pockmarked Bee Tree mountaintop removal site. An idle drill rig sat fifty feet away from the tree line, and we made our way to it, walking carefully so as not to fall into the holes drilled for ammonium nitrate explosives, which would blast even more of this West Virginia mountain apart. The massive drill pointed vertically toward the sky. One organizer locked himself to it, his face pressed so firmly against the cold metal that when the police cut his locks and removed him hours later, his cheek was smeared with black dust. I climbed into the operator's cab, took a seat in the chair, and pulling thick chains and a lock from my backpack, secured myself to it.

Then I waited.

Miners discovered our presence half an hour later and lightly heckled us—asking us where we were from, and why we were doing what we were doing—as they waited for the head of security for Massey Energy (the company that in 2009, owned Bee Tree) and state police to show up. The head of security got there first, and approached the two people acting as support for the two of us locked down. I'd interacted with the head of security at previous protests; he had a gray beard and red face, and

/

somehow managed to be jolly even while orchestrating the arrest of direct actionists. I leaned forward and, despite the glass window and dozen feet separating us, managed to make out what he was saying.

"Who drove you up here?" he asked.

"We walked," one of the supporters replied. They held a banner that read, simply, "Save Coal River Mountain"—a banner that would later be used to charge us with littering.

"Yeah, right," he replied. From where I sat, I could see him crack a smile.

But we *had* walked. We walked all night up Coal River Mountain and through the November forest, thick with twisting rhododendron limbs and fallen tulip poplar leaves the size of dinner plates. It was so dark in those woods that the only illumination was the moon and lights from a mine several ridges away; it was so still that the only noises were our footfalls along with the clanks and jangles of equipment from that same mine. It sounded like a mix between a dirge and battle cry: the loud thumps of mining cut by the soft, patterned steps of four people determined to stop further destruction. The scurry of small animals, crisp night air, and forest canopy studded with stars felt purposefully placed, as though the mountain itself wanted us to know exactly what was being lost before we climbed up on that drill rig. My lungs felt full. In their cavities, sadness mixed with awe.

*

WREN AWRY

/

106

I ended up in southern West Virginia the way I did most places in my early twenties: haphazardly. Inspired by an environmental justice course in college, I spent a week at Mountain Justice Summer Camp, which turned into another week helping the media team with the first action in Climate Ground Zero's campaign against mountaintop removal to result in arrests. I was hooked. I spent the summer in the Coal River Valley, and when autumn came, faxed in my college withdrawal papers from West Virginia.

That was 2009, the year I turned twenty. Adulthood was new to me, and working on a direct action campaign in Appalachia felt like just about the most exciting way to leave adolescence behind. And it *was* exciting, but also difficult, and sometimes heartbreaking. The year I lived in the Coal River Valley—as well as the several years afterward when I returned for parts of the summer—became a sort bildungsroman, a coming-of-age accompanied by all the requisite growing pains.

I don't remember many of the civil disobediences and protests from that year. The only action I recall in great detail is my own, although I was a core media team member and worked on most of the twenty-something actions that Climate Ground Zero supported in 2009 and 2010. I remember being surrounded by orange-striped mountaintop removal miners at a permit hearing at the Charleston Civic Center—they screamed "Where you from?" and "Get outta here tree hugger!" and I escaped by crouching down and sneaking between their feet—but I don't remember which mine site the hearing was about. And I often skipped rallies, opting to work on media for those events from afar instead.

What I recall best are details of my life in southern West Virginia, the things I saw and experienced on a day-to-day basis. How, in winter, snow and bare trees along the ridges made the hills look like line drawings, and in summer, a canopy of tulip trees, maples, oaks, and elms exploded across the mountains in dense, variegated greens. I remember eating hunted venison— rich and earthy, cooked into stroganoff, or sautéed up with garlic and onions—in fall, and sharp ramp onions in April. I recall, too, some of the practical knowledge I accrued: how to write a press release, the history of union organizing and strip mining, the proper way to make cowboy coffee (pour in two cups of cold water and tap the pot with a metal spoon to sink the grounds), and the proper way to pronounce *hollow* ("holler"). How, when I was interning for local nonprofit Coal River Mountain Watch, I once eavesdropped on its director, Judy Bonds, as she took a conference call. A spitfire, she presented her ideas to bigger environmental organizations based in Washington, DC, and California with a plucky, lyric drawl and unparalleled sense of resolve; they didn't think her particular plan was viable, and she didn't care. Sitting in an adjacent room, I stared at the list of phone numbers I was supposed to call for a fund-raising drive, too socially anxious to pick up the receiver and dial.

WREN AWRY

/

Bonds lived most of her life in Marfork Hollow—now just a ghost town on the road that leads to Alpha Natural Resources' mining complex on Coal River Mountain (Alpha took over Massey in 2011, after Massey ran into legal trouble following the Upper Big Branch disaster in which twenty-nine out of the thirty-one miners on-site were killed). She grew up fishing and swimming in the nearby creek, and raised her daughter in the hollow. When Massey started blasting apart ridges above Marfork, the air became thick with dust. Still, Bonds stayed. But then fish started floating belly-up in the creek, her grandson developed asthma, and Bonds found out about plans for the Brushy Fork impoundment—which replaced the Brushy Fork portion of the mountain with a 25,100-acre-feet lake of toxic mining by-product. It was time to move. Although Bonds relocated to a nearby town north of the impoundment, she didn't forget the catastrophe that she had experienced in Marfork Hollow. Her sorrowful anger transformed into a life of organizing against mountaintop removal, and she cofounded Coal River Mountain Watch in 1998.

Bonds slept with a shotgun next to her bed—organizing in southern West Virginia could be dangerous, especially for a local—and offered to teach me to shoot—an offer that I never took her up on. It was just one of the opportunities that I let slide by when I lived in the Coal River Valley. I was too caught up in my own anxiety and sense of isolation to put myself out there, to say yes, to develop the relationships that many of the out-of-state organizers I lived and worked with had so successfully built. Too awkward to be taught to drive an ATV through the mountains or read a topographic map, and missing the car and driver's license that would have given me a certain freedom of mobility, I filled my time by noticing and collecting—in my mind and worn spiral notebooks—the ephemera and ritual of our lives. I held onto the smallest moments of community and connection like they were rare fossils, dug out of a secret spot deep in the hills.

*

This is an essay about collective grief, and how that grief appears in the middle of resistance, or catalyzes into resistance, right? It could be about Larry Gibson's funeral, where hundreds of people packed the Charleston Municipal Auditorium to honor that late, great West Virginian, who turned his family's land into a trust to prevent it from being mountaintop removal mined—despite being offered millions of dollars by coal companies—and then toured the country proselytizing about the dangers of strip mining. Or about the March on Blair Mountain, during which three hundred people walked fifty miles through southern West Virginia over five days in remembrance of the 1921 Battle of Blair Mountain—the largest armed labor insurrection in US history—and protest of mining permits that threatened to eat up the mountain. Or about listening to the testimonies of Appalachians impacted by mountaintop removal at rallies and protests—testimonies that touched, inevitably, on things that had been lost. Yeah, I was there for Gibson's funeral, Blair, and many speeches and rallies, but others have written powerfully about such moments, and they're not the ones I return to again and again when I think about my time in West Virginia.

Rather, I viscerally recall ephemeral instances of grief, shared between fewer people. Those small moments of connection I held so dear. Like quietly driving down a rural state highway with another person, both of us staring out the window at the crumpled hills and small, half-shuttered towns, one of us breaking the silence to say "It's so beautiful" and receiving a wistful sigh in response. Or sitting at the kitchen table of a family that had us rough-and-tumble out-of-state organizers over multiple times a week for coffee, biscuits, and chili—never minding, it seemed, that we smelled, were covered in dirt, and had substandard table manners. While conversations were usually lighthearted, they sometimes veered into stories about our friends' late father, whose arms were badly scarred from working with chemicals in a coal-processing plant. After the Upper Big Branch disaster claimed those twenty-nine lives just up the road in April 2010, sometimes that tragedy came up for discussion, too; the family knew a few of the miners whose lives had been lost.

Collective grief meant not just holding hands in eulogistic prayer but also liking a Facebook status that quoted Mother

Jones's "Pray for the dead and fight like hell for the living," when yet another older West Virginian organizer had passed on prematurely from cancer or a heart condition. It meant singing around the campfire in the backyard of the organizing community I lived in—residents there ranged from eighteen to eighty-one—where we changed the words of songs to fit the current fight against mountaintop removal in southern West Virginia. We replaced "Muhlenberg County" with "Raleigh County" (our county) and "Mister Peabody" with "Mister Blankenship" (the conniving former CEO of Massey Energy) in John Prine's "Paradise," written about a community destroyed by strip mining in Kentucky. Singing wasn't necessarily a solemn event—it was usually accompanied by laughter and cans of cheap beer—but the songs themselves conjured loss and grief. And when we let the coals die down and went to bed, wood smoke stuck to our skin like myrrh.

These moments filled up the space between active resistance, between meetings, rallies, phone banking, and civil disobedience. They allowed me, at least, to process how difficult it was to live somewhere where blasts rang out from the mountaintops daily, where strip miners screamed at our houses and asked us hard questions we didn't have good answers to, where we knew West Virginians—young and old—suffering from gallbladder disease, asthma, and cancer. In an intensely focused organizing community where few conversations strayed away from environmental destruction in Appalachia, and working hours stretched from morning coffee to midnight, it was easy to feel more like an automaton than a human, and forget the emotional reasons why I was engaged in working to end strip mining. Time taken to grieve communally reminded me of the gravity of the situation, and of the lives, communities, and eco- systems that were being lost. It reminded me that the press re- leases I wrote, meals I made, and presentations I gave had tan- gible impacts—and that I should try my best to do my work with commitment and love.

*

While we weren't driven up Coal River Mountain that day in November 2009, we were driven down it. As I sat in the back of a police car, handcuffs scraping against my wrist bones, I felt filthy, exhausted, and badass. I'd participated in the direct action that had been, since I'd arrived in West Virginia, what I'd most been looking forward to—the culmination of several months of learning and listening. The short ride from the mine to the police station took us past Marfork Hollow, where Bonds once lived along a creek whose water was clean and whose fish were edible. I'd never seen Marfork before, and I studied its emptiness, trying to imagine the neatly kept double-wides that had once stood in the grass, the dogs who once ran up and down the road barking, the children who had once played tag by the creek.

There were a lot of things I didn't know that morning in

2009. I didn't know that less than a year later, Bonds would be diagnosed with a fast-acting brain cancer and would pass away in January 2011. Or that later that same day, in jail, my bravado would melt into social anxiety and I'd spend the forty-eight hours at Southern Regional hiding in my cell from my (friendly) fellow inmates under the pretense of reading a pulp Western about a female horse jockey. Or that when I moved away because life in a direct action campaign proved too difficult, I took the idea with me that you can't struggle against something without also leaving space for mourning—and that sometimes the most powerful acts of collective grief are quiet, unnamed, and ephemeral. Or that nearly seven years later and two thousand miles away, when I sat down to write this in Tucson, what I'd remember most about the action was the walk we took the night before—a hike through an enchanted forest, to the timbre of the nearby mine. What I recollect most are the bright punctuations of the stars, our soft footsteps on fallen leaves, the crisp autumn air that filled my lungs with sadness and awe.

*

Wren Awry lives and writes in Tucson. They're a contributor to and founding editor of Tiny Donkey, *a journal of fairy-tale nonfiction affiliated with* Fairy Tale Review. *Their work has been in* Rust + Moth, Essay Daily, Anarcho Geek Review, filmmakermagazine.com, *and elsewhere, and their zine* Baba Yaga Burns Paris to the Ground *was published by Strangers in a Tangled Wilderness in August 2015. Wren would like to ac-*

WREN AWRY

/

114

knowledge the amazing friends and organizers they have worked with during their time in West Virginia as well as John Washington, who read over and gave feedback on multiple drafts of this essay. If you're interested in the struggle to end mountaintop removal mining in Appalachia, Wren strongly encourages you to check out rampscampaign.org.

TO THE LIGHTS
THAT NEVER
WENT OUT

NATASHA TAMATE WEISS

For the places we have called home, and the people who loved them.
For Detroit, a city that never went away, and therefore cannot come back.

*

Long after we have gone from this place,
after the new stakes plunged into our ground and
the structures they call structurally sound
and the thievish look of gold in the streets
and the wiping clean of the mess that was the passion of our
    lives:

i thought i saw the smoke still rising
from the fire we made
the one we set alight to burn
every item we could not bring with us

in the garden
where winged insects had rippled against my body
and green shoots had sprang up overnight,
we set ablaze the evidence of our existence

not to destroy, never to destroy
but to return to the sky and earth

/

our ash that held so many meanings
swirling out the mouth of the young crater we created
a shrine, a tomb, a sorrow, a celebration.

Some fires are so mighty they stay awake
beneath the ground where the earth loves them
where nothing has a name but everything is known

and after many days of rain
thirsty monsoon drowning the basement mushrooms
washing machines bobbing like swans
someone swept out to sea and never found

i see the smoke rising
out of that circle of ash, where we seared our love into the
    ground—
you are not coming back; you never left
you never left,
did you.

*

*Natasha Tamate Weiss (DEFIANCE aka Little Riverbank) is a Shintofutur-
ist poet, taiko drummer, energy healer, sister, and filmmaker. Her people come
from the Abukuma River hamlets of Japan's Fukushima Prefecture and Ash-
kenazi Jewish communities. Born in the homeland of the Muwekma Ohlone*

people known as San Francisco, Natasha currently lives in Detroit, homeland of the Anishinaabe people, learning from lifelong Detroiters about land-based practices and intelligences, studying healing touch and Reiki, and writing her way back into her own bones.

TO THE LIGHTS THAT NEVER WENT OUT

/

RAGES OF FUKUSHIMA AND GRIEF IN A NO-FUTURE PRESENT

MARI MATSUMOTO,
INTERVIEWED,
TRANSLATED, AND
WITH A PROLOGUE
BY SABU KOHSO

In the history of nuclear disaster, Fukushima stands out in its singularity—a singularity that resists dissolution by the power and knowledge presently known to humans. It is ongoing, endlessly releasing radioactive nuclides across the entire planet. Fukushima announces the advent of the age of new catastrophe. Therein two kinds of disasters were intermixed: the earthquake/tsunami, and the nuclear explosion. On March 11, 2011, nature and civilization collapsed in the worst imaginable manner. The first catastrophe was tragic enough—with 15,894 deaths, 6,152 heavy injuries, and 2,561 missing persons (as of March 2016). Then came the radioactive contamination. It would be liable for the creeping development of illness, dying, and death among an increasing number of the populace, and for *xxx* number of years ahead. If it had been just the so-called natural disaster, it might have been possible for us to materialize a paradise built in hell or mutual aid society amid the zone of devastation, hand in hand with its natural resilience. But the second disaster instantaneously deprived us of all power to intervene in the radioactive terrain.

As the two interviews with Mari, a Japanese feminist, anticapitalist activist, and writer, attest to, this is a new challenge not only for antinuke discourses and movements but also anar-

/

chism or antiauthoritarian politics in a broad sense. When the first interview was recorded, June 12, 2011, three months after the disaster, an anarchic sensibility was dramatically in evidence among a large part of the populace, arising from the complexity of people's emotions: grief (over the losses), fear (of the coming devastation), panic (due to uninformed dread), rage (against nuclear capitalism and the state), and even joy (tied to the possibility of a regime change). In ensemble, this affective power created a wide range of grassroots organizing, from everyday struggles such as do-it-ourselves radiation monitoring and voluntary evacuation, to all sorts of antinuke actions, to legal disputes against Tokyo Electric Power Company (TEPCO) and the Japanese government. This collective impetus demonstrated that people's power and self-initiative could change society, but only for two years—until the Ōi nuclear plant was restarted (it went off-line again later), despite the mass direct action to blockade its operation, and because of the pronuclear and proarmament Abe administration of the Liberal Democratic Party that came into power.

In the second interview, which took place on July 1, 2016, Mari explains what happened to the affective climate during the time in between. Our discussion explores the fissures that opened up within the entire society. On the one hand, there was a radicalization of the collectively shared grief, panic, and rage, which in turn encouraged a number of projects aimed at protecting people's well-being against the government policy to na-

MARI MATSUMOTO AND SABU KOHSO

/

tionalize radioactive contamination. On the other hand, a massive obliviousness to the devastating situation settled in, allowing for the continuation of business as usual. It is this obliviousness that constitutes the main obstacle for the struggle to achieve what many expected: a strong movement that confronts the postnuclear disaster governance.

The complexity of the emotions, once collectivized in an ensemble, could be the strongest weapon for organizing this movement. But by the time of our second interview, they had been overshadowed by the nationalist empathy for the industrial and commercial reconstruction of Fukushima. The difficulty facing affective politics in terms of gathering a powerful force of resistance is largely due to the conformism that has long dominated Japanese society, wherein the nation is assumed to be a big family ruled by the emperor, to which family, township, municipality, and civil society are deemed subunits. In this familial society, national mourning has been an indispensable part of the state apparatuses, as exemplified by the Imperial Shrine of Yasukuni, dedicated to soldiers who've died in wars of aggression. Even the annual Hiroshima commemoration is not totally free from nationalism.

Yet Mari believes that post-Fukushima affective politics still sustain potency to decompose the nationalist production of empathy due to the magnitude of people's sufferings. In order to achieve that, however, the struggles must shift their perspective: from shortsighted political goals to aims related to the enduring quality of radiation contamination, whose temporality continues irregularly and astronomically, and whose spatiality expands into a complexity that any sort of causality cannot always grasp. It is necessary to commit ourselves to the persistent self-documentation of illness, dying, and death as part and parcel of processing the loss, grief, and resistance. Mari implies that there is yet the possibility of organizing a strong movement by way of sharing "a new history of feeling" (in the sense of Alexievich Svetlana) and precise information on the shifting course of this unending disaster.

JUNE 12, 2011: FEMINIST(IC) SELF-DOCUMENTATION OF LOSS

SABU: *Yesterday, June 11, was a global day of antinuke action, and there was a large demonstration in Tokyo, in which we participated. Can you talk about other types of actions besides street protests?*

MARI: First of all, keep in mind that I am not aware of all kinds of activities during the past three months. As of today, it has been three months since the nuclear accident, and right now we have a new series of actions among women that is less visible compared to protests in the street and around governmental buildings. We can say that this is a new movement of parents—largely mothers—who are committed to reproductive labor on

MARI MATSUMOTO AND SABU KOHSO

/

a day-to-day basis. Even here in Tokyo, 250 kilometers away from Fukushima, this kind of movement has begun.

During the past three months, we have come to realize that we can no longer rely on our government, which has totally neglected to take adequate safety measures for the people, and we can no longer trust the safety myths spread by the nuclear industry. So the parents who grew concerned about their environment for raising kids started exchanging information, organizing study groups to learn about radiation, and buying their own Geiger counters to monitor radioactivity in their neighborhood such as in parks, kindergartens, sandboxes, and so on. They are also negotiating with local schools to start monitoring the radioactivity of schoolyards and school lunches.

Learning from Chernobyl, it is certain that the effects of radioactivity are several times more harmful to children and youths than to adults. This is even a consensus among such institutions as the World Health Organizations. But the Japanese government managed to ignore it by setting up lax measures for children. Its decision was a horrifying one. In April, a grassroots organization took samples of breast milk from nursing mothers in Tokyo, and radioactive particles were detected in some of their milk—even from mothers in Tokyo! This group, based on its experience after the Chernobyl accident, immediately tested those mothers with the help of physicians. It called for various testings "in order to correctly understand the circumstances in which you and your children are put."

RAGES OF FUKUSHIMA AND GRIEF

/

SABU: *How did such movements start in the first place?*

MARI: To my surprise, these movements have grown from autonomous and grassroots activities. Both national and local governments have no appropriate measures to take; their priority is to cover up the effects of radiation on one's health. Therefore, previously unorganized parents and supporters began working together to investigate their living environment in detail. From the viewpoint of labor unions and protest movements, it seems to be difficult to understand this kind of grassroots movement engaging itself in reproduction, but the grassroots movements against industrial pollution and neighborhood associations formed in the 1970s helped to cultivate it. Also, it was aligned with the practices of the antinuke movements that flourished in the 1980s following Chernobyl. In fact, some activists from that era are working to support today's actions. In this sense we can call it a revival of the social, collective experience of the past. We are now witnessing the wisdom and collective memory operating together with the recent need and desire to know accurately the living conditions affected by the nuclear disaster.

I was impressed to see how the two factors are developing actual projects one after another. In Chiba Prefecture adjacent to Tokyo, several "hot spots"—areas randomly irradiated more highly than others—have been found. In the city of Kashiwa, parents have already collected more than ten thousand signatures to petition the city for a better safety measure. I assume that in every one of Tokyo's twenty-three wards, there must be at least a few grassroots groups to monitor neighborhood radioactivity. These groups, however, are still isolated from their neighbors and local communities, and even spoken ill of, as being "too worrisome," or "anxious" and "hysterical" about radiation—notwithstanding their indispensable contributions to revising the safety measures of the local communities by discovering hot spots in sandboxes and swimming pools. In addition, some nongovernmental organizations have started monitoring radioactivity in food with their sophisticated Geiger counters, which are too expensive and technically difficult for laypersons to handle. We have seen support groups arise to help pregnant women, children, and single mothers in affected areas; meetings and networks are being organized among evacuees from Fukushima and surrounding areas. If you visit any of these meetings, you get to hear in detail and be filled with various personal stories as to how the nuclear disaster affected their ways of living as well as how it changed their everyday routine.

SABU: *So it is that we are witnessing the way everyday struggles are arising with tremendous intensity and variety. How are they seen through the lens of feminist points of view?*

MARI: The antinuclear movement first rose up in Japan in the 1950s, then again from the late 1970s into the 1980s at the time of Chernobyl. During those periods, the main motivation for women to be involved in the antinuclear energy and armament movements was largely dependent on the standpoint of a mother. Thus the term *mother* was overrepresented in the scene. The kind of feminism that stressed the individual independence of women was highly critical of this tendency. In short, the criticism was that it might maintain and reinforce the division of labor by gender role and patriarchal authority, and by making a political claim from the vantage point of "as a mother" and "for our children."

Indeed, there is the historical fact that during the 1950s, a part of women's movements played a favorable role in the development of energy by the state, due to the vantage point of simplifying and modernizing housework. Certain organizations of mothers supporting the peaceful use of nuclear energy also appeared. If you look further back, there is the historical fact that organizations of "mothers" were led by and collaborated with the state. At the time of World War II, mothers were hailed as the "bearer of children—soldiers of the future." Women's liberationists sometimes endorsed the state policy and were incorporated into the war. Thus generally, feminism in Japan is cautious of women voicing their opinion and participating in politics from a mothers' standpoint.

Following the current nuclear accident, too, we have observed a similar kind of criticism by feminists. Many are doubtful of phrases such as "save children" that put emphasis on a mother's point of view. I think that this kind of criticism is missing the point, considering the particular circumstances after March 11, 2011. Because for one thing, the state and government in the meantime are plainly exposing children to danger, let alone *not* "saving" them from the disaster by giving them proper safety measures. Nor are they taking a protective measure for pregnant women in light of reproductive health. On top of that, the authorities are trying to take control over the data collected from children and pregnant women, in order to underrate the effects of radioactive contamination and maintain the nuclear industry. Basically, the nuclear industry and state of Japan, even after the Fukushima disaster, have not given up their intention to stay with nuclear energy and continue exporting the nuclear reactors overseas. For this purpose, they are desperately seeking to deny the fact that the lives of people in Tohoku and Kanto area are in danger. Accordingly, they have not had children and mothers evacuated but instead raised the maximum allowance of radioactive intake up to twenty milli-sieverts per year—twenty times higher than the international standard. They also continue to spread propaganda like "there are no immediate health effects" and "worrying about radiation is worse for your health." This is the situation where the patriarchal state, far from protecting children and mothers, has in actuality abandoned them, and is about to coax and tame them.

Following the experience of Chernobyl aftereffects, German feminists Maria Mies and Claudia V. Verhoff wrote a book called *Chernobyl Changed Our Lives: Why Women Have Had*

Enough. I noticed that in this book, the same phrases—"no immediate health effects" and "worrying about radiation is worse for your health"—have repeatedly appeared as propaganda used by the governments of Germany and other European countries to calm down people's anxiety over radiation. These are the precise words employed by the driving forces of nuclear power and as the manual of social control after nuclear disaster. Therefore, demands such as "save children" and "give priority to evacuation for pregnant women" are gradually becoming a means of protesting against the state and nuclear industry, especially in the circumstance inverted by negation.

SABU: *If we regard the ideological and historical context too highly, it is hard for us to grasp what is in front of us. Theorists tend to do this from time to time.*

MARI: That's probably true. During the last twenty years that I have been involved in feminism, I have never seen such a significant number of parents, mothers to be precise, actively mobilizing themselves. Women and mothers are standing up without theory or even feminism. In Japanese society, however, the term *mothers* tends to be implied only as love of and emotional connection to children. Media is eager to depict "desperate mothers fighting to protect their children" with a sense of ridicule. But the point I would like to emphasize is that "parents" are reproductive laborers for raising their children and domestic works.

Since the nuclear accident, people have been spending enormous amounts of time on reproductive labor and related obligations. As an easy example, you don't want your children to drink tap water because it might be contaminated with radiation, so you would have to go and buy two or three bottles of water per day, each of which costs you about three hundred yen. This is about the necessary amount in a household with one child. It probably weighs four to five kilos; to carry this would be tough labor. If you want to feed your family with safe food, you'd need to spend a lot of time finding and choosing ingredients. I think this is an issue of "labor" enforced on people by the nuclear state. Yet I still see some feminists just repeating their theoretical claims by ignoring the subtle yet significant changes in reproductive life taking place on a daily basis. I must ask, Whom are the feminists trying to help, and with whom are they seeking to connect?

SABU: *In the context of a parents' movement, can you speak about the siege of the Ministry of Education on May 23?*

MARI: Many people assembled at the Ministry of Education, Culture, Sports, Science, and Technology in central Tokyo, demanding withdrawal of the "maximum allowance of twenty milli-sieverts per year for children." Among them were Fuku-shima parents, who attempted a direct action by presenting their demand to the minister in person, but he would not meet with them, and the withdrawal of the "twenty milli-sieverts" did not take place that day. The people from Fukushima certainly left a strong impression by having made a trip all the way to Tokyo, however. Thereafter, the ministry, even though passively, began considering the cleaning of contaminated areas and revised the maximum allowance of radiation dosage. We saw progress. And gradually no longer just parents but many supporters started showing up. Fukushima residents and children have since been directly expressing their demands and negotiating with government officials. So the government has no other choice but to hear Fukushima's voice in a formal manner. I think there has been a bit of change in power dynamics since the May 23 siege. This all goes back to the initiative of the people—parents, children of Fukushima, and nongovernmental organization supporters—who stood up amid the severe living situation. A little sad thing is that we didn't see many from younger activist circles in the Tokyo metropolis joining this action. In addition, there seems to be a separation between the movement of the people struggling around reproduction issues, the one mentioned earlier, and demos and protests in the street.

SABU: *Why so?*

MARI MATSUMOTO AND SABU KOHSO

/

MARI: You can't blame anybody for not being able to get involved in all kinds of actions at a time. But one reason, if any, might be that the tasks we have to tackle have expanded so widely that the traditional sense of social movement can no longer embrace them all, as if parallel to the expansion of radiation. In fact, even if you politically appeal for "antinuke" and "de-nuke," you aren't necessarily concerned with or interested in such micro issues as those concerning medical care, body, food contamination, or children's right to live. This is a little unfortunate, though, because these issues are directly related to your own body. The radioactive contamination after Fukushima nuclear accident will continue for decades, and will expand more widely. So you will have to have a wider scope for your action.

Tokyo is a city that wants to cling to the myth of "safety" as it tries to maintain the function of capital, keep the economy alive, and continue holding onto real estate values. It is, as it were, the stronghold of the nuclear safety myth. Neither the government nor the residents would want to acknowledge the radioactive contamination too easily. In addition, we will need a spatiotemporal imagination in order to envision how we are going to live in the post–nuclear disaster climate. To do so, we will need a different position and different thinking from the activisms centered on street demos and protests in a traditional sense—those that act in a shorter span of time. Hereafter the

RAGES OF FUKUSHIMA AND GRIEF

/

people will have to live with radiation for decades to come. Even if Japan decides to phase out nuclear energy or shut all nuclear reactors, the effects of the accident will persist and stay with us a great deal, for a long time. We cannot seal it off as if it had never happened. How do we live with the "rupture" of time and space that was brought up by this event?

Although neither Tohoku nor Tokyo would happily admit, we will most likely have to live "together with radiation." Under such circumstances, we will have to consider how we are going to create resistance from within the aspects of life's necessities: food, clothing, shelter, living space, cohabitation space, and our own bodies. Three months have passed since the accident. We seem to be at a turning point now, and our tasks will keep changing in half a year, one year, and five years from now.

SABU: *With that in mind, do you have any model movements in terms of forms of practice and engagement?*

MARI: Personally I was inspired by some of the AIDS activism like ACT-UP in the early 1990s. Of course, we need to be careful not to mix up the effects of radiation and HIV virus, but I think we can find important hints in ACT-UP! While being two different substances, virus and radiation are both the cause of danger that gets enclosed within a society. Under such circumstances, members of society would strongly oppose discrimination against people in high-risk groups, but at the same time, try their best to distance themselves from, say, the HIV virus itself. We must prove in practice that there is no contradiction in stating "we accept that we have to live with radiation scattered after the March 11 accident" and "we have to keep ourselves as far away as possible from the radiation."

We also need to create layers of thought and speak out. In order for us to do so, the total disclosure of medical and health care information and knowledge is crucial. The effects of radioactive contamination will bring various changes to human bodies, not limited to Fukushima but in surrounding areas, too, in different degrees. Hence by acknowledging the radioactive effects to their own bodies, adults are going to need to use this knowledge, especially, to protect children who have the most risks in the future. AIDS activism has a thorough resistance against health care authorities and pharmaceutical companies, which is exemplary for us.

Lastly, I would like to stress that no matter how many fissures we create among ourselves, we must not forget that the entire responsibility for and cause of this disaster falls to the nuclear industry and TEPCO. This short period since March has only been the tiny part of a preface to a long, long beginning "after" the Fukushima disaster. Looking at the results of Chernobyl, changes in people's and children's health conditions will became more prominent in five-, ten-, and twenty-year sequences after the accident. A single event of the nuclear accident has made huge changes in the environmental conditions—in soil, air, ocean, and food. Plus, tens of thousands of people have had to move out of their homes whether forcibly or voluntarily because of the effects of the nuclear disaster. What effects are we to expect on the horizon of human lives, and how do we resist them, and how do women put their creativity into practice in the reproductive territory? While the public deems women's resistance "hysterical" and "oversensitive," I would like to *not* cast away any anxiety and dilemmas that women are experiencing in the field of reproduction.

JULY 1, 2016: MOURNING
IN THE APOCALYPSE

SABU: *It has been five years since the disaster. And this is our second interview. How has the situation changed?*

MARI: It has taken five years for the public to know how criminal the responses of the government have been. In part this has to do with the temporality of the nuclear disaster, which necessitates time for the victims and evacuees to settle in and reflect on their situations. Around 2013, the nuclear disaster was finally acknowledged as a "man-made disaster" by the government.

MARI MATSUMOTO AND SABU KOHSO

/

Meanwhile, thanks to journalists' tireless investigations, the fact was clarified that TEPCO had totally neglected measures to protect against the effects of a tsunami for over ten to twelve years.

After the earthquake, a tsunami with a fifteen-meter wave hit the reactors. TEPCO was not unaware of such a possibility. It repeatedly ignored warnings by specialists. In fact, up until four days before the accident, the discussion concerning the need to take measures had gone back and forth between TEPCO and government agencies. The international code for nuclear policy states that it must be prepared for even a situation that may arise once in ten thousand years. TEPCO not only ignored it but also made special efforts to do away with it. Even after the accident, the government has subtly covered up the evasion. All in all, the people realize they have been consistently tricked and deceived by the authorities. It was some independent bloggers, journalists, lawyers, and reporters who strived to reveal all this. With the retrospective revelations, the victims were naturally infuriated. In this sense, the five years have been spent preparing evidence for lawsuits—forty-some cases with over ten thousand plaintiffs. So criminal actions, too, will follow. Although the legal fight has its limitations, this development requires attention.

SABU: *What is the situation of the evacuees' movement?*

RAGES OF FUKUSHIMA AND GRIEF

/

MARI: In October 2015, the voluntary evacuees, who are scattered across the country, got together and established the Association of Voluntary Evacuees (Jishu-hinansha-no-kai). It is as if those who had scattered in diaspora met again in a new platform. The core group consists of voluntary evacuees from across Fukushima Prefecture—namely, those who are from outside the designated evacuation zone. At the same time, however, the members include the forced evacuees from the designated evacuation zone, and voluntary evacuees from Tokyo and other neighboring prefectures; the point is not to privilege Fukushima natives only.

What is the significance of this? The categorizations of forced evacuees and voluntary evacuees as well as those from Fukushima and otherwise are the divisions set by the government—not by the people who suffer from the disaster and intend to protect their well-being. Therefore, they intend to unite as "one and the same refugees," and seek to connect themselves even with those who remain in Fukushima.

SABU: *All in all, the government has done nothing for the disaster victims, or has even harmed them.*

MARI: In the first place, the government refuses to count the number of—if I may use this term—the refugees. It has to do with its intention not to define who are the refugees. The problem is that the category of those who are desperately migrating in fact and the legal category of refugees are not in synchronicity. This is because the Japanese government, if it grasped the actual number, would not be able to deal with the enormity, unless it gave up "business as usual." Therefore, it would rather underestimate the number by refusing to accept the reality. By paying attention only to the forced evacuees, it chooses to ignore the voluntary evacuees from Fukushima, not to mention those from Tokyo, and even treats them like "illegal immigrants."

SABU: *Meanwhile, radiation-related illnesses have been increasing, haven't they?*

MARI: Yes. Children's thyroid cancer has evidently increased. Even the government acknowledges it, although adding a strange proviso that more cases may be discovered because of its obsession to nitpick. But we all know that at some point in the future, the government will be forced to admit the reality. So far, it has looked into the situation only in Fukushima, but not in adjoining prefectures. So the people have been investigating the cases by themselves; for instance, in Kashiwa City in Chiba Prefecture, there are as many as 173 cases. In addition, leukemia among the nuclear workers has drastically increased. As someone has said, radiation is an ideal poison, because of the difficulty of proving causality in the court.

RAGES OF FUKUSHIMA AND GRIEF

/

SABU: *My friends and I, both in and outside Japan, imagined that a radical change would come inevitably. But in five years, the situation is going in the opposite direction, toward the reinforcement of pronuclear and pro-rearmament nationalism. And yet the disaster continues—since March 11, the majority of people have become disaster victims in different ways and degrees. Not only in Fukushima but also Tokyo, an unprecedented number of residents have been and will be affected by radiation. The fact is made more and more invisible, however, buried in the psychological inattention. What do you think is creating this situation?*

MARI: There are many factors on both personal and social levels. Those who live with dangerous contamination don't want to think about, admit, and confront the fact, though they know it in their subconscious, because acknowledging it would force them to join along with a radical change in all existential dimensions. Reinforcing the denial is the sense of equilibrium that has been socially shared in the postwar period. Among many things that have been said vis-à-vis catastrophe in the contemporary history of disaster, the most dreadful aspect of this particular experience is the revelation that the seeds of the catastrophe had been embedded in the midst of the everyday life of the highly consumerist society; the possibilities of planetary catastrophe have been so deeply internalized in the high-consumerist and controlled society called Japan. And

MARI MATSUMOTO AND SABU KOHSO

/

to say it in reverse, even a catastrophe of this magnitude is quickly absorbed into the everyday process of social reproduction.

SABU: *When I visit Japan, walk around the city, and watch television, I am shocked by the normalness of consumer life as well as the images of joy in embracing it—of food, technology, culture, and tourism—coexisting with the radioactive contamination. That is to say, tragedy certainly coexists in various respects. What are the status as well as features of people's emotional responses—say, rage, sorrow, dread, anxiety, and so on?*

MARI: One thing I can say is this: there are certainly physical losses, such as health, home, family, subsistence, and so forth, but public discourses often emphasize the "loss of home" or "deprived community"—namely, the loss of what cannot be reduced to a monetary value. All in all, these expressions are saying that invisible things that are indispensable for constituting individuals—a place to live and act, mutual relations, and the ways and means of life—are largely destroyed.

What can one do when this happens? There are no formulas to deal with such situations. So people must continue to record what happens, how the situations changes, and how they feel about it. For instance, it took twenty-some years for Michiko Ishimure to begin writing her magnum opus *Paradise in the Sea of Sorrow*, after her engagement in the Minamata mercury poisoning. The power of the novel, involving real enunciations and events of the victims along with their movement, exists in her persistent documentation and memorization of the everyday of endless purgatory for oceanic lives, animals, children, farmers, fishers, and so on. Only by this strategy of persisting in the unbearable temporality, even the events of absurdity that refuse interpretation can spark resistance from time to time. The Fukushima nuclear disaster, too, is very much an event of temporality and feeling. And our strategy to confront it must be based on collective, persistent recording and memorializing.

In the entirety of social apparatuses, forces are in full gear to make us forget about and nullify all the events around the accident. The coming Tokyo Olympics 2020 is the symbolic machine for a nationwide obliviousness, but in the larger picture, the civilian use of nuclear power has always involved such effects, from the outset. Nuclear accidents and the resulting illnesses involve a time lag that does not follow clean-cut regularity, from which oblivion effects are made to develop.

The nuclear disaster doesn't have an end, and therefore healing by mourning is out of the question at this point. What unites us is rage, which is the basic weapon to organize ourselves in order to fight against the nuclear capitalism and state. But in the five years after, rage seems to have been replaced by counterparts—apathy and resignation—leading to a passive onlook-

MARI MATSUMOTO AND SABU KOHSO

/

ers rather than engagement. Mourning is solidly shared among the earthquake and tsunami victims, who have physically lost homes, families, and means of subsistence. Still, in this case where the nuclear disaster immediately followed, another spatiotemporal dimension that is unthinkable for us was imposed, spreading like a social cancer and depriving us of any cathartic solution. In the second dimension, mourning is bracketed, because the effects of radioactive pollution are hard to prove as causality. We need time—until an undeniable number of clinical cases appear, probably after ten, fifteen, or twenty years, and nobody can then deny the effects as data—or the cathartic phase, which involves a full and massive attack against the nuclear regime, won't come.

At this moment, the cancer patients along with their families focus more on cure than political action—that which can be organized based on a solid causal recognition. For that matter, the victims of Hiroshima/Nagasaki are still fighting for recognition even today, seventy-some years after the bombs. They are still suspended in devastation. All in all, for the struggles against nuclear power, the crux is how we manage to confront the unbearably long temporality, based on observations and recordings of the situational and sensual mutation. Therefore, at this moment in the struggle against radioactive pollution, sorrow and mourning seem to be futile.

SABU: *What are you going to do from now on?*

RAGES OF FUKUSHIMA AND GRIEF

/

MARI: There are many things to be done. But I believe the basis for all projects is to patiently observe what is going on and listen to people's voices. It seems to me that what is lacking is the will to see through the event: what it involves, where it leads, what are the effects to whom and what.... Generally speaking, perspectives of the social and political movements are too shortsighted.

After Fukushima, we saw a dramatic upsurge of the antinuke movement for two years. But after the Ōi nuclear plant was restarted in spite of the mass direct action to blockade it, the movement quickly stagnated. The ultraconservative Abe administration came into power, realizing the reform of the US-Japan security treaty toward Japan's militarization. Thereafter it has been doing almost whatever it wants to do. No protest movements and no progressive politics have been able to stop it. Its policies are centered on a kind of shock doctrine and the politics of spectacle that constantly shift its ostensible focus in order to fade from our attention. In order to fight against this, we should not just respond to its move but also construct multilayered strategies based on the nonspectacle developments of events—such as the increasing number of people getting sick or refugees having lives like fugitives—that are invisible in the media and incalculable in statistics.

Even before Fukushima, nuclear problems were always made to be obscure, as exemplified in the issues of nuclear workers and radioactive contamination. As analyzed in the inspiring book by Olga Kuchinskaya, *The Politics of Invisibility*, in the political situation after Chernobyl, nuclear politics is based on invisibility instead of open debate on scientific truth. In Japan, various safety standards have been set and reset after Fukushima, which have nothing to do with scientific consideration, but are pure political decisions tacitly for the benefit of nuclear industries.

SABU: *How would you describe the situation people face in Japan after Fukushima?*

MARI: A phrase from the book *Voices from Chernobyl* by Alexievich Svetlana speaks to it well:

> Something occurred for which we do not yet have a conceptualization, or analogies or experience, something to which our vision and hearing, even our vocabulary, is not adapted. Our entire inner instrument is tuned to see, hear or touch. But none of that is possible. In order to comprehend this, humanity must go outside its own limits.
> A new history of feeling has begun.

Ungraspability or spatiotemporal indeterminacy exists at the core of nuclear accidents and radioactive contamination. Radioactivity, which is invisible, omnipresent, and everlasting, has come to determine our future. In my adolescence, the so-called no-future thing was in fashion, yet it has now become reality. After Hiroshima/Nagasaki, during Japan's postwar period, an obsession with apocalyptic imagery—such as in *Godzilla*, *Japan Sinks*, and *Akira*—flourished in mass representation. But I think that in order to confront the post–Fukushima disaster situation, we need a much longer view: a planetary history. In this sense, I am interested in the recent debates on the Anthropocene.

Political discourses circulating around today's Japan, including those of the sociopolitical movements, even feminism and anarchism, avoid dealing with the crux of the event. I would see an ultimate potency for emancipation—if not healing—not in these discourses but instead in the rumors and panics—the fundamental power to awe—deriving from people's dread and rage. This is to initiate our thoughts about what is really troubling or unsound. This is the only basis for resisting the status quo, which is constantly seeking to absorb the endlessly expanding accident. As Yu-Fu Tuan stresses in his *Landscape of Fear*, a community that has lost the power to fear will perish.

Meanwhile, as evident with the so-called anarchists in today's Japan, claiming to be an anarchist and confronting a life in anarchy are two different things. Those who grasp people's autonomous actions after the disaster as anarchy and go along with them anarchistically are limited. According to my observation, I can see anarchist practice in those who have been actively engaged in people's autonomous projects to deal with irradiation rather than those who have organized a large-frame antinuke movement.

I myself am a feminist, but when I see those who take care of the health of their families or more straightforwardly "mothers" struggling so radically, I feel embarrassed to think in the name of feminism. Those people who live the anarchic situation don't know the isms such as anarchism, Marxism, and feminism.

There is one good example in Japan of someone who was most consciously engaged in an anarchic situation anarchistically: the anarchist activist and poet Ko Mukai (1920–2003). He organized anti–nuclear power actions from within everyday life, with the group called Fubarai-ren (Coalition for Nonpayment), which sought to take back the initiative of electricity users to choose the amount and kind of electricity by refusing to pay the bill using various tactics. He said that by choosing the issue of nuclear power, he was able to talk to everyone; by scrutinizing nuclear power, his life became inexorably anarchic, since the network of life, consisting of electricity bills, energy, food, urban infrastructure, and so on, is thoroughly objectified as the moment of struggle. Around 1986, after Chernobyl, an antinuke movement arose in Japan, and it organized a series of mass direct actions with performative interventions in urban space; the conventional anarchists bashed the movement as a deviation.

RAGES OF FUKUSHIMA AND GRIEF

/

Mukai was one of the organizers. Without nitpicking the political ideology of the movement, he embraced the anarchic situation in order to fully accelerate it. In today's situation, Mukai's practice must be a good point of reference.

SABU: *With Mukai in mind, can you speak a bit more about the popular radiation-monitoring movements, such as around food?*

MARI: Now that the contaminated areas are identified, the most effective means of protection is to purchase food according to its productive origin. Most of us buy rice, vegetables, and so on, from Kyushu and other western parts. We also choose grocery chains that are selective.

An important point is that the consciousness about food has been made to change by the contamination and development of protective measures. One thing is that some of us have stopped spending as much money as before, and that's due to the development and sophistication of selective consciousness as well as the sense of satiation—enough is enough—about the consumerist society itself. The so-called high culture such as gourmet food and fashion come to appear as vanity, nothing but part of the same system. After Fukushima, many people have thrown away a lot of their belongings—a new phenomenon. This is less moral judgment than refusal, with the awareness that the desire produced in the consumerist society has become an obstacle for us to confront the event.

MARI MATSUMOTO AND SABU KOHSO

/

In a similar sense, even the conventional protest with a general antinuke slogan has become an obstacle; it is mostly organized as an alibi for big social movements that they are doing something, without concrete prospects for achieving anything other than supporting election campaigns for liberal or progressive politicians. What is crucial for us is to create ways to confront this event.

First of all, we have to recognize the fact that Fukushima is close to Tokyo. Tokyo is closer to Fukushima than it is to Nagoya in the west. It is shocking. Perceiving this nearness, the residents of Tokyo have to accept the deadly situation in which they live. In front of them, though, is this ordinary and peaceful everyday landscape, which incapacitates us from keeping and polishing the critical sense. We have learned the sheer fact that the status quo can nullify the event as long as the urban function appears to be working normally.

Fisheries in Fukushima have restarted operations. The marine products that have passed the lax standards of radiation monitoring are being sold in the market. At one point, they were fishing mainly to measure radioactivity, but now they are fishing exclusively for selling. If they don't continue operations, they won't get compensation for the damage. When TEPCO announced it would release contaminated water from the reactors to the ocean, the fishers' union strongly objected at first. But it has finally accepted it, because of security money.

Here exists one of the most crucial issues: the problem of

radio-contaminated water is seen only in terms of fishing rights. This is the way nuclear capitalism and state see the ocean itself. The ocean is a vast domain that is the source of all living beings and affects the entire ecosystem, which involves all sorts of concerns. But the modus operandi of the government is to reduce it to the issue of fishing rights that are directly convertible to profit. This is also the way to make the locals—of Fukushima and even Japan—silent on the serious damage to the entire planet.

Another shocking turn of events is that the government (the Ministry of the Environment) has determined to use the radioactive soil, which has been overaccumulating from decontamination work, for public enterprises such as building materials and road construction. Before the Fukushima disaster, the regulated level of radiation for such use used to be less than a hundred becquerels, but it has now been raised to lower than eight thousand becquerels. This desperate measure of the government will spread radiation across Japan. This tells us of the advent of a new age of apocalyptic infrastructure.

SABU: *In your first interview, you spoke of the "movement of mothers." What does that stand for now, after five years?*

MARI: All in all, this means "care workers" or "reproductive workers." But now I could point to the increasing population of people who get ill as well as who takes care of them. To say it more broadly, those who live an existentiality that is different from capitalist productivity; those who live their own sociality autonomously; those who live by expanding the realm of autonomy; those who disregard conventional divisions of political ideologies—these modes of existence are increasingly crucial at this juncture. What is at stake is whether to become part of this impetus and accelerate it, or just interpret and correct this impetus according to isms.

The practice of these modes of existence is voluntary—namely, self-paid, or that is to say, they take charge of all the debt, derivative of the nuclear disaster and imposed by the patriarchal society. Precisely in this sense, nuclear workers and mothers are in the same position. This is why these two modes of existence are important. Right after the disaster, the main discursive tendency quickly divided them: the former being the most oppressed form of labor, and the latter being part of the habitude of the petit bourgeois middle class. I believe that this way of thinking is futile. These two are the form of existence that has been supporting capitalist production, while being excluded from it. They are the people who are exploited, in layers, by sovereign power, productive system, and within the family; they are paying off the debt of the entire society, in the invisible structure of exploitation.

SABU: *I see that in the exploitation of these existences, there exists the political core of the Fukushima dilemma. If so, it is necessary to dis-*

RAGES OF FUKUSHIMA AND GRIEF

/

cover the moment in which to transversally connect these modes and practices of existence. Would that be possible? As you emphasize, is patiently recording and observing radiation and illnesses—or a certain strategy of information and collective intelligence—helpful for that?

MARI: That has to be done, but we don't know how to do that precisely yet. But the problem is that the discursive realm on the Fukushima disaster, including journalism, media, and academia, has proven futile in terms of dealing with the situation that internalizes the invisible exploitation of these existences. It is a sine qua non to break out of the form of conventional method and thought in order to tackle the problematic, and then share the results widely. This incapacity has revealed the institutional limit of discourses. People point out the power of what's commonly called the "nuclear village," the network of pronuclear authorities, stretching out in the central and local governments, bureaucracy, companies, industries, academia, and media, which constantly discredits and incapacitates the spreading and exchanges of critical information. But according to my observation, a village-like network where all anomalies are immediately silenced or ejected entraps all realms of political and intellectual practice in Japan, even before the conspiratorial operations of the nuclear village

I value works of some independent bloggers, researchers, and journalists who dedicate themselves to analyzing what is happening. But I feel the need of more collaborative efforts to-

MARI MATSUMOTO AND SABU KOHSO

/

ward building a collective intelligence and information-sharing network to fight against the pronuclear status quo. It is necessary to analyze the present situation, involving the incapacitated sociopolitical movements and complexity of sovereign power. We need, to repeat, patient observation and sharp analysis. If we can share them, we can rise up for rebellion, together with nuclear workers and care workers. Trusting the potency of the people and sharing information/analysis would be the best means of organizing. It goes without saying that demonstrating and campaigning for election are far from enough. What's necessary is less about stronger protests than a rebellion on wider, existential dimensions.

For one to two years after 3/11, the majority experienced the state of anarchy with fissures running across the social space and everyday life. People were enraged, feeling ferocious, with a desperate need to exert justice. The defeat of the movement was due to the organizers who could not tolerate the state of anarchy beyond their control. They could not deal with people's power to live, grudge, rage, and panic. They sought to direct the mass impetus toward a well-mannered organization, a civil institution, with enlightened attitudes on politics and science. This was responsible for the stagnation today.

Now it is evident that the waste from the melted core of the Fukushima Daiichi reactors cannot be removed. This has long been known, but now it is being revealed bit by bit by the authority. But the people don't seem to be infuriated any longer.

RAGES OF FUKUSHIMA AND GRIEF

/

"Oh, we had known it"—this sense of *dèja connu* seems to prevail among the public. This is the scariest thing. This is precisely the extension of the mechanism inherent in nuclear power that Günther Anders (1902–92), a German philosopher and antinuke activist, pointed out in terms of "apocalyptic blindness" (*Apocalypse-Blindheit*). So it is necessary for us to be shocked, to fear anew. My hope is then to be enraged together— more than ever.

*

Mari Matsumoto is an activist and writer based in Tokyo. Since the early 1990s, she has been active in the antiauthoritarian sector of feminism, anti-globalization organizing, and anarchism, while writing articles on women's roles and issues in social movements. After March 11, 2011, she organized the group No Nukes, More Feminism, and her writing appears on its website at nuclearfeminisms.wordpress.com. Recently, Mari has been affected by frequent outbreaks of cancer among her close friends, especially her own partner. She plans to instigate a mutual aid group of the victims of the Fukushima nuclear disaster, including younger cancer patients, living in Tokyo.

Sabu Kohso is an activist, writer, and translator based in New York City. His work is focused on anarchist thought, the formation of urban space, and the postwar politics of nuclear disaster in Japan. He has published three books in Japanese on these topics. Sabu has translated books by Kojin Karatani and Arata Isozaki into English from Japanese, and David Graeber and John Holloway into Japanese from English. He is the cofounder of the platform Japan—Fissures in the Planetary Apparatus, which promotes global ex-

change between thinkers, artists, and activists to address issues arising in the aftermath of Fukushima. Sabu is a frequent contributor to various journals and platforms, including through europe, e-flux, borderlands, and boundary 2. He is currently working on a book, Radiation and Revolution, to be published in the series Thought in the Act edited by Brian Massumi and Erin Manning.

CRACKS IN
MY UNIVERSE

A. J. WITHERS

2005

I got my friends back the day I was diagnosed with cancer.

I had spent three years getting increasingly sick, and as I was less and less able to do organizing work and go out of my house, I became increasingly isolated. I watched people try to stay in my life. I watched people slowly fade out of my life until there was just me and the three closest people, ... and then two. Every day, I grieved for those friends I lost to the crack in my universe.

It all happened slowly, over a few years. I had already identified as disabled, so for a long time, people just thought my chronic pain was getting worse. I got so tired, and then I got even more tired. Slowly I stopped being able to sit up a lot of the time because it was too painful. Then I stopped eating (or nearly). I had a constant, grinding pain in my abdomen that penetrated every action I engaged in and every thought that I had. Then the nausea came. It came in waves of hours to days, and sometimes it felt like it subsumed my entire existence. When it was really bad, I would have to sleep on the floor because the motion of my own breathing caused the bed to feel intolerable. I began taking opiates to handle the pain. They were helpful but

/

left me more out of touch with the world around me. The pills also gave me short-term amnesia and other cognitive problems. As the life I knew faded away, I became increasingly sad about it. Sometimes, when the pain and nausea weren't debilitating, my sorrow stopped me instead. In between the bad days, there were good ones. Yet as time went on, there were fewer and fewer, until there were none.

All of my doctors and many of my friends treated me like everything was in my head. Even after a surgeon told my doctor I needed surgery—two weeks before I found out it was cancer—my doctor told me it was psychosomatic.

I was a queer, gender-nonconforming youth on social assistance. The public health system didn't give a fuck about me. My doctors routinely treated me like I was a drug-seeking malingerer and/or crazy. My friends, for the most part, didn't know what to do with me: I had less and less to talk about, I was boring because I was isolated, and was almost always incredibly high. Like me, my friends were all organizers so we didn't have much to talk about when I wasn't going to meetings and was becoming increasingly out of touch with what was going on. Most of us had so little balance in our lives that there was just nothing else to chat about. And what did I have to contribute to conversation, having only watched *Buffy* that day and the day before?

I began reading, when I could, about disability history and theory. There was almost nothing available about disability politics so I tried to do research to help contribute to the ways my radical community understood disability and disablism. This was as much a selfish pursuit designed to prove my worth to my vanishing universe as it was about broader social justice work. It backfired. On a tearful phone call to my friend Loree, I said, "I'm not even a useless eater because I can't even eat." I was referencing the Nazi propaganda line calling disabled people "useless eaters." She firmly told me that I needed to stop reading about eugenics for a while.

Loree couldn't visit me in my house because it wasn't wheelchair accessible. I couldn't really go out. So we had a long-distance relationship in the same city. Sometimes she would travel across Toronto (taking 1.5 hours, much longer than most because of inaccessible transit) to visit me, sometimes with groceries. So many wouldn't make the twenty- or thirty-minute trip to see me, but she understood disablism, internalized eugenics and isolation, and the importance of mutual support.

So most of my friends—my community—disappeared. In some ways, I don't fault them. I was a hard person to love in those days. I was incredibly angry and deeply traumatized from having been a teenaged runaway. I was angry at disablism, at patriarchy and its cousins, cissism and heterosexism, and at capitalism and the social assistance system. That anger was legitimate. At the same time, my anger didn't have an impact on those oppressive systems—just on me, and the people around me who I took it out on. So for a lot of people, I think, it was an easy exit to just let me fade away.

CRACKS IN MY UNIVERSE

/

It wasn't easy for me, though. At first, when people started leaving, I was so angry at those individuals; then I was just angry. Because my isolation happened so slowly, I had almost normalized it. I didn't really process the individual losses of my friends or the loss of what I thought was my community. Rather than feel that sadness, rather than grieve, I became harder and more jaded.

2002-3

A few years prior to this, my friends and I had set up a care collective to help me meet my basic needs. It was born out of another serious illness, again with inadequate and incompetent medical care, during which I needed round-the-clock observation because I stopped breathing from time to time. It was scary. As I recovered, my need for help (which I will call "care shifts" from here on out) decreased, and things became slightly more organized, with me coordinating shifts as needed.

It can be hard to organize your own care. It took a lot of e-mails and phone calls, coordinating and delegating. Also, when you aren't going to eat until someone shows up, it is a big deal when they don't. For me, the material impact was not as significant as the emotional one. When someone would come late or not at all, I would feel deeply sad and rejected. But because it was me, and it was back then, it would emerge out of me as rage.

A. J. WITHERS

/

This rage protected me from feeling my grief for my disappointment in much more than those individuals—in how far we are from and inept at creating anything like the world we want to be living in. It also meant that I couldn't engage with or process it. And when you are asking people if they will take on a shift to help you, most of the time people say "no." Even if those responses are the most reasonable, legitimate, and sincere in the world, they still hurt. Eventually I learned to have a coordinator as a buffer—to ask people and hear the "no" for me, and only tell me the "yes" replies and talk to people on my behalf about problems that arose.

This is not to erase the care that I did get—the care that sustained me. That care included pushing me up the stairs so I could go to the bathroom when I couldn't make it up on my own, making me food, doing emotional support, getting groceries, doing laundry, getting me out of the house to go to the corner store, and holding my hand for doctors' appointments, hospital visits, and hard moments. There was so much love in those acts, which doesn't negate that it was work, too. Care work, paid or unpaid, can be rewarding. It can also be exhausting and trying, and sometimes those things all at once.

I also don't want to reinforce the binary of the helper and helped. Disabled people do a tremendous amount of care work, which is often rendered invisible. Most of the care I give and get is informal. While I have a care collective sometimes, I have been in such groups supporting others as well. In my care shifts,

CRACKS IN MY UNIVERSE

/

I am also giving, whether it is through conversation, advice, legal information, television suggestions, or just the intimacy of care itself. And we teach each other about the practical, tedious, and tender parts of love.

Then, too, I don't want to erase the fact that some, or maybe most, of those people who vanished were doing a lot of care work elsewhere, and/or had their own health issues and crises. It is largely for this reason that I don't assign individual blame to people (at least for the most part) because this was a collective failure. My intent in telling this story certainly isn't for those who were around to feel bad. Rather, it is to lay bare my broken heart in the hope that more hearts won't break.

And while I felt entirely abandoned by everyone but my two closest friends at one point, things ebbed and flowed in my life. When I broke up with my partner, I got new roommates as well as new neighbors, and they helped me in the ways they could.

At one point, around 2003, thirty of us came together to set up a bigger care collective with more people, and one that could support people who only needed help once in a while or just needed to know that it was available. We even did a training day on mental health and the politics of care collectives. It fell apart, though. I'm sure people would tell the story of why that happened differently. My theory is that it was because of interpersonal dynamics: some people didn't want to deal with other people, and we didn't have ways of talking about it or figuring it out. Moreover, I think a lot of people didn't understand the commitment that this kind of work can take and backed off when they realized it. Eventually the larger collective shrunk into my own care collective.

Then Loree moved here. Loree Erickson is a femmegimp who moved to Toronto to go to grad school. We knew each other a little bit before she came here and quickly became good friends. She uses a wheelchair, and needs people to help her go to the bathroom, get food, get into and out of bed, and do some other stuff. Neither a citizen nor permanent resident, nor rich, Loree couldn't get paid attendant workers (although many people deemed to have sufficient immigration status also can't access attendant care because the government shamefully underfunds such programs). She needed to put together a care collective with enough people to do at least three shifts a day. She drew much of her care collective out of my care collective and the broader group that had disintegrated.

Both Loree and I were trying to meet our basic needs within our communities because we didn't have the financial resources to do it any other way. But we also (and independently, as two disabled organizers among mostly nondisabled people who also made the political decision to use the term *care collective*), came to the conclusion that care collectives are (or at least can be) an important part of prefigurative practices. Care collectives, ideally, are ways that community members can come together to support one another, and that involves recognizing that those relationships are reciprocal. The people doing the care also get things out of those interactions and help build a network that will support them when they need it.

Quite quickly, Loree had enough help (for the most part, although it was still difficult to coordinate and took a lot of work), and I didn't. Some people stopped doing care shifts for me and joined Loree's care collective (a few of those people also went on to bail on her, though). I couldn't get new people because no one wanted to join my collective. Loree and I both felt like the people who were doing the support work were making decisions about whom they viewed as legitimate as well as whose needs they thought were more significant. This isn't to equate our needs, but it is to say that we are the people who should have been making those decisions. The imbalance in numbers made us both uncomfortable, politically and personally.

Nondisabled make decisions about our legitimacy as disabled and our needs all the time—this is one of the key ways that disablism functions in our lives. Some times people talk about this in terms of the invisibility and visibility of disability; my disability was (often) invisible while Loree's was visible. But it is a little more complex and relational than that. Loree and I had different needs—sometimes hers were easier to meet, and sometimes mine were. Sitting on the bus, I get derided for being a "young kid who has no respect for old people" from time to time for not giving up my seat. My need for a seat is only legitimized if I show my cane (if I have it). But it isn't the visibility of the cane that makes me need the seat. I need the seat, and sometimes I use my cane when I don't need it because I know I will need a seat on public transit. Within the disablist logic that nondisabled people know what our needs are and get to decide who is (most) legitimate, it made a lot of sense that people would leave my care collective for Loree's.

I also think that there was another reason that Loree could fill her shifts when I couldn't: a lot of the time Loree was a ball of sunshine, and I was a ball of steel wool.

There are two crucial reasons why I lost people in my life and, especially, couldn't get my care needs met—reasons I touched on earlier. Both of them speak to the ways that systemic oppression gets reproduced at microlevels even when we are working to eliminate those systems. First, I was profoundly angry as well as difficult because of my experiences of oppression and in particular sexual violence. It would be irresponsible and untrue to say that I don't need to be accountable for the harm I have caused because of that, or that some individuals would not have been fully legitimate in choosing not to do care work with me. It also isn't to say that Loree isn't deeply impacted, too, and in some ways, constructed by the oppression she has experienced. Nevertheless, it saddens me that this group of well-meaning people who were committed to antioppressive work largely made individual choices about care provision that worked to alienate someone who was reacting to their experiences of oppression. Individually, many of these choices would not have been problematic, but collectively they are oppressive.

CRACKS IN MY UNIVERSE

/

INCITE! Women, Gender Non-Conforming, and Trans People of Color Against Violence, writing about transformative justice in its "Community Accountability Working Document," asks the question, "What if we presume there is no 'outside' our community?" I think about this quote a lot. I also try to resolve the contradiction in myself that believes that the twenty-four-year-old me, like all of us, deserved to have people doing their care work, and that work is an elemental part of doing community organizing, and that knows that there are certain people who I just don't want to do that work with. There are some people I know who no one wants to do that with. How do we take care of one another beyond the boundary of who fits in?

The second point is that I feel like one of the reasons I didn't get the support I needed was because people thought I was crazy. I have two equally weighted responses to this. The first is that it doesn't matter how others perceive my mental health; the needs that I articulate are my needs. They are no less significant than someone else's. The second is that of course I was crazy. I felt like I was under siege by the world. And I was in incredible pain that people kept telling me wasn't real. Because I only felt rage—which I now understand to be a cover for or protection from my grief and sorrow—my responses to things that were hurtful were inconsistent. I was stilted, dramatic, fiery, withdrawn, or any number of other adjectives that others understood as bizarre. I don't think that crazy is inherently bad or inherently good; it is just a way of being (or more aptly, many

A. J. WITHERS

/

172

different ways of being). It is where I was, and it makes perfect sense that I was there. And again, being crazy doesn't mean that you shouldn't be able to get the help you need.

And then the cancer diagnosis came. Everything changed (except for me—for my body and my needs).

I got my friends back. People got in touch, made plans, arranged care shifts, and brought me food. The people who had vanished started doing all the things that I needed all along. My number of care shifts increased, and there was no shortage of people to fill them, even when I needed them daily. The medical-industrial complex legitimated my experiences and needs.

My cancer went away, but my disability didn't. I would still spend about a week every month in bed from pain. My community stuck around, however, at least for a little while. Slowly, both my needs and me faded into illegitimacy once again; most of the people who had been doing care shifts and support work with me went with them. Here again, I felt a terrible loss, yet I didn't grieve for myself, or for my validation or friends. I raged. Again.

2012

Nearly ten years later, in early December 2012, I had top surgery. I created a schedule in advance for care shifts. I needed help and wanted to make sure that the labor didn't fall on the same couple of people, especially because so much of it would

CRACKS IN MY UNIVERSE

/

fall on my partner since we lived alone together. It felt relatively easy: this was going to be a short-term situation, and no one would question the legitimacy of my needs.

The recovery was harder and took longer than I was told it would. Then my partner got sick and spent time in the hospital.

By this point I had been doing disability organizing in radical movements for more than a decade. My book about disability had recently come out, and I was on the bottom rung of the ladder of Canadian left-wing celebrities because of my writing and organizing around disability, including care collectives.

I couldn't extend my care collective. I couldn't ask for more help (aside from a couple of really close friends). I just couldn't. I was simply emotionally incapable of it. My long-buried grief invaded every attempt I made to access the networks that I had worked so hard to build and support others in building. I let myself become more and more isolated rather than tell more people what was going on and ask for help. I did this, I think, so that it would be my choice—so that I could still believe we could collectively support one another, so I wouldn't feel abandoned again. I felt a deep sorrow for the gap between the politics that I promote and believe in versus my own capacity to practice them. And shame, so much shame.

I needed to put a care collective in place again. I told one of my best friends that I felt guilty about asking for help given that I had had a care collective so recently. This was the friend who, when I had cancer (including my prediagnosis), would get me to

A. J. WITHERS

/

walk the quarter of a block to the corner store with him every night even though it took forty-five minutes. It took me a few years to realize that those trips weren't for the light bulbs, chocolate, and toilet paper that they claimed to be but instead to get me out of the house, to keep me moving, to get me talking. Years later, in a moment of kitchen-table honesty that was so hard for me to say, I revealed that I didn't feel deserving of taking up so many resources. I knew my admission laid bare the gap between what I said and what I did. It also wasn't even the whole truth. I didn't tell him that I couldn't do it before and was only trying to talk this through now because I felt like I needed a care collective so badly that I had no choice.

"Fuck off," he told me. It was followed with something about how I knew it was bullshit, I should get over myself, and I would never ever think that of someone else. And he was right.

So the care collective was formed. Two months later, almost no one was around anymore. Six months later there were just a couple of close friends holding things down and helping out, plus a couple of peripheral folks who checked in and helped when they could. People were there for the short run, but when the immediate crisis was over and we still needed support, they were gone. This story of people leaving, I think, is the more common narrative of support than my cancer story, where people come back.

Some of those people never came back. It was "too hard" to be my friend. I tried to feel the sadness of these losses, to grieve

CRACKS IN MY UNIVERSE

/

and move forward, but it was incredibly hard for me. It *is* incredibly hard for me.

For me, writing about this period of my life means writing into a broken and unhealed heart. It also means navigating some tricky waters. There are two normatively permissible identities for disabled people: tragic and super. The tragic or pitiful is the most common one, including in radical spaces—the site of gratitude and warning. The super—the supercrip or able disabled—are the sites of inspiration—the plucky folks who "overcome" their "challenges." Dominant, mainstream disability activists generally have responded to this by refusing to tell either story, and instead presenting tales of banality and contented normalness. At the same time, disability activists tend to both critique the notion of overcoming and supercripdom while requiring it, or at least its facade, of one another.

There has been some pushback over the past thirty years against this pressure not to tell our stories about the hard parts of our lives, but that tension still feels real for me as well as for many disabled people. This is why I typically talk about the need to create space for people to talk about the hard parts of disability, although I rarely actually do it. I don't do it because there are certain kinds of vulnerable that I don't like to be in public. I also don't do it because it is scary, even with the long-standing work done by disabled people. I am afraid that people will use my honesty against me. Inside of this bind, there is both a paradox and sadness. In the name of liberation, I am bound—

A. J. WITHERS

/

and I bind myself—not to show who I am, even though liberation means making the space for people to be who they are, and for all our diversity and difference to be recognized and celebrated.

Despite the fact that I articulate a politics in which there is no contradiction between what I am fighting for and how I get to be in the world, that isn't where I am. This is a prefigurative failure, and I am in continuous mourning for who I can't be. But creating the space for us to be who we are, for me to be who I am, requires so much nuance and complexity that most people (at least those who aren't disabled, or aren't intimately and regularly involved in a disabled person's life) don't have. Not having that space, though, means swallowing my secret sadness and shame. Upholding the practice of not talking about these things means that I have never been able to go through the process of grieving because my acceptable public disability identity has consistently delegitimized and erased my feelings.

2016

I am recovering from a six-month-long back injury that has kept me in bed for three of those months. This is the first time that I have been in a pain that has made me scream regularly and often. While I am getting better now, I am once again on opiates and other medication with significant cognitive implications, including short-term amnesia (although the pain does that too). I also know that things could easily get worse again as I await my surgery. (While public health care is essential and everyone should have access to it, the Canadian system is frustrating. My surgery is probably months away.)

The first day that this particular pain started, I was in the library. I wrote to push through the pain while waiting to see a doctor:

I am in so much pain that I really can't get any work done. I can't think about anything else really. A few minutes ago, I laid down on the floor thinking that would help (this is one of the forbidden acts in the Toronto Public Library system. Another is removing your shoes, which I also do often because of pain). It didn't really help. Then I couldn't get up easily, and it was all quite horrible and ridiculous.

So I am writing this to be able to focus on my pain in a way that isn't destructive. Being able to focus through my pain is the only thing I seem capable of right now, so that is what I am doing.

I am terrified of the two blocks I will have to walk shortly and by the fact that the super strong painkillers I took seem to be ineffective. Last night I went to the ER because my heart problem was acting up. I got there and it was fine, but my blood work came back with a potential kidney problem so I have to go to the doctor again tomorrow. With that appointment, I will have had to go to

A. J. WITHERS

/

seven different medical appointments this week. This is far from the norm; I rarely go to the doctor that much, thankfully, but there isn't a week that goes by that I don't have to make time for at least one appointment. Right now, my experience of my body is entirely and only awful.

In a few days or weeks, I will be able to tell you about the positive things that come from this experience, as I have been able to do with so many past ones. Maybe that will be new ways I understand the library or my body because of this experience. But I don't know what that might be yet. I do find it reassuring, though, that I know that there is still value in this experience even if it is so shitty right now.

This latest health crisis for me—this hard part—is real, and it is a real part of me living in my disabled body, and it sucks. For some disabled people, their experiences don't suck. Some disabled people's lives suck for other reasons altogether, or only as a result of oppression and so on. But for me, and for lots of people, there are times when things are just shitty, and we experience that through our disabilities.

So here I am in bed with incredible back and leg pain. Once again, my entire world has collapsed into my bedroom. I like having company but find it exhausting. I am unbelievably high most of the time. This high would be a lovely afternoon, yet it is a near-intolerable long-term state. I can't meet my basic needs and need help doing everything, but I am too scared to try to put together a care collective. I call a friend to tuck me in when my partner is working a night shift (I can't turn out the light on my own) or help me sit up when I get stuck. This crisis and the sporadic help that I do arrange are, understandably, overwhelming for my partner, who I live with. But I just keep putting off asking for help and am so ashamed that I can't ask.

One day, my partner was at the hospital doing a shift supporting a mutual friend, as had been planned. She left early. I woke up and looked around. I had about twenty sour cream and onion Pringles, a rice cake, and a quarter bottle of water in my bed with me; because it was so hard to move, I would just sleep with random stuff. It was going to be another five hours before my partner came home. I could survive but it would suck. So I texted someone who lives in the neighborhood. I've known him a long time and like him, but we've never hung out together. I had texted him and asked if I could put him on my list of people for short dog walks (the walks are short—but the dog is short too) a week earlier. Now, I texted him and asked if he could come over for fifteen minutes and make me breakfast. In twenty minutes I was eating oatmeal with blueberries. He offered to hang out and do chores, and we chatted for quite a while. It was lovely.

This was a simple act of caring, yet it opened a door that my heartbreak had forced closed. I set up my care collective again and had someone come in every day to help. It is still hard. I am still ashamed that it is hard. So much of this shame is rooted in

A. J. WITHERS

/

my feeling of failure. Grief, like pain in general, can be an important teacher. I hope taking the space to allow myself to talk about the realities of my life as it is rather than how it should be will help me process my grief for who I have lost along with the disablism at so much of the heart of my pain and my lack of care. In building this space (and I am certainly not claiming that I am alone in doing so) and refusing to hide my grief, I can move forward, and can understand and celebrate what has been won.

*

A. J. Withers is an antipoverty organizer and author in Toronto. They are the author of the radical disability blog stillmyrevolution.org and Disability Politics and Theory *(Fernwood, 2012) as well as* The Healing Power of Domination: Interlocking Oppression and the Origins of Social Work *with Chris Chapman (forthcoming). A. J. would like to thank Loree Erickson and Laura MacDonald for their feedback and ongoing support, and is also grateful to everyone in their circle of care, past and present, along with the makers of the podcast Hugwolf for creating space for hard conversations about care.*

CRACKS IN MY UNIVERSE

/

IN SELF-DEFENSE,
IN DEFENSE
OF MEMORY

MIRTHA LUZ PÉREZ ROBLEDO,
TRANSLATED AND WITH
A PROLOGUE BY SCOTT CAMPBELL

For nearly ten years I have been translating texts from Spanish into English, primarily relating to social movements, resistance, and repression in Mexico. But few of the pieces I've worked on have moved me to the degree that the following letter by Mirtha Pérez did. In it, I found an emotional resonance absent from most documents with a radical perspective—documents that often limit themselves to discussing facts and analysis, even when grappling with horrific and intimate violence. Her words grabbed me with a quiet strength that demanded to be heard. I saw a woman and her solitary pain, a morsel of which rose through me and lodged behind my eyes. I too felt hurt, betrayal, and outrage. There was a sense of overwhelm at the vastness of the despair created by the cruel loss of a singular person as well as a fear of succumbing to the whirlwind of accumulated grief such as is now being experienced over and over again in that one section of the globe called Mexico. This sensation was more than I felt capable of holding alone. So, as she did through writing, I tried to give it expression through a loving translation.

On July 31, 2015, this pain was cast on Mirtha when her daughter, Nadia Vera Pérez, age twenty-two, was murdered in a Mexico City apartment. Also killed were Yesenia Quiroz Alfaro, Mile Virginia Martín, Olivia Alejandra Negrete Avilés,

/

and Rubén Espinosa Becerril. Nadia, a social justice organizer and human rights defender, and Rubén, a photographer and journalist, had both fled the state of Veracruz after receiving death threats for their work. Before her murder, Nadia stated that if anything should happen to her, it would be Javier Duarte who was responsible. Duarte was governor of Veracruz from 2010 to 2016, renowned for his corruption and human rights abuses, including the deaths of at least eighteen journalists during his rule. He resigned six weeks before his term ended as a result of legal proceedings against him, and at the time of this writing, is a fugitive. The state's investigation into the murder of Nadia and the four others has been condemned as full of irregularities, as outlined in Mirtha's piece.

Most texts I have the opportunity to translate, I do so from the perspective that the information they contain merits circulation to a wider audience, as they offer accounts or analysis not typically available in English-language discussions on Mexico. Yet when I came across Mirtha's piece, written on the eve of the one-year anniversary of her daughter's murder, more than *knowing* it would be worth translating, I *felt* it had to be translated. I found compassion and rage, mourning and indignation, in her writing. It revealed the solitude of being one more drop of anguish in a world brimming with pain, dammed in by official indifference and impunity. What it stirred in me was more than ideological or ethical affinity. It struck a somatic chord that echoed up my spine, opening a door to another layer of under-

MIRTHA LUZ PÉREZ ROBLEDO

/

standing. It gave me access to what all that I've been translating and writing about Mexico felt like to those living it. My hope in translating her words into English is that they move others as they moved me.

The intangible ache created by profound loss, coupled with the seemingly insurmountable futility of achieving any resolution via the mechanisms of the Mexican state, frequently lead many to mourn in private. Fostering this impulse toward isolation and alienation is the additional latent threat that those who do otherwise, those who make noise, are often silenced themselves. In spite of all this, Mirtha has chosen to speak. In written correspondence, she explained to me that it was these very circumstances that led her to raise her voice:

> I don't know if it is to share the pain, I don't know if it is to defend memory, but I believe I needed to speak in the face of such indifference, impunity, and negligence, to say that I am here, living this unending pain, that I am a person who thinks, analyzes, and reflects. I am saying to them, "You are not doing your job, what we pay you for.... Don't insult my intelligence with all these lies." Maybe that's why I write, because I've misplaced my words and I'm trying to find them. Given their many wasted words, writing letters such as the one I wrote is a way of resignifying them.

For Mirtha, writing publicly is the avenue open to her to affirm her experience and reality, a refusal to be subsumed by the narrative proffered by the state. It is a countermove of reclamation and recuperation, layered with facts and emotions all the more poignant for their concision. "From the start, I knew this would happen," she told me. "Because in this country, that's how it is. I write because it's a way of releasing a little bit of this pain that doesn't fit in my body. This rage, this impotence. That which remains after they take what you loved most."

While it goes unmentioned in her letter, another act of redefinition that Mirtha contributes is bringing the focus to Nadia. Following the murders, and even to this day, most of the attention centered on Rubén as the one male and most well-known person of the five. Only subsequently was it directed to Nadia, and even less so to Yesenia, Mile, and Olivia. This can be partially understood given that Rubén and Nadia were the intended targets, while Yesenia, Mile, and Olivia had the tragic misfortune of being present when the assassinations were carried out. With limited discussion of Nadia's social justice work, and mentioning Rubén only in passing, Mirtha pierces through the constructs of patriarchy and social status to reveal the unhealable wound that occurs simply when a loved one, any loved one, is stolen so unjustly.

Yet at the same time, Mirtha carries forward the outrage and disquiet that propelled Nadia's activities when she was alive. In such an acknowledgment, she succeeds not just in connecting with the public in general and those in mourning in particular but most specifically those who feel moved to act in life, as Nadia did, and know that the cost of resistance can be the ultimate price. In that holding, Mirtha signals to that community that while a life has been stolen, the work that life was undertaking continues, and that others will continue to speak for it.

Along with Mirtha's public signaling to her and Nadia's community, the community has signaled back. It is this reciprocal communication around grief that allows us to shift the loss of Nadia and so many others away from narratives of senselessness or pointlessness. Rather, that loss, when acknowledged among accomplices in the struggle for a more just world, can assist in both tending to wounds and building together to prevent further wounding. Mirtha wrote of how this support has helped her personally: "This broken, divided, aching heart; this heart wants to thank, thank all the love it has received, all the light that you've sent me in this darkness that has invaded me."

The sharing of her grief publicly also serves to mobilize. When asked what her aspiration was for the impact of her words, she shared,

> I wrote with the hope that a wind might carry my voice beyond borders, that someone might hear me ... and you heard me. If foreign outlets can know what the relatives of the victims have to say, maybe, just maybe, it will help to pressure the authorities to do their job, to exhaustively investigate, and if that happens, the truth will be arrived at, and as the saying goes, "the truth will set you free," the truth might bring a little bit of peace.

IN SELF-DEFENSE, IN DEFENSE OF MEMORY

/

In our exchange and her writings, Mirtha frequently returned to the question of what remains following the deep loss she has suffered. And of what can be done with the grief she now holds. Her path brought her to give expression and form to that loss, to present it so it may be shared collectively, and in doing so, offer it in the service of something greater. Mirtha wrote to me,

> When almost nothing remains, what remains is to defend memory, what remains is to not become desensitized to the normalization of violence, of this damned violence that sometimes seems so far away and other times slaps us in the face. What remains is to turn our backs on the individualism imposed by the market's logic, on this ridiculous "everyone for themselves." What remains is solidarity.

Be it in grief or resistance, solidarity can only manifest in the collective. As it inspired Mirtha's word, it inspired this translation. May that solidarity grow.

*

When they wrest what we love most from us, the possibility of justice no longer exists.

When the word justice loses meaning, all that remains for us is the defense of memory, of self-defense.

MIRTHA LUZ PÉREZ ROBLEDO

/

Country-hell, country of police.
Long weeping river, wide painful sea,
Republic of angels, lost homeland.
Country of mine, yours, of everyone and of no one.

—EFRAÍN HUERTA

From this country that sustains itself on pillars of misery, injustice, impunity, corruption, and crime,

From this country whose great society towers like a hostile court to judge all through lenses tarnished with prejudice and double standards,

From this country where the "man with money rules,"

From this country where they use the same rationale for every investigation into violent incidents,

From this country where victims are revictimized and criminals are protected,

From this country where judges leave the citizenry in a state of helplessness with their deliberate omissions, allowing criminals to go free, arguing that they didn't have due process or that "they didn't know they were going to commit a crime,"

IN SELF-DEFENSE, IN DEFENSE OF MEMORY

/

From this country where prosecutors exemplify the injustice system, incapable of preparing solid cases or attending to the growing number of them that accumulate one after another,

From this country in which a government's political interests don't allow it to look at the escalating violence, and where it becomes a neglectful or complicit authority capable of obstructing a criminal investigation,

From this country where to open your eyes every day and discover you're still here is more than a miracle,

From this country of crossfire, of defenders of the rights of criminals,

From this country where they create the illusion of freedom of movement and freedom of expression,

From this country where institutional negligence and inability rule,

From this country where most of the media are "city fish who lost their guts amid a shoal of whitebait,"

From this country where they persecute you, harass you, threaten you,

MIRTHA LUZ PÉREZ ROBLEDO

/

192

From this country where criminal violence follows institutional violence,

From this country where they erase you, they take away hope,

From this country where it seems that the only safe place is in a book,

From this country where our words do nothing in the face of their bullets,

From this country my voice tries to leave, to rise up and be carried by the wind to resonate beyond borders to condemn the pain that has invaded me for the murder of my daughter, Nadia Dominique Vera Pérez, it joins with the pain of knowing that:

In one trip of the earth around the sun—that is, one year since the massacre,

There is no clear motive.

There is no one in authority interested in conducting a serious, fair investigation free of political or personal interests, without making money for doing it—a clear, diligent, exhaustive, effective, and scientific investigation.

IN SELF-DEFENSE, IN DEFENSE OF MEMORY

/

Those truly guilty for leaking the case file have not been punished.

Those who took the victims' belongings have not been investigated.

The friends, relatives, and neighbors who wanted to provide information have not been allowed to make statements.

The weapon used in the crime has not been sought out.

The chain of custody has not been kept, the scene and objects have not been properly safeguarded, and no one in authority prevented the altering of the crime scene.

Protocols were not followed during interrogations of the Veracruz government, which received preferential treatment, downplaying the significance that five people were murdered.

Nadia Vera's activities as an activist and Rubén Espinosa's as a journalist in the city of Xalapa were not considered as evidence of them being in a vulnerable situation.

The government of Veracruz has not been investigated (whose plainclothes state police detained, beat, and robbed Nadia Vera; pulled her into a van and threatened her for her political activi-

TO MOURN
AND STRIKE

PROLOGUE AND
INTERVIEWS BY
JEFF CLARK

In French, *faire grève* means "to strike." It's first seen with that meaning in an 1805 police report, and is linked to Place de la Grève in Paris, where unemployed people seeking work would gather. The grève in Place de la Grève refers to *gravier* (gravel in English), which in turn probably refers to the Latin *gravare* (to be burdened).

Our own word *grief* is etymologically linked to gravare; when we mourn, our hearts are burdened. And amazingly, our term *grievance*, in French, is "grief."

Faire grève (to go on strike) and *to grieve* (mourn) are thus ultimately etymologically connected. But that doesn't mean that people didn't make the link when the syntagm faire grève appeared. One could imagine a person at the time saying (as a play on words) that people seeking jobs on Place de la Grève were burdened (*gréver*) by the misery of unemployment.

The public artists in the pages that follow have made of grieving a grievance—a visual strike—proving it's possible to transmute some of the weight of mourning those murdered by the state into an act that is simultaneously memorial and protest.

/

JOSE CRUZ

Once your artwork or action has been publicly mounted, what are you hoping will transpire?

Hope, dreams, solidarity, commitment, consciousness, idealism, rebellion, and autonomy. We will keep retaking and defending our spaces.

Do you imagine your ideal audience as the perpetrators of murder, those grieving it, and/or someone else?

I think that it is for everyone. It's a reminder to our brothers and sisters that we are with them, we support them, that they are not alone. It is also for those who have no idea as to what is happening and why it is happening. Lastly, it is directed at those committing the atrocities, to tell them that we are no longer afraid and that we are going to keep screaming: we will not forget.

Because the most beautiful of the arts is that of collective support.
—SUBCOMANDANTE INSURGENTE MOISÉS,
Mexico, July 29, 2016

Our work as graphic designers must become a generator of critical thought and action. There is no other option but this one—though the ways in which this may manifest itself are diverse.

/

FACING: Jose Cruz, *Where Are They?* 2015.
Spray paint and stencils, San Francisco.

/

WHERE ARE THEY?

43

ABEL GARCIA

#IT WAS THE STATE
#AYOTZINAPA

LAPIZTOLA

Do you imagine your ideal audience as the perpetrators of murder, those grieving it, and/or someone else?

For us, the audience is the general public. Having said that, specific sectors may feel more interpellated than others. For some populations, perhaps our work will have no effect. Nonetheless, the idea is that our image makes others reflect.

FOLLOWING SPREAD: Lapiztola,
Libertad Extinta, 2015. Mural, Mexico City.

/

MELANIE CERVANTES
AND JESUS BARRAZA

Once your artwork or action has been publicly mounted, what are you hoping will transpire?

We hope that the visual works that we create, particularly the portraits of people who have become ancestors too soon at the hands of the state, interrupt the violence of forgetting that silences and negates our history. The pieces we create can be visual aids for political education and discussion; they can be used as public declarations of grief, and are both figurative and literal signs of a larger public memory project that resists dominant narratives that seek to criminalize and villainize the victims of police and state violence.

Do you imagine your ideal audience as the perpetrators of murder, those grieving it, and/or someone else?

The work we create is made primarily for our community as a sign of solidarity and, as with the Oscar Grant piece, for the people grieving the losses of their folks. Through the use of portraiture, we elevate the images of the people whose lives have been taken, convey the loss of a precious life, and participate in a process of healing through remembering.

/

/

216

I AM OSCAR GRANT
AND MY LIFE MATTERS

OREE ORIGINOL

*Once your artwork or action has been publicly mounted, what are
you hoping will transpire?*

The application of my artwork online or in public spaces is
meant to promote the conversations that hopefully lead to action against racism and police brutality by individuals who encounter my work. The creation of this project is to serve as a
tool to continue shaping culture specifically in the way we imagine what justice means in our society.

*Do you imagine your ideal audience as the perpetrators of murder,
those grieving it, and/or someone else?*

My portraits are pieces of information to be processed by
everyone. From the police who murder to those grieving it. The
translation of my portraits by the viewer will differ from one
another, but the general projection in each piece is to present
them with dignity and humanity that any other human should
recognize and uplift.

FACING: Oree Originol, *Justice for
Aiyana Jones*, 2016. Digital illustration.

/

Sakia

BY
TATYANA
FAZLALIZADEH

/

TATYANA FAZLALIZADEH

Once your artwork or action has been publicly mounted, what are you hoping will transpire?

I hope this mural incites a sense of empowerment and comfort to those who knew Sakia, and any women and girls like Sakia. I painted her with the intention of saying that a young, poor, black, masculine-of-center, queer girl is important. Her life was important, and it's important that we remember her, and remain aware of her life and death.

Do you imagine your ideal audience as the perpetrators of murder, those grieving it, and/or someone else?

The audience for this work is the community in which she grew up. This piece was a part of a large mural project in Newark, NJ, where dozens of artists were invited to create pieces about Newark. When we think of who gets to represent cities, we don't think of people like Sakia. So this work is for Newark, for her community, for anyone who looks like Sakia. It is not for the perpetrators of her death; their gaze is not important here. It's for her loved ones.

/

ZOLA

Once your artwork or action has been publicly mounted, what are you hoping will transpire?

I hope for many things. Mostly, I hope that the ones who are grieving in the face of injustice will feel like people have their backs. We have a collective responsibility to remember together and support each other. Solidarity art, in that sense, is a way to take up public space and stand in solidarity. I hope my piece participates as a link in the broader net of collective support.

I wanted to say a tiny bit about Colten. Colten Boushie was twenty-two years old, from Red Pheasant First Nation. He was shot dead by a rural Saskatchewan man when he and his friends pulled their car into his yard for help with a flat tire. The shooter pleaded not guilty to second-degree murder and was granted bail. Colten's family is asking for justice. This young indigenous man had his whole life in front of him. He was training to be a firefighter and was a fire keeper in his community.

FACING: Zola, *Justice for Colten*, 2016.
Wheat pasted illustration, Montreal.

/

JET CHALK

Once your artwork or action has been publicly mounted, what are you hoping will transpire?

I want the complicit to encounter Aura Rosser's name and have it circulate permanently in their psyches. I want the noncomplicit to be reminded that they're part of a permanent movement.

Do you imagine your ideal audience as the perpetrators of murder, those grieving it, and/or someone else?

All of them. Cops and their allies on city council and in courtrooms should know we'll never stop reminding Ann Arbor, Michigan, that Aura was murdered by an employee of that city. To Aura's kids, siblings, loves, and advocates, we owe much of this kind of memorial labor. To anyone comfortable and content in Ann Arbor: you had a finger on that trigger, too.

FACING: Jet Chalk, *Aura*, 2016. Spray paint on concrete, Ann Arbor, Michigan.

/

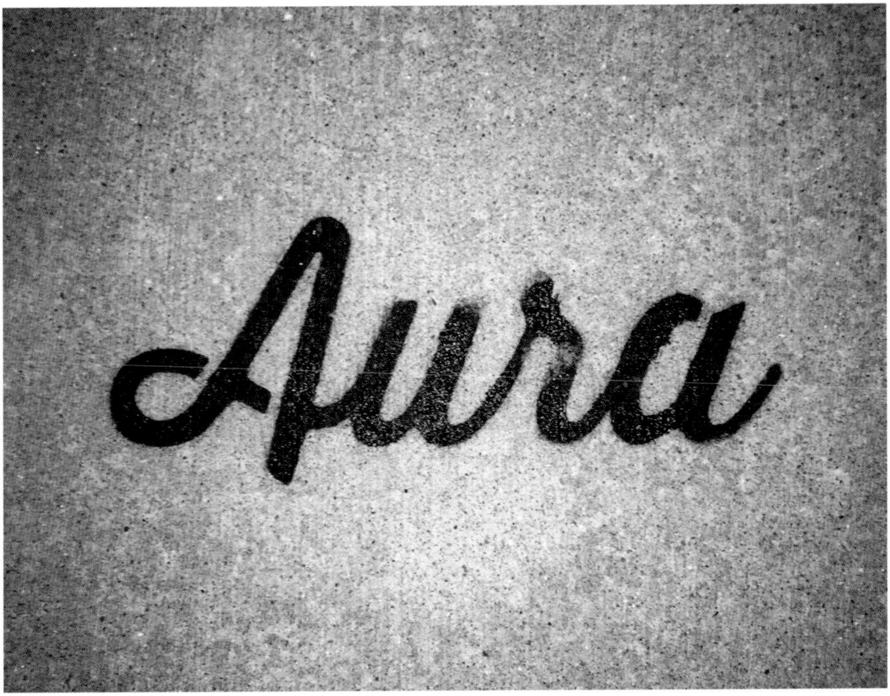
Aura

MICAH BAZANT

Once your artwork or action has been publicly mounted, what are you hoping will transpire?

First I am hoping that the art will surprise and interrupt them. I love being in a city, or anywhere, and finding unexpected art and beauty. It's one of the pleasures of life. It's a very moving spiritual experience for me, that has a different impact than visiting a museum or gallery with expectations and guides. It feels unmediated and connected to the flow of my life.

With the memorial portraits, I'm hoping they create a human connection with the figure in the drawing. We love to look at all faces, make eye contact. So many of us are so isolated. I'm often nervous to make eye contact as a gender-nonconforming person in public—it sometimes leads to more harassment. People are usually staring at me in public and I'm trying to block it out. And other gender-nonconforming people are sometimes nervous to acknowledge each other in public, because the danger of violence immediately increases when there's more than one of us and cis people feel more threatened.

The memorial drawings always intentionally show someone making intense eye contact, confronting the viewer with their spirit and humanity. I want people to be forced to connect with someone who has literally been erased in life and death, and

/

considered disposable and less than human. I think dehuman-ization is one of the primary ways that people are persuaded to harm each other. These memorial portraits are a small opportu-nity to remember and honor our own humanity, including our commitment to fight violence, and honor the humanity of trans women and femmes of color.

Do you imagine your ideal audience as the perpetrators of murder, those grieving it, and/or someone else?

My ideal audience would include everyone. Ideally I would love for everyone to see art that humanizes black trans women and treasures their lives. In reality I think my memorial por-traits are mostly for the victims' families (especially their trans family), friends, and extended networks of trans and racial jus-tice activists. The first of these posters were requested by local Bay Area #BlackLivesMatter activists to make sure that trans women and femmes were being included in #SayHerName pro-tests. After that I started getting more requests from other black trans activists and family members.

Every murder is so devastating, and many of them are so ex-tra violent. Like trans women being shot over and over and over, or being dismembered—usually by cis men in their own communities. And the white LGBT media and organizations do not give a shit. If this were happening to white gay people—if the average life expectancy for white gay people was thirty-five years old—they would be declaring a state of national emer-

/

gency. As a white trans artist, I hope it makes some impact on other white queer and trans people, and makes them think about whose lives are valued and how they can take action to support black trans people.

After hearing about a murder, I sometimes have a hard time feeling things. I think there's a reason that humans have marked our deaths with ritual and art for tens of thousands of years. Ceremony and art opens something in me, and allows me to weep and grieve. These are offerings to the spirits of those who've been killed. And to all the trans folks who need to grieve, especially other black trans women and femmes. To say you're not alone. You're not the only ones who see and feel what's going on. How you're in the cross hairs of white supremacy and transmisogyny everyday. Some of us will support and honor you in death and life.

FACING: Micah Bazant, *Keisha Jenkins*, 2016. Graphite illustration.

/

KEISHA JENKINS

BLACK TRANS LIVES MATTER

Jeff Clark is a graphic designer in Ypsilanti, Michigan.
Thanks to Alejo Stark for his translations from Spanish to English.

JUSTICE AND LOVE FOR ALEX NIETO

REFUGIO AND ELVIRA NIETO,
TRANSLATED AND WITH
A PROLOGUE BY
ADRIANA CAMARENA

WITNESS TO GRIEF

Since the killing of Alex Nieto on March 21, 2014, by four officers of the San Francisco Police Department (SFPD), I have been a witness to Elvira and Refugio's journey of grief and struggle to hold up high the name of their son in defiance of the state machinery that pursued character assassination at every turn. The Nietos and their surrounding community for two years responded with murals, storytelling circles, films, actions, protests, community gatherings, articles, essays, and theater productions about Alex Nieto, as his own person and one of us. A federal civil trial was also filed in summer 2014, and was lost two years later, in March 2016. Long before that legal loss, though, the district attorney had dismissed murder charges in 2015.

These were the painful but unsurprising results of having pitted ourselves knowingly against an unjust system. But they were useful experiences too, because with evidence on record, community members (from organizers to artists) took the opportunity to deliver an alternative narrative based on the same crime scene evidence and expose the corruption of the formal justice system. A sentiment of unaccountable wrongdoing was

/

left lingering from the shooting and trial evidence. This, coupled with the vital experience of community members who knew that Alex was not capable of the actions claimed by the officers who killed him, and who themselves have experienced the brutal effects of systemic racial bias, helped his parents win their son's story. Ben Bac Sierra, a close friend of Alex's and principle organizer of the cause for "Amor por Alex" (love for Alex), claimed our victory on the evening of the jury verdict by saying, "We did it better and more creatively than they did!"

A few days later, after the trial verdict, on March 21, 2016, on the second commemorative celebration of the life and death of Alex, a double rainbow shimmered across the sky following a spring shower at sunset over Bernal Heights. At this same time, community supporters flocked to the Mission Cultural Center for Latino Arts for a programmed celebration. The first-ever mass protest march against Alex's killing had departed from this location a week after his death, and here now, two years later, the sole eyewitness to Alex's shooting, Antonio Theodore, a black Jamaican singer who was badgered and belittled in court as a biased and allegedly unreliable witness, stepped onto a makeshift stage to belt out an a capella song that he had composed to the man he saw murdered by police. This was the testimony that would heal community that night.

The dust of the trial soon settled, but then from the quiet realm of family grief emerged two parents again, this time requesting community help to achieve the most personal of their demands: a permanent memorial for their son, permitted by the city at the site of his killing on Bernal Heights that would outlast even them. Our coalition was in a late stage of burnout, but the Nietos, assisted by other community members, rallied us into one last effort. On September 13, 2016, we held an action in front of city hall in which the Nietos asked the board of supervisors to issue a resolution for a permanent altar and memorial in honor of Alex. Speaking in front of city hall, María Villalta, a friend of Alex's and original cofounder of the Justice and Love for Alex Nieto Coalition, reminded the supervisors of the importance of altars in Latino culture:

> Establishing a memorial altar at sites of tragedy is a sacred tradition of Latino communities with deep ancestral and spiritual roots. An altar is a sacred place for sacrifices and gifts offered up to God, Our Creator. It is a place to show love toward our deceased....
>
> To begin mending broken trust with the Nieto family and their community, the minimum the mayor and board of supervisors could do is to provide the permits and resources to establish a permanent memorial for Alex Nieto on the hill. Have it be an act of restoration of all the trauma SFPD has caused the brown and black communities decade after decade. Let it be a protected space where we can safely grieve.

There at the hill, at the site of his killing, the Nietos, María, Oscar Salinas, Ely Flores, Yaya (Alex's girlfriend), Ben, myself, and many known and unknown family, friends, and community members kept a community altar after his death. There was a time in 2014 when a vandal would attack the site, and we would hold all-day and all-night vigils to prevent its defacement. During a nighttime restoration of the altar after an attack is when our sole eyewitness, Antonio, reached out personally to say what he had seen. Refugio, in particular, was tortured by the trashing of the altar on the hill, but after each act of hate, an act of kindness would follow—words, flowers, banners, and people gathered on the hill—that helped mend the shredded heart muscles.

Soon after our petition to the board of supervisors, I left the Justice and Love for Alex Nieto Coalition over what I'll call "irreconcilable differences." My departure was nothing short of a traumatic tearing of a tight, 2.5-year bond with the Nietos, the loss of which I deeply grieve. I hope one day to restore lost trust with the Nieto family, but in the grand scheme of struggles my feelings are not important in this matter. Unlike them, I did not lose a child to lethal police violence—fifty-nine shots fired, to be precise—so I remain an admirer of their resilience and resourcefulness for fighting for every square inch of permanent acknowledgment for their child.

On December 13, 2016, the board of supervisors voted in favor, nine to one, of an ordinance that mandates that the city install a permanent memorial for Alex in Bernal Heights Park. I know activists might guffaw at this achievement vis-à-vis the long road ahead toward ending police impunity, and maybe one day, even abolishing this armed force that perpetuates state violence, but there are three great things about the memorial. The first is that Alex's parents have requested this memorial from the start, and its achievement is an inch gained toward restoring their peace of mind that they have done right by their son. The second is that the permanent memorial for Alex represents defiance of the criminal and civil justice system that denied the Nietos justice and determined that officers acted lawfully. Just sit with that thought. The board of supervisors of San Francisco nearly unanimously sided with community sentiment of wrongdoing and our need for restoration despite what the formal justice system determined. Defiance of a justice system that systematically favors police and exudes racial bias is a critical step. Our job is to erode its credibility. The approval of the memorial marks a cultural shift from city officials toward police shootings in San Francisco by acknowledging that independent of any legal justification, a police shooting is violence in the community and a killing by police is harm done by the city. The third is as María stated in originally addressing the supervisors: we will have a permanent place to mourn Alex.

On this journey of grief and struggle for restoration, the Nietos have had translators and surrogates to deliver messages to move hearts and minds. Most consistently over the years, that has included Ben and myself as well as Oscar, María, and Ely, and most recently, María Cristina Gutierrez, Mary Mendoza, Paul Flores, Isabel and Marco Gutierrez, and others. Below is a writing that I facilitated for the Nietos. It began as an exercise in La Victoria Café in which I asked them to remember their son and tell me the message they wished to deliver to their supporters on the first anniversary of Alex's killing by SFPD. I then collated their words and messages by prefacing each with the first-person voice of the parent who spoke, so that the reader could identify them. The accidental result was a prose poem of grief and gratitude for Alex and the struggle for justice.

I once asked them, knowing that justice by the law was not possible, what justice would feel like for them. Refugio was quick to answer: "I want the names and faces of the officers who killed Alex to be known all over the world." He wanted those officers to face the inescapable truth that they had taken a life and that we—community, a world community—held them accountable. On that day in February 2015 when District Attorney George Gascón announced that he would not press any criminal charges against Alex's killers, I wrote a brief statement titled "No Consequence, No Confidence":

> The lack of a criminal indictment does not mean a lack of consequences for the officers who killed Alex Nieto. Today begins the public trial and public shaming of his killers and their accomplices:
>
> Lieutenant Jason Sawyer, you are a killer.
>
> Officer Roger Morse, you are a killer.

ADRIANA CAMARENA AND THE NIETOS

/

Officer Richard Schiff, you are a killer.

Officer Nathan Chew, you are a killer.

Chief of Police Greg Suhr, you are an accomplice to killers.

District Attorney George Gascón, you are an accomplice to killers.

Mayor Ed Lee, you are an accomplice to killers.

You are declared guilty by the people, guilty by our community.

We will continue to shine light on this broken system until police officers who kill are made personally accountable by standards satisfactory to the communities in which they kill.

This public trial will not end until the system that doesn't work is fixed.

No consequence, no confidence.

WORDS FROM REFUGIO AND ELVIRA NIETO ON THE ONE-YEAR COMMUNITY COMMEMORATION OF ALEX NIETO

Here we are, and it seems incredible that a year has transpired since Alex was taken from us.

I, Refugio, miss his jokes. Sometimes in the morning, he'd enter quietly into our room and rip the covers off of us. I also remember that he would squeeze me, hugging me from behind, and when I'd get mad at him, he'd smile and say, "Don't get grumpy, old man." Now, I wake up stiff. I must be missing his hugs.

I, Elvira, remember that he loved to eat: enchiladas, tacos, fajitas, barbequed goat, pork in green chile sauce, pinto and black beans, everything. I remember he would grab his belly, the rolls of fat, and say, "Mami, I'm going to exercise to lose weight!"

I, Refugio, remember that before Alex died, we trusted in the police and the city government, but after Alex's death and seeing the lies they told of him, we lost all trust. These days I think often that Alex was excited to go to Mexico in September to visit our town. It is the greatest and most painful sorrow that that journey did not take place.

I, Elvira, remember that the district attorney told us he was going to help us and in the end he said nothing could be done for us.

I, Refugio, remember in those first days after the death of Alex that his friends arrived—Ben Bac Sierra and María Villalta —to offer their help. Then Joey Vaez and Adriana Camarena.

I, Elvira, of those first days, remember nothing.

I, Refugio, remember that more of Alex's friends gathered to help. I had never been to marches and I felt like I wanted to escape. I felt out of place in the crowd. Reporters and people greeted me, and I felt confused. It took me months to understand why I was there. In those days, I would hear the doorbell ring late at night: Alex returning from his night shift. I would hear it clearly, but when I looked out the window, he would not be there.

I, Elvira, in those early days, would not even leave the house. We had never been to those protest things, despite Alex loving to support justice causes. I would wake up and ask, "Is this a dream?" I felt he was there, but he was not. I ask myself if it is worse to suffer the death of a loved one with a prolonged illness, but being able to see them, or an abrupt death such as Alex's.

I, Elvira, remember that he was about to enter his internship at the Juvenile Hall to counsel youths. It was his great, greatest aspiration.

I, Refugio, remember that he had just completed his exams to take that job, but to motivate him I would say, "I don't believe you. The facts will speak for themselves when you bring me your certificate."

I, Elvira, remember when after his death, we received his certificate of graduation from City College in time for Mother's Day.

I, Refugio, remember telling Alex, "Forgive me, son, for having doubted you."

I, Refugio, gradually learned that it was important to march. Even though they gave us nothing, we were distracted from our anguish.

I, Elvira, realize that the police want us to stay real quiet, but protest marches are meant to awaken people. Since I was told that the officers who killed Alex will not face a criminal trial, the marches have become even more important.

I, Refugio, think that we have met so many very beautiful people at those marches. It was a pleasure to feel so much love for Alex. I would even put my hand on my chest to feel my heart flutter. I thought maybe I would die and would tell Elvira, "If I die, you have to carry on." I would even feel embarrassed by so many people wanting to greet me. Those hugs would reach so deep inside me that sometimes tears would flow. It was and continues to be so lovely to see the people who are still accompanying us.

I, Elvira, see that we have met so many people who knew Alex, of whom we had no prior knowledge. I feel such pride that Alex was so loving and friendly with all people.

I, Refugio, feel it would be just for Alex's killers to face trial and to be fired, but feel that justice might not be found by formal means. The only thing left to do is to continue learning who killed him. Let their faces be known.

I, Elvira, feel it should be known who are those officers and their exact reasons for killing Alex.

I, Refugio, want to see a change in the process, even if small, so that a sincere and unbiased investigation can be carried out. Why did they have to shoot him so many times as he lay on the ground?

I, Elvira, want to know exactly what happened that day and let the public know the type of police we have.

I, Refugio, give thanks that you still believe that we can have

ADRIANA CAMARENA AND THE NIETOS

/

justice, and ask not to let yourselves be intimidated, since we do not know when this will end. It is not for us; it is for Alex and the entire community, so that we learn to hold unity.

I, Elvira, give you thanks for helping us and continuing on with us.

*

Refugio Nieto and Elvira Rodriguez (now Elvira Nieto) were born a year apart in the little town of Tarimoro, Guanajuato (Mexico), known for its agricultural and handmade brick businesses. Elvira ventured out to California in 1973, following her brother and sister to the Mission District of San Francisco. Refugio headed out to California in 1978 to become a lechugero *and* tomatero *in the fields close to San Jose. Refugio and Elvira fell in love in San Francisco, and married in 1984, making a home on Cortland Street on Bernal Hill. In 1985, Elvira got a job as a housekeeper in a small tourist hotel. After their two young sons were born, Refugio became their primary caretaker and also worked as a temporary dayworker. Elvira retired shortly after their eldest, Alex, was killed by the SFPD. Today the Nietos are widely acknowledged representatives of the Latino grassroots struggle for police accountability.*

Adriana Camarena is a Mexican writer and researcher living in San Francisco. Since moving to the Mission District in 2008, she has documented the stories of this neighborhood's traditional Latino and poor residents. Adriana is also a community advocate against police brutality, working closely with Elvira and Refugio as well as the family of Luis Góngora Pat, a Mayan Mexican man killed by SFPD on Shotwell Street on April 7, 2016.

JUSTICE AND LOVE FOR ALEX NIETO

/

THE
GENTRIFICATION
OF AIDS

SARAH SCHULMAN

Key to the gentrification mentality is the replacement of complex realities with simplistic ones. Mixed neighborhoods become homogeneous. Mixed neighborhoods create public simultaneous thinking, many perspectives converging on the same moment at the same time, in front of each other. Many languages, many cultures, many racial and class experiences take place on the same block, in the same buildings. Homogeneous neighborhoods erase this dynamic, and are much more vulnerable to enforcement of conformity.

AIDS, which emerged as gentrification was under way, is an arena where simple answers to complex questions have ruled. "Keep it simple" only works if you are an alcoholic who doesn't want to take another drink. In most other areas of life, complexity is where truth lies. AIDS has been bombarded by simplification since its beginning. *The people who have it don't matter. It's their fault. It's over now.* Easy to blame AIDS on the infected, and much more difficult to take in all the social, economic, epidemiological, sexual, emotional, and political questions. Even treatments have turned out to be combination medications, not a single pill that just makes AIDS go away.

The relationship of gay men to gentrification is particularly interesting and complex. It is clear to me, although it's rarely

/

stated, that the high rate of deaths from AIDS was one of a number of determining factors in the rapid gentrification of key neighborhoods of Manhattan. From the first years of the epidemic through to the epicenter of the AIDS crisis, people I knew were literally dying daily, weekly, regularly. Sometimes they left their apartments and went back to their hometowns to die, because there was no medical support structure and their families would take them. Many, however, were abandoned by their families. Sometimes they were too sick to live alone or pay their rent, and left their apartments to die on friends' couches or in hospital corridors. Many died in their apartments. It was normal to hear that someone we knew had died and that their belongings were thrown out on the street. I remember once seeing the cartons of a lifetime collection of playbills in a dumpster in front of a tenement, and I knew that it meant that another gay man had died of AIDS, his belongings dumped in the gutter.

In the early years, people with AIDS had no protections of any kind. Homosexuality itself was still illegal—and sodomy laws would not be repealed until 2003 in the Supreme Court ruling *Lawrence v. Texas*. There was no anti-discrimination legislation, no gay rights bill in New York City, no benefits, no qualifying for insurance or social services. There were no treatments. Particularly gruesome was that surviving partners or roommates were not allowed to inherit leases that had been in the dead person's name. Everett Quinton, the surviving lover of theater genius Charles Ludlum, famously fought eviction from the apartment the two of them had shared after Ludlum's death. ACT UPer Robert Hilferty was evicted from his apartment in the mid-1980s when his lover, Tom—the leaseholder—died of AIDS. And this policy was true in public housing projects as well as in private rentals. So for every leaseholder who died of AIDS, an apartment went to market rate.

While, of course, AIDS devastated a wealthy subculture of gay white males, many of the gay men who died of AIDS in my neighborhood were either from the neighborhood originally and/or were risk-taking individuals living in oppositional subcultures, creating new ideas about sexuality, art, and social justice. They often paid a high financial price for being out of the closet and community oriented, and pioneering new art ideas. Indeed, many significant figures in the history of AIDS, like iconic film theorist and West Village resident Vito Russo, died without health insurance. So the apartments they left were often at pre-gentrification rates, and were then subjected to dramatic increases or privatized.

In my own building, our neighbor in apartment 8, Jon Hetwar, a young dancer, died of AIDS after our tenants' association had won a four-year rent strike that resulted in across-the-board rent reductions. After his death, his apartment went from $305 per month to the market rate of $1,200 per month. This acceleration of the conversion process helped turn the East Village from an interracial enclave of immigrants, artists, and longtime residents to a destination location for wealthy diners and drinking spot for Midtown and Wall Street businesspeople. Avenue A went from the centerpiece of a Puerto Rican and Dominican neighborhood to the New York version of Bourbon Street in less than a decade. I similarly observed the West Village change from a longtime Italian and gay district with an active gay street life into a neighborhood dominated first by wealthy heterosexuals and then by movie stars, as new gay arrivals shifted to other parts of the city. Now you have to be Julianne Moore to live in the West Village. The remaining older gay population is so elite as to have an antagonistic relationship with the young black and Latino gay men and lesbians and transgendered kids who socialize on the streets and piers of the West Village. Organizations like FIERCE (Fabulous Independent Educated Radicals for Community Empowerment) had to be formed to combat harassment of young gay kids of color by wealthy white West Villagers. Gay life is now expected to take place in private in the West Village, by people who are white, upper class, and sexually discreet.

Strangely, this relationship between huge death rates in an epidemic caused by governmental and familial neglect along with the material process of gentrification is rarely recognized. Instead, gentrification is blamed on gay people and artists who survived, not on those who caused their mass deaths. We all know about white gay men coming into poor neighborhoods and serving as economic "shock troops," buying and rehabbing properties, bringing in elite businesses, and thereby driving out

SARAH SCHULMAN

/

indigenous communities, causing homelessness and cultural erasure.

While the racism of many white gay men and their willingness to displace poor communities in order to create their own enclaves is historical fact, gentrification would not have been possible without tax incentives for luxury developers or without the lack of city-sponsored low-income housing. That the creation of economically independent gay development is seen as the "cause" of gentrification is an illusion. We need to apply simultaneous thinking to have a more truthful understanding of the role of white gay men in gentrification. It is true that like many white people, many white gay men had a colonial attitude toward communities of color. Yet at the same time, it is helpful to think about why white gay men left their neighborhoods and homes to re-create themselves in black, Latino, Asian, and mixed neighborhoods. It seems clear that heterosexual dominance within every community does not aid and facilitate gay comfort, visibility, and autonomy. The desire to live in or create gay enclaves was a consequence of oppression experiences. Only gay people who were able to access enough money to separate from their oppressive communities of origin were able to create visible, gay-friendly housing and commerce as well as achieve political power in a city driven by real estate development. This does not excuse or negate the racism, or the consequences of that racism. And these observations in no way negate gays and lesbians of color living successfully and unsuccessfully in black, Latino, Asian, and mixed neighborhoods. But if all gays could live safely and openly in their communities of origin, and if government policies had been oriented toward protecting poor neighborhoods by rehabbing without displacement, then gentrification by white gay men would have been both unnecessary and impossible.

It is crucial at this point to understand how overt and vulgar the oppression against gay people was at that time. There was not even a basic gay rights anti-discrimination bill in New York until 1986. I remember being on a date with a woman at a restaurant called Kenny's Castaways on Bleecker Street circa 1980. We were kissing at the table and the waitress came over with a distressed expression.

"I don't know how to tell you this, but the manager says that you are going to have to leave."

In the same period (1979–82), I was with a group of lesbians at a Mexican restaurant, Pancho Villa's on pre-gentrification Broadway and Ninth Street. We were sitting on each other's laps and again were told to leave.

It was perfectly legal to deny public accommodations (restaurants and hotels) to gay people. And these events both took place in Greenwich Village!

It took the disaster of the AIDS crisis for New York queers to win the right to legally kiss in a restaurant unmolested. This helps us understand how the implementation of gentrification policy could have been invisible to the average New Yorker, while the presence of openly gay men rehabbing a building was extremely visible.

Although I have spent thirty years of my life writing about the heroism of gay men, I have also come to understand their particular brand of cowardice. There is a destructive impulse inside many white gay men, where they become cruel or child-like or spineless out of a rage about not having the privileges that straight men of our race take for granted. They have grief about not being able to subjugate everyone else at will. Some-times this gets expressed in a grandiose yet infantile capitula-tion to the powers that be—even at the expense of their own community. Professor John Boswell stopped the Center for Lesbian and Gay Studies (CLAGS) from coming to Yale be-cause he insisted that its board be composed entirely of full pro-fessors, in an era in which there were no out-of-the-closet les-bian or nonwhite gay full professors in the country. CLAGS refused, and was moved by its founder, Martin Duberman, to the City University Graduate Center. Boswell died of AIDS, abandoned by the social system he so strongly defended. Or Daryl Yates Rist, who wrote a piece condemning ACT UP in the *Nation* for being "obsessed" with AIDS, of which he too later died. Media pundit Andrew Sullivan produced one of the lowest moments in AIDS coverage, one we are still paying for, when he claimed in the *New York Times Magazine* on Novem-ber 10, 1996, that we had reached "the end of AIDS." No lie could be more dear to the dominant culture than that "AIDS is over." For from the moment that the *New York Times* told us that AIDS was over—even though it was and is a phenomenon so broad and vast as to permanently transform the experience of being a person in this world—its consequences no longer needed to be considered.

We still have to work every day to assert the obvious: that in fact, there are two distinctly different kinds of AIDS that are not over.

1) There is AIDS of the past.

2) There is ongoing AIDs.

Neither is over, although they are treated quite differently in the present moment.

Ongoing AIDS is both maintained and addressed by globalization—a sort of worldwide gentrification in which specificity of experience, understanding, and need are glossed over by a homogenizing corporate net, and existing knowledge—about medicine, water, housing, and food—existing methods of education, and existing international resources are denied human beings in huge numbers so that a small group of privileged people can enjoy happiness.

Those of us still living who witnessed the early days of the crisis know that had the US government risen to the occasion (as many of our dead begged them to do), there would not be a global epidemic today. As well, we know that the obstacles— lack of clean water, economic underdevelopment, lack of health care, the high price of treatments, and so on—are sustained by lack of political will above all. The need for our side of the world to live off the other, and maintain them in poverty, dependency, and underdevelopment, is HIV's best friend. And this divide is as powerful internally to the United States as it is globally.

The confluence of gentrification and ongoing AIDS has been a true spectacle. Marketed as "AIDS in Africa," ongoing international AIDS has inspired a kind of insipid charity mentality in the citizen who expresses her opinions through the products she consumes. Gentrifying chain stores like the Gap, which have replaced many independent businesses while creating homogeneity of dress across regions, have instigated programs where purchasing a particular shirt results in a donation, lower than sales tax, to "AIDS in Africa." Instead of sharing the world's riches, the United States has responded with programs both governmental and corporate that fluctuate in their level of support, and fail to address the underlying issues. In her book *Dead Aid*, Zambian economist Dambisa Moyo explains how George W. Bush's AIDS fund delivered twenty cents on the dollar to its intended recipients—a rate typical of most international and domestic AIDS bureaucracies.

Regarding ongoing AIDS at home, the March 15, 2009, *Washington Post* reported that 3 to 4 percent of Washington, DC, is HIV infected—a higher rate than many West African countries. While death rates have declined domestically, infection rates are increasing. The failure of US prevention programs to raise their percentage of effectiveness gets addressed with the gentrified cure-all: marketing. Periodically changing subway ad campaigns and alternating slogans abound. Offering young men of color free metro cards to come to "prevention counseling" doesn't change the fact that they are economically, politically, and representationally pushed aside. But the larger problems—the United States' refusal to destigmatize and integrate gay people on our own terms, treat drug users effectively, support reasonable public education, provide health care, and stop incarcerating black males—these policies are what keep infection rates high. As long as prevention is the US gay man and straight woman's private problem, it will continue to be a public disaster. The insistence on bootstrap prevention has produced prevention campaigns for "men-who-have-sex-with-men" because we recognize that homophobia is so punitive that calling homosexual sex *homosexual* will keep people who are having homosexual sex from the support that they need to avoid HIV infection. We decide to replace truth with falsity, to *gentrify* the truth about sex in order to save lives. Lying becomes constructed as "saving." Telling the truth, that "men-who-have-sex-with-men" are having homosexual sex, is assessed as ineffectual and therefore destructive because the prejudice that creates this environment is considered to be unchangeable. Yet this capitulation to and (thus) prolongation of homophobia has not shown statistical success in lowering infection rates....

Ongoing AIDS also involves refusing to accept that educa-

SARAH SCHULMAN

/

260

tion and job training that give people an interesting, valued social role are the best prevention against drug abuse. That getting
into effective rehab should be as easy as getting into jail. That
needle exchange should be as pervasive as liquor stores and—as
Linda Villarosa pointed out on the front page of the *New York
Times* in 2004—that the incarceration of black men has created
a generation of unpartnered, heterosexual black women, thereby rendering them more vulnerable to unsafe sex and AIDS infection. Finally, ongoing AIDS means recognizing that people
become infected, as art critic Douglas Crimp said about his own
sero-conversion after twenty years of AIDS activism, "because I'm human."

Here, however, I am mostly concerned with past AIDS. I am
driven by its enormous, incalculable influence on our entire cultural mind-set and the parallel silence about this fact. Do you
know what I mean when I refer to "AIDS of the past"?

I am talking about the plague (the overlapping period between perestroika and gentrification). The years from 1981 to
1996, when there was a mass death experience of young people. Where folks my age watched in horror as our friends, their
lovers, cultural heroes, influences, buddies, the people who
witnessed our lives as we witnessed theirs, as these folks sick-
ened and died consistently for fifteen years. Have you heard
about it?

Amazingly, there is almost no conversation in public about
these events or their consequences. Every gay person walking

around who lived in New York or San Francisco in the 1980s and early 1990s is a survivor of devastation, and carries with them the faces, fading names, and corpses of the otherwise-forgotten dead. When you meet a queer New Yorker over the age of forty, this should be your first thought, just as entire male generations were assumed to have fought in World War II or Korea or Vietnam. Our friends died and our world was destroyed because of the neglect of real people who also have names and faces. Whether they were politicians or parents, as people with AIDS literally fought in the streets or hid in corners until they too died or survived, others—their relatives, neighbors, "friends," coworkers, presidents, landlords, and bosses—stood by and did nothing.

As of August 16, 2008, 81,542 people have died of AIDS in New York City. These people, our friends, are rarely mentioned. Their absence is not computed, and the meaning of their loss is not considered.

On 9/11, 2,752 people died in New York City. These human beings have been highly individuated. The recognition of their loss and suffering is a national ritual, and the consequences of their aborted potential are assessed annually in public. They have been commemorated with memorials, organized international gestures, plaques on many fire and police stations, and new construction on the site of the World Trade Center, all designed to make their memory permanent. Money has been paid to some of their survivors. Their deaths were avenged with a

SARAH SCHULMAN

/

262

brutal, bloody, and unjustified war against Iraq that has caused at least 94,000 civilian deaths and 4,144 military deaths.

The deaths of these 81,542 New Yorkers, who were despised and abandoned, who did not have rights or representation, who died because of the neglect of their government and families, has been ignored. This gaping hole of silence has been filled by the deaths of 2,752 people murdered by outside forces. The disallowed grief of twenty years of AIDS deaths was replaced by ritualized and institutionalized mourning of the acceptable dead. In this way, 9/11 is the gentrification of AIDS. The replacement of deaths that don't matter with deaths that do. It is the centerpiece of supremacy ideology—the idea that one person's life is more important than another's. That one person deserves rights that another does not deserve. That one person deserves representation that the other cannot be allowed to access. That one person's death is negligible if they were poor, a person of color, a homosexual living in a state of oppositional sexual disobedience, while another death matters because that person was a trader, cop, or office worker presumed to be performing the job of capital.

In 1987, ACT UP's affinity group Gran Fury created an installation in the window of the New Museum in New York City. It may have been the first work about AIDS in a major art institution. The installation was called Let the Record Show. Employing the politics of accountability at the root of ACT UP's ethos, the show featured photographs of real-life individuals who were causing the deaths of our friends. People like North Carolina senator Jesse Helms. Helms had just said that the government should spend less money on people with AIDS because they got sick as the result of "deliberate, disgusting, revolting conduct." In the background of the installation was a photo of the Nuremburg trials. The implication was that the specific people who caused our friends to die would one day be made accountable. They would be reduced from their undeserved grandeur into wilted, hovering little people like Nazi Rudolf Hess wasting away in prison in Spandau, Germany. In the end, though, our public enemies—people like Cardinal Joseph Ratzinger, who called homosexuality "an intrinsic moral evil," Mayor Ed Koch, President Ronald Reagan, and others—all got away with it. No one was ever made accountable. Our friend Sal Licata spent nine days on a gurney in the hallway of a New York City hospital. He never got a hospital room. And then he died. No one has ever had to account for this. When Helms died, his life was marked benignly. His crimes against humanity were barely mentioned. The names of our friends whom Reagan murdered are not engraved in a tower of black marble. There has never been a government inquiry into the fifteen years of official disregard that permitted AIDS to become a worldwide disaster.

Where is our permanent memorial?

Not the AIDS quilt, now locked up in storage somewhere, but the government-sponsored invitation to mourn and understand, equal to designer Maya Lin's memorial in Washington, DC, to the dead in Vietnam? Where is our wall of white marble with the names of every New Yorker who died of government neglect, and blank tablets with room for more to come, surrounding a white marble fountain spouting water the color of blood? . . .

Where is our material aid to survivors and damaged communities?

Where are the children of people who died of AIDS? There must be hundreds of thousands of them. Most children of murdered parents coalesce into some kind of community, but not these. I fear that the descendants of people who died of AIDS do not fully understand that their parents perished because of governmental and societal neglect. Not because they were gay or used drugs. Where is our catharsis, our healing? Where is our post-traumatic stress diagnosis? Where is our recovery?

The period I address here is the confluence of the waning of the epicenter of the AIDS crisis and the stabilization of gentrification and gentrified thinking. This is when the radical direct action expression of gay liberation began to be overwhelmed by assimilation—one of the principal consequences of AIDS. But I think that day one of the triumph of gentrified thought was actually November 10, 1996, the morning when the people who ran the *New York Times* (or "New York Crimes," as Gran Fury called it) decided that of all the lesbian and gay thinkers and activists in the vast nation, of all the LGBT leaders who had bravely built our communities for fifty years . . . the person who should be given a platform was . . . author Andrew Sullivan. That he was the person who made them the most comfortable. He was the most "Timesy," as an editor there once told me. So they chose him to say in the "paper of record" (the same paper that ignored the AIDS crisis until ACT UP forced it to acknowledge it) (the same paper that would not mention people's surviving partners in their obituaries) (the same paper that would not print the word *gay*) that we had all come to a time that would be known as "the end of AIDS."

Andrew then went on to become the gay spokesperson of choice for the ruling class for almost fifteen years. This statement, one that every queer person whom I knew in 1996 understood to be wrong, absurd, and stupid—this crazy, diabolical, and poisonous statement—earned Sullivan credibility with the power elite. It allowed him to eclipse the actual queer and AIDS community, their organically evolved leadership, and become the gentrified PWA (person with AIDS)—the gay man with AIDS who would lie and therefore replace all the AIDS activists who were telling the truth. Gentrification had to be in place for someone like him to be put into power. He is a symptom.

Eight months later, in 1997, the Key West Literary Seminar focused on the literature of AIDS. It was a gathering of most of the surviving pioneers of AIDS literature, including Mark Doty, Larry Kramer, Edmund White, Tony Kushner, Dale

Peck, and myself. The list of names of the pioneers of AIDS literature who were already dead by 1997 is five times as long as those who lived. At one point during the conference, critic Michael Bronski shared a startling insight from the stage. He said that the rubric "AIDS literature" is itself an expression of homophobia, because without denial, oppression, and indifference, these works would be called "American literature." The cultural apparatus was instructing people that those works telling the truth about heterosexual cruelty, gay political rebellion, sexual desire, and righteous anger were not to be recognized. It was a living reenactment of Frankfurt school philosopher Herbert Marcuse's insight into what he called "repressive intolerance," in which communities become distorted and neutered by the dominant culture's containment of their realities through the noose of "tolerance." The dominant culture doesn't change how it views itself or how it operates, and power imbalances are not transformed. What happens instead is that the oppressed person's expression is overwhelmed by the dominant person's inflationary self-congratulation about how generous they are. The subordinate person learns quickly that they must curb their most expressive instincts in order to be worthy of the benevolence of this containment.

Milan Kundera's masterful novel *The Book of Laughter and Forgetting* engages the ways that pretending away the truth diminishes the integrity of both individuals and nations. The very privilege of supremacy—the ability to deny that other people are real—becomes the fatal flaw keeping us from collective integrity as a society. Thus, pretending away the deaths of 540,436 adults and 5,369 children from AIDS in the United States alone (as of 2008) becomes a mammoth action of self-deception, with enormous consequences for our decency. Ignoring AIDS as it was happening, and then pretending that past AIDS has no impact on survivors or perpetrators, allows us to pretend that ongoing AIDS is inevitable, sad, and impossible to change.

There is something inherently stupid about gentrified thinking. It's a dumbing down and smoothing over of what people are actually like. It's a social position rooted in received wisdom, with aesthetics blindly selected from the presorted offerings of marketing, and without information or awareness about the structures that create its own delusional sense of infallibility. Gentrified thinking is like the bourgeois version of Christian fundamentalism—a huge, unconscious conspiracy of homogeneous patterns with no cognizance of its own freakishness. The gentrification mentality is grounded in the belief that obedience to consumer identity over recognition of lived experience is actually normal, neutral, and value free.

It is helpful in this moment to think back to ACT UP's politics of accountability: if someone hurts you, you have the right to respond. Your response is the consequence of their violating action. Pharmaceutical executives, politicians who have pledged to represent and serve the people, religious leaders who claim moral authority—anyone who interfered with progress for people with AIDS was made to face a consequence for the pain they caused. To do this, ACT UP had to identify what needed to be changed, identify the individuals who were obstructing that change, clearly propose courses of action that were doable and justifiable, and then force the people with power—through the tactic of direct action—to do something different than what they wanted to do. Making people accountable is always in the interest of justice. Those who are dominant, however, hate accountability. Vagueness, lack of delineation of how things work, the idea that people do not have to keep their promises—these tactics always serve the lying, the obstructive, the hypocritical.

I've noticed through my long life that people with vested interest in things staying the way they are regularly insist that both change and accountability are impossible.

"It's never going to change," a wealthy, white, male, MFA-trained playwright told me about the exclusion of women playwrights from the theater in the United States. "And if you try, people will say you are *difficult*."

On the other hand, Audre Lord—black, lesbian, mother, warrior, poet—told me, "That you can't fight city hall is a rumor being spread by city hall."

As we become conscious about the gentrified mind, the value of accountability must return to our vocabulary and become our greatest tactic for change. Pretending that AIDS is not happening and never happened, so that we don't have to be accountable, destroys our integrity and therefore our future. Ignoring the reality that our cities cannot produce liberating ideas for the future from a place of homogeneity keeps us from being truthful about our inherent responsibilities to each other. For in the end, all this self-deception and replacing, this prioritizing and marginalizing, this smoothing over and pushing out, all of this profoundly affects how we think. That then creates what we think we feel.

*

Sarah Schulman is a novelist, nonfiction writer, playwright, screenwriter, journalist, and AIDS historian, and the author of eighteen books. A Guggenheim and Fulbright fellow, Sarah is a distinguished professor of the humanities at the City University of New York, College of Staten Island. She cofounded the Lesbian Avengers as well as MIX: New York Queer Experimental Film Festival, and was active with both ACT UP and the Irish Lesbian and Gay Organization. This piece is excerpted from the original version, reprinted from The Gentrification of the Mind: Witness to a Lost Imagination *(Berkeley: University of California Press, 2012) by Sarah Schulman with permission of the author.*

SARAH SCHULMAN

/

GRIEF AND ORGANIZING IN THE FACE OF REPRESSION

/

THE FIGHT AGAINST AIDS IN PRISON

DAVID GILBERT,
INTERVIEWED AND
WITH A PROLOGUE
BY DAN BERGER

Prison is a grievous institution. Grief and loss surround it, physically and conceptually. The loss of people and freedom, the devastation of communities and relationships—prison would seem, through its nature of physical removal and containment, to deny the existence of a public. Any access to prison is tightly controlled through armed guards, government bureaucrats, and thick walls of concrete.

And yet prisons are never as far removed from the rest of society as some might like to think. People in prison constitute a public unto themselves—a fraught and limited one, riven with institutionalized barriers, no doubt, but a public nonetheless. Incarcerated people retain connections to friends, family, acquaintances, and others outside prison. Most people who are incarcerated leave at some point, even if briefly. Ideas and social networks, disease and violence, are not contained within prison. Rather, they pass between jail, prison, and neighborhood with an ease that belies the heavy security of the individual institution itself.

Prison is a paradox. It is at once public and sequestered, isolated yet connected. Living within it, or working against it, and especially doing both, requires a certain intimacy with grief. In his book *Live from Death Row*, journalist and political prisoner

/

Mumia Abu-Jamal called prison a "second-by-second assault on the soul, a degradation of the self, an oppressive steel and brick umbrella that transforms seconds into hours and hours into days." Mumia's recognition of the slow-burn violence of incarceration, written inside the death row of a maximum-security prison, adds another layer to the paradox: How do people survive within an institution predicated on their suppression?

The prison's daily assault on body and soul, and the prisoner's struggle to survive and contest it, is especially evident in the realm of health care. A legion of testimonials, recorded in lawsuits and interviews as well as the kitchen-table stories of loved ones living and dead, reveal the combination of benign neglect and malicious disregard that is the US prison health care system. Diseases routinely spread through jails and prisons. Officials ignore early warning signs that could save lives. Medical workers are often unsympathetic to treating "criminals," and even if they are compassionate, lack adequate resources to help. People are cramped in tight, frequently unsanitary quarters. Conditions are ripe for the spread of viruses and infections, which can then become epidemics. Add to that the stigma, racism, and homophobia characterizing the government's pitiful response to the rise of HIV and AIDS, and it's self-evident why so many people died of AIDS-related illnesses during the 1980s and 1990s.

The punitive environment of prison exacerbated (and still does) the hostility that people with AIDS (PWAs) faced outside prison in those years (and since). Officials fear any kind of organizing among prisoners. Homophobia governs the sex-segregated world of incarceration, often among prisoners as well as staff. Within men's prisons, this combination nurtures a self-censoring of most emotional expression.

In the early days of the epidemic, AIDS activists around the world worked to mobilize grief into action. The prison context was no different in that respect. Yet as HIV and AIDS spread throughout US prisons, those who first rose up to fight it had to confront the everyday obstacles of life and death in prison while also challenging the larger systemic failures to treat a disease that largely affected injection drug users along with queers of all racial and ethnic backgrounds.

The AIDS crisis emerged alongside and as part of two other political-economic crises in the United States: the unprecedented buildup of the world's largest incarceration system and the divestment of resources from inner cities. This confluence of what scholar-activist Ruth Wilson Gilmore has called the "organized abandonment" of capitalism and "organized violence" of the state especially ravaged working-class black communities. Many on the Left, too, failed to confront this brutal convergence.

Yet the AIDS movement, primarily coming out of queer communities, practiced a radical politics of care in its effort to save lives and force the government to act. And like all mass movements, the fight against AIDS created space for people to locate themselves within a broader collective. In prison, several political prisoners from revolutionary movements of the 1960s and 1970s took the lead in developing campaigns to stop the spread of the virus in the mid- to late 1980s. Working with other respected prisoners, they developed multiracial, black- and Latino-led programs of peer education and direct action.

David Gilbert was one of those people. A former member of Students for a Democratic Society and the Weather Underground, Gilbert was sentenced to serve seventy-five years to life in prison for his role working in solidarity with the Black Liberation Army in a 1981 robbery of a Brink's truck that went horribly wrong, leading to shootouts in which two police officers and a security guard were killed. After the death of his co-defendant and comrade Kuwasi Balagoon, Gilbert cofounded the Prisoner Education Project (PEPA) on AIDS. PEPA and similar efforts—including one in a women's prison in New York State founded by other codefendants of Balagoon and Gilbert— saved countless lives in a period of official indifference and hostility to the AIDS crisis.

They provided a positive example of prisoner initiative to build on as the growing AIDS movement outside prison created pressure on the Department of Correctional Services (DOCS) to institute programs throughout the system. As Gilbert describes below, the functional end of the program constituted its own kind of loss: the breakup of a certain support collective among people in prison. Officials tried to stymie the organizing efforts at every turn. Once they could no longer do so, they launched their own programs and shut down the prisoner-led ones. The fight against AIDS has advanced considerably—the fight for people, in prison and out, to take control of their lives continues.

This interview was conducted by mail in 2015 and 2016, with additional edits supplemented through phone calls. It builds on almost two decades of friendship and occasional coauthorship in which we have discussed grassroots organizing and radical movements over the twentieth and twenty-first centuries. I have been especially keen to hear David reflect on his work combating HIV and AIDS in prison. In fact, I have been far more interested in hearing about it than he has been in talking about it. That organizing, which we explore below, saved an untold number of lives through grassroots and intersectional radicalism. It is a stark example of a revolutionary commitment to confront state violence through a transformative politics of care.

The fight against AIDS constituted a rare level of collectivity inside prison that David has not experienced since. While prisoners in different parts of the country have staged a series of labor or hunger strikes since 2010, New York State prisons have seen little activism. The culture of life in prison remains institutionally bleak. In recent years, Gilbert has prioritized dialogue with contemporary political activists outside prison. His investment in social movements, in and out of prison, remains

GRIEF AND ORGANIZING

/

undaunted. We engaged in this conversation to record an all-too-frequently unacknowledged history in the struggle against mass incarceration, with the hope that it might prove useful to today's battles.

*

DAN: *In the 1980s, you cofounded the first comprehensive prison-based peer education program around HIV and AIDS. Saying it that way sounds too official, like it was planned all along. But it in fact emerged from chaotic, difficult circumstances. You started the project after the death of a close friend and comrade. Can you say more about who Kuwasi was, and the context of his illness and death in prison?*

DAVID: Kuwasi Balagoon was an incredibly wonderful human being—creative, courageous, principled. In 1969, he had been part of the New York City Panther 21, the most notorious case of the police bringing false criminal charges to suppress political organizing, and before that, he was a light-heavyweight boxer in the army and sparkling poet who read on the same programs as the Last Poets (considered the 1960s' precursors to hip-hop). Kuwasi, with incredible daring and brilliance, had managed two different escapes from New Jersey State prisons. Each time he was out and clear, and only got caught later because he continued to try to free other comrades. In our time together at Auburn Correctional Facility, Kuwasi whistled jazz tunes, painted surreal watercolors, and got up at 5:00 a.m. to

DAVID GILBERT AND DAN BERGER

/

work in the kitchen because that afforded him the opportunity to bake for friends—Kuwasi, my comrade and best friend. We shared a deep commitment to stand firm in upholding militant struggle against this antihuman system, and yet at the same time to openly admit and analyze errors so that those in the movement could draw needed lessons. He was writing a piece that both upheld basic principles and analyzed errors when he died.

DAN: *How did other prisoners respond to his death?*

DAVID: Kuwasi's death was so sudden and unexpected. How could it be that vibrant Kuwasi, with the workouts everyone admired, was dead at the age of thirty-nine? He had been transferred to an outside hospital ten days before he died. And even more surprising was the diagnosis: Pneumocystis pneumonia as a result of his having AIDS. This was December 1986, and we still didn't know a lot about AIDS, although months earlier Kuwasi and I had talked about the few prisoners known to have it, supportive of them and upset about the lack of sympathy in the prevailing homophobic culture. We hadn't yet recognized AIDS as a major human rights battle, let alone that it would become a scourge in prison.

The outpouring of love and respect for Kuwasi was for me like bathing in a warm ocean. Dozens of prisoners, many of whom I'd never met before, came up to me to express sorrow and condolences. And not just black prisoners but Latinos and

GRIEF AND ORGANIZING

/

whites too, at a time when social bonds and networks were mainly segregated. Even I was surprised by how widely respected and loved he'd been.

In terms of how people processed it on an intellectual or emotional level, the main reaction among prisoners, especially among black prisoners, was that the state killed him, infected him in some way. There were good reasons for that response: the long and brutal history of white supremacist America's assassinations of radical black leaders—including a period fifteen years earlier when close to forty of Kuwasi's Black Panther comrades had been killed. Those who were sure that it had been murder also were well aware of the wider, nefarious history of the Tuskegee syphilis "study" and various unethical experiments on prisoners. Dozens of them urged me to have our people conduct an investigation, and I agreed. Our staunch and dedicated lawyer, Susan V. Tipograph, had flown up to see Kuwasi in the outside hospital in Buffalo. She was working to get our own doctor in to see him, but time ran out before that could happen. She did get to speak with Kuwasi, and he said that years ago he had some activities now identified as risky. With Kuwasi, who was a free spirit in many ways, it could have been anything. Given that history of possible transmission, we couldn't charge that the state had killed him. (And what I learned about AIDS over subsequent years made that increasingly unlikely.)

DAVID GILBERT AND DAN BERGER

/

Now I had this daunting task to tell all these prisoners who were sure he had been assassinated that "no, we can't charge that; good chance Kuwasi unwittingly contracted it." Several of the black prisoners involved were highly nationalist, not used to taking the word of a white guy, yet they showed great respect in coming to me because I was Kuwasi's codefendant and comrade. I could see the disappointment, so visible in their faces, when I wouldn't confirm what fit with their passionate and legitimate belief—generally valid, but not applicable in this instance. My credibility with many took a big hit. It was terribly tempting to tell people what they wanted to hear, what *sounded* the most radical. But as a revolutionary I had to tell people the truth as I understood it. That first month I was caught up in a swirl of conflicting currents: an intense sense of loss, yet feeling the warmth of our community's love for Kuwasi, but aware of how my stance was terribly disappointing to many of them.

DAN: *The fight against AIDS looks so different now. We seem on the verge of possibly curing AIDS, or minimally, managing it as a chronic condition rather than a death sentence—at least for people of some means in Western countries. It can be hard, then, to recall the fear, panic, and hostility that marked the early days of the epidemic. What did it mean to learn about HIV and AIDS in prison? How many people showed signs of either condition? How was the institution responding?*

GRIEF AND ORGANIZING

/

DAVID: At this time, there were few prisoners with visible signs of AIDS. At the Auburn Correctional Facility, there were three identified PWAs, out of a population of sixteen hundred, and they were held separately, in the facility's infirmary. So there wasn't much sense of the ravages of AIDS. But I was engulfed in grief and turned that into studying AIDS, almost obsessively. As I did, it started to dawn on me that we were on the cusp of a major epidemic within the New York State DOCS. Its public position in 1986 was that AIDS was not a problem because drugs and sex were prohibited. Yet at the same time, I was reading about astronomical rates of infection among intravenous drug users in New York City, and I knew that something like 50 percent of New York State prisoners had a prior drug history. Even with a long, if not yet pinned down, incubation period, waves of deadly sickness would soon be on us. And despite the rules, drugs and sex were common enough that transmission within prison had to be a significant problem.

DAN: *Clearly there are a lot of barriers to organizing in prison. How did you go from studying the disease to getting a peer education program off the ground?*

DAVID: I felt it was an urgent matter of life and death within our community, and it couldn't be left to official indifference. Two different good friends of Kuwasi's came to me to see if we could develop a constructive approach. Mujahid Farid was a jailhouse lawyer with an outstanding record of fighting for prisoners' rights. Angel "Papo" Nieves had been at the heart of efforts to develop programs for Latino prisoners. We found a few positive examples of compassion. Prisoners at Green Haven and the women's prison at Bedford Hills were volunteering to visit with AIDS patients in the infirmaries (this at a time of widespread fear of casual transmission); some at Sing Sing made an educational video, *AIDS: A Bad Way to Die*. But the epidemic was about to mushroom. Was there more we could do? We were acutely concerned about the need for prevention—for prisoners and the communities to which many would be paroled.

In my studies, the most effective approach I'd seen was the inspiring initiatives by gay activists to have peer (homeboys and homegirls) educators working with folks in their community. The peer approach was doubly, maybe triply, needed in prison —where not only do people completely distrust the authorities but also the very activities that had to be discussed frankly, sometimes in detail, could subject people to disciplinary sanctions. At the same time, the stigma around AIDS and widespread homophobia undercut the sense of solidarity we so sorely needed to move forward as a community. While there was no way to make homophobia instantly disappear, Farid, Papo, and I agreed that the work had to be based on respect for every person involved.

The three of us put together a simple, one-page proposal for a comprehensive Prisoner Education Project on AIDS (PEPA;

GRIEF AND ORGANIZING

/

see appendix at the end of the interview). We faced a giant chasm: a population that completely distrusted the establishment, including the medical authorities, yet the urgent need for prisoners to access and assimilate new and in some ways technical information. The bridge over the gap would be to develop trusted and well-versed peer counselors, with the training to be done by an outside of DOCS, community-based AIDS organization.

I'd already been working informally with some guys I knew. That experience showed that in the context of mutual trust and respect, consistent and day-to-day counseling could foster changes away from high-risk practices. We wanted PEPA to be more thorough and ongoing than a one-shot movie or assembly. Our proposal included sessions that would reach the whole population, and we wanted enough counselors so that every prisoner could find someone he respected for private, confidential discussions about all the ins and outs of drug and/or sexual practices. At the same time, we educated against fears of casual contact and advocated for any institutionally isolated PWAs to be let into general population activities.

We had come to this approach by studying what seemed to work in practice, but it also turned out to provide a paradigm of the difference between the political Right and Left. The former uses such crises to impose restrictions and repression from above, even though that never solves the problem. We responded with education, organization, and mobilization from below, encouraging the oppressed to take control of their own lives.

Several prisoners who were experienced in fighting for programs warned me that DOCS would be hostile and that I should expect to get shipped out of the facility. Outside friends were incredulous that the authorities would oppose such a humanitarian project, but "corrections" is all about control, and they react viscerally against prisoners' organizing. Our focus on developing peer counselors from every sector of the population— not just black, white, Latino, and native, but also the major different national, religious, and social groupings within that— evidently conjured up to DOCS its nightmare of prisoner unity.

We had prepared by developing outside support, which led to an outcry when DOCS rejected our proposal. What followed was a long and involved battle, too complicated to recount here. The main weapon deployed was prisoners' fear of casual contact. There were some tense moments, but the combination of the informal education we had done, especially that there was no danger of casual transmission, and some fast footwork thwarted the potentially violent reactions. As soon as we succeeded at that, I was shipped out to Clinton Correctional Facility, a restrictive "disciplinary" facility (most get sent there after disciplinary violations) near the Canadian border, as far away as possible from supportive outside organizations. They moved me three days before Christmas, so none of our outside supporters were in town to raise a fuss. They immediately took

GRIEF AND ORGANIZING

/

away my family reunion visits, a great New York State DOCS program that allows overnight visits on the prison grounds with immediate family—a program that played such an important role in my relationship with my son. I managed to get the denial overturned on appeal. That transfer was the opening to a bit of a personal odyssey; over the course of thirty-three months, DOCS had me moving in and out of twenty-one different cells in four different prisons. I tried to start a PEPA in every place I went.

Nonetheless, the PEPAs back at Auburn managed to complete a training that graduated fifteen peer counselors in February 1988. That first class of graduates included Nuh Washington, an ex-Panther and political prisoner deeply respected throughout the population. The peer counselors weren't allowed to implement anything nearly as extensive or intensive as the initial PEPA proposal, but just having these highly knowledgeable guys in the population made a difference. More important, PEPA was not alone. By early 1988, AIDS Counseling and Education (ACE) was up and running at Bedford Hills (two of the key initiators there were also longtime comrades and codefendants of Kuwasi and me), which went on to be the outstanding nationwide example of a successful program. Inspired by PEPA and ACE, prisoners at a few facilities started the very worthwhile Prisoners AIDS Counseling and Education.

By the 1990s, the pressure from a strong outside AIDS movement led New York State to mandate that every prison have "peer" education on AIDS. In practice, many of these were paper programs with little outreach, but overall it made some difference, saved some lives. This result was not at all a straight-out victory since in many, and maybe most, the approach was bureaucratic, with no program for systematic outreach. But in several facilities, especially those closest to New York City that could find committed community sponsors, there have been serious programs that have made a difference, and with the many transfers that happen, much of that understanding then permeated throughout the state. Not a pure or simple victory, but a significant advance.

At its peak in 1995, the AIDS epidemic took 258 lives in just one year among DOCS' relatively young population of some 60,000 people. The year 1996 brought a dramatic breakthrough of new, effective treatments that started saving lives. We still ache at the loses—valiant Kuwasi and the many other dear friends I and other AIDS counselors saw taken away by this terrible epidemic fostered by social neglect. At the same time, it is heartening that so many prisoners responded to grief and fear with grassroots organizing to give people ways to take care of themselves and fight for our communities.

DAN: *The problems to confront were not merely among the administration. You've written elsewhere about the harms caused by homophobia and general ignorance of HIV and AIDS among people in prison in the early days of the epidemic. Later, this gave rise to AIDS conspir-*

GRIEF AND ORGANIZING

/

acy theories in prison. You've said that both issues led to a number of deaths through people's inaction or aversion to proven harm reduction strategies (like safer sex). Given that context, how did you and the other PEPA cofounders approach your work?

DAVID: Well, when I first asked prisoners what they thought, back in 1987, the almost-universal response was, "We have to keep those people away, don't let them work in the mess hall, etc." But as soon as we educated people about that, once those suffocating weeds of fear had been uprooted, people's humanity flowered. Within a month of when we started, several different individuals came up to me and said, "Tell those guys in the AIDS ward that they can come out without any fear because *I'll* be happy to walk the yard with them." After we broke that initial stranglehold, we got some of the most respected guys in the facility to sign up for the training.

Of course, the disdain and fear was intertwined with the backward, predominant homophobia. While we were a small counterforce in terms of respect for all and commitment to saving lives in our prison community, we didn't turn that deep and prevailing bias around. As the epidemic emerged, it became clearer that the overwhelming majority of prisoners with AIDS had contracted it via drug use, so homophobia receded as a main issue.

By the early 1990s, fear of casual contact was no longer a significant factor. Our educational work may have played a role, but mainly it was because by that time, almost every New York State prisoner had a family member or friend with AIDS. That individual connection humanized the issues, and everyone had already had casual contact. But a new and pervasive obstacle had arisen within prison culture, as you just mentioned: AIDS conspiracy theories. Most prisoners, especially black prisoners, were convinced that AIDS was created by the CIA to attack those the government deemed "undesirables"—gays, drug users, blacks, Latinos. (By this time, people recognized that it wasn't just a "gay disease.") This view was kind of a collective version of what had happened individually around Kuwasi. Again, there were very good reasons to believe it—there's an extensive and sordid history that even most radicals don't know of medical experimentation on prisoners, biological warfare on Cuba, radiation exposure on Indian reservations, the Tuskegee syphilis "study," and other examples of scientific and medicalized white supremacy. And of course, mass incarceration itself, which began to take off in 1973, was a form of warfare against the black and Latino/a communities. When I first read accounts of how HIV was created in a lab, they sounded plausible enough to me.

But these beliefs were also a giant obstacle to our work. If the government created it, the information about prevention was undoubtedly bogus, and the medications offered probably harmful. In a way, those most at risk were the most adamant; so I guess it was a convenient form of denial. So I felt I had to study

GRIEF AND ORGANIZING

/

the issue. Fortunately I had a really good friend, Janet Stav-
nezer, who was a microbiologist, and she, along with literature
she got me, showed that creation in a lab was impossible. Scien-
tists didn't even know that retroviruses could affect humans until the mid-1970s, and also didn't have the sophisticated methods
of gene engineering needed until then. But HIV was found in
blood samples from the 1950s, and there were a few medical case
histories going back to the 1930s that indicated those patients
had had AIDS.

Most AIDS programs dealt with the conspiracy theories by
saying, "We don't know how HIV got here, but we need to focus on prevention." While that helped, I didn't think it was
enough—because the theories circulating in prison discouraged
people from prevention and treatment, and also scared people
about casual contact with gays. So I felt we had to counter it
more directly. And you know, as bad as all the real conspira-
cies have been, far, far more oppressed people have been killed
and damaged by lack of access to the type of health care that
middle-class whites enjoy, so the theories were like a red her-
ring that diverted attention from the much bigger issue. So I argued all this directly and eventually wrote a substantial pamphlet about it. Once again, my credibility took a big hit with
some of the most radical prisoners. A big help was provided by
an outside researcher I worked with, *Covert Action Quarterly*'s
Terry Allen, who found that the main source prisoners were
reading, Dr. William Douglass, had a history as a white su-

premacist. We have to wonder why (closeted) white suprema-
cists were circulating literature to black youths that discounted
prevention and treatment, and promoted homophobia. Exposing him, even more than the technical information, had some
impact, but I don't know how much. I think these theories began to recede after the 1996 breakthroughs that came up with
effective treatments.

DAN: *The hostility is one thing. But even among people who were re-
ceptive to your efforts, there must have been a lot of fear, sadness, or
anger about the disease along with the accompanying neglect or violence. How did you help people grieve, mourn, or otherwise process
these feelings?*

DAVID: When I first started working with PWAs, some had
been suicidal—the combination of the grim health prospects
with the stigma. But the emergence of education and support
efforts provided needed encouragement. Many PWAs were fu-
riously angry—at the medical establishment overall and prison
health services in particular. As understandable as that anger
was, it was eating people up. When we developed ways for
them to fight for their own needs—like the successful effort to
get nutritional supplements—the anger was transformed into
positive energy, and people felt better about themselves; a few
PWAs became some of our most effective peer educators. And
again, once the more effective treatments came out in 1996, and

GRIEF AND ORGANIZING

/

in New York State, prisoners got immediate access, people did a lot better.

We didn't have good community ways to grieve in the men's prison, at least the four I've been at. The closest we came to that was the tremendous outpouring of love and respect for Kuwasi. And about a hundred of us sent a message to the outside memorial for him, while two recent parolees represented us there. Otherwise there wasn't much. Maybe a couple of guys would talk wistfully about a mutual friend who had passed away, or if he had been part of a religious group, they might have held a small memorial. The two barriers were the prevailing culture that "strong men" didn't show their feelings and even more so the severe limits on collective gatherings in the men's maximum prisons. Women prisoners at Bedford Hills found beautiful ways to commemorate those who had died. They were more expressive, and the institution allowed them to be more expressive, so their gatherings were less limited than ours were.

DAN: *Your organizing saved a lot of lives. Still, you had to deal with a steady experience of loss. The experience seems both inspiring and demoralizing. How did that dynamic impact the culture of people around you in prison?*

DAVID: I don't know how much we impacted the overall culture. In a way we were a bubble, but only able to be a small one, of counterentropy of people working together in a constructive way for the community. I vividly remember the glow on the faces of peer educators after they did a successful presentation. But we were too constricted to have a major overall impact. Similarly, while we maybe attenuated the prevailing bias, I regretted not being able to more directly and fully challenge homophobia.

Although there is no way to count, I know that we saved many lives, which is great. But it also was frustrating that we were handcuffed from doing more. I loved doing work that combined grassroots organizing with public health, but my dream of developing a strong and sustained organization that worked around all aspects of prisoners' health was never realized. (Although, thankfully, I was able to get hepatitis C added to our curriculum in the late 1990s.) And honestly, for all my skepticism about establishment medicine, the breakthroughs on treatment became vastly more important than our work. Still, I think that the experience shows that even in the face of tremendous losses, fear, and sadness, to the degree we can break the chains, education, organization, and mobilization of and self-activity by the oppressed can make a tremendous difference. Health care in prison remains atrocious, and the system still fears organizing inside. As always, the struggle continues.

GRIEF AND ORGANIZING

/

APPENDIX: PROPOSAL FOR A PRISONER EDUCATION PROJECT ON AIDS

This proposal was the first in the country for a comprehensive prisoners' peer education program on AIDS. Three good friends of Kuwasi Balagoon—Mujahid Farid, Angel Nieves, and David Gilbert—wrote this proposal in April 1987 and submitted it to the Auburn Correctional Facility administration that June. As brief and simple as this proposal was, thirty years later few prisons have programs with anything like the scope of outreach proposed here and still so sorely needed. This proposal was reprinted in David Gilbert's 2004 collection of essays, *No Surrender: Writings from an Anti-Imperialist Political Prisoner.*

BACKGROUND

AIDS is now by far the main cause of death in the New York State prisons. Yet many prisoners remain woefully uneducated about the true nature of the disease and how it is spread. On the one hand, there is periodic panic over forms of contact that don't transmit the disease; on the other hand, high-risk practices continue. The front line of defense has to be education. For such education to be effective in changing high-risk practices, it must be thorough and ongoing, and involve (with proper training and direction) considerable inmate-to-inmate counseling.

DAVID GILBERT AND DAN BERGER

/

294

The main purpose is to save lives by providing inmates at Auburn Correctional Facility with health education on how AIDS is spread and how to prevent it. With systematic and qualified prisoner-to-prisoner education, we can significantly curtail the spread of AIDS among inmates as well as to the outside community to which most prisoners eventually return. A related goal would be to provide counseling and support for inmates already afflicted with AIDS.

SPECIFIC GOALS AND PROGRAM

a) Have a number of inmates trained as AIDS education counselors.

b) Set up specific and thorough seminars with appropriate groupings of prisoners (e.g., the various inmate organizations).

c) Develop an educational presentation that would become part of the Auburn Correctional Facility orientation program and thereby eventually reach every inmate at Auburn.

d) Sponsor special educational programs such as movies, slide shows, skits, and speakers.

GRIEF AND ORGANIZING

/

e) Prepare a special pamphlet that speaks directly to prisoners—about their concerns and in their language.

f) Write articles for the *Auburn Program*.

g) Establish an information and counseling office.

h) Work with prerelease in its efforts to provide information and encourage a sense of responsibility among released prisoners.

i) Coordinate AIDS educational work with existing substance abuse programs.

j) Provide counseling and support for those inmates already afflicted with AIDS.

k) Fulfill other needs and goals that will emerge from these initial efforts.

CONCLUSION

Because of the urgency of the situation, we hope that this project can be approved and commenced as soon as humanly possible so that we can stop today's ignorance from sowing tomorrow's death. This proposal is very simply about saving lives.

*

DAVID GILBERT AND DAN BERGER

/

David Gilbert, an antiracist and anti-imperialist activist since the early 1960s, has been a prisoner in New York State since 1981. He is the author of *two books,* No Surrender: Writings from an Anti-Imperialist Political Prisoner *and* Love and Struggle: My Life in SDS, the Weather Underground, and Beyond.

Dan Berger is an assistant professor of comparative ethnic studies at the University of Washington Bothell. He is the author or editor of several books on US social movements, including most recently Captive Nation: Black Prison Organizing in the Civil Rights Era. *A longtime antiprison activist, Dan is cofounder of Decarcerate PA.*

With thanks to all who have been part of the struggle against AIDS.

GRIEF AND ORGANIZING

/

POSTCARDS

FROM AMERICA

/

X RAYS

FROM HELL

DAVID WOJNAROWICZ

Late yesterday afternoon a friend came over unexpectedly to sit at my kitchen table and try to find some measure of language for his state of mind. "What's left of living?" He's been on AZT for six to eight months and his T-cells have dropped from one hundred plus to thirty. His doctor says, "What the hell do you want from me?" Now he's asking himself, "What the hell do I want?" He's trying to answer this while in the throes of agitating FEAR.

I know what he's talking about as each tense description of his state of mind slips out across the table. The table is filled with piles of papers and objects; a boom box, a bottle of AZT, a jar of Advil (remember, you can't take aspirin or Tylenol while on AZT). There's an old smiley mug with pens and scissors and a bottle of Xanax for when the brain goes loopy; there's a Sony tape recorder that contains a half-used cassette of late-night sex talk, fears of gradual dying, anger, dreams and someone speaking Cantonese. In this foreign language it says: *"My mind cannot contain all that I see. I keep experiencing this sensation that my skin is too tight; civilization is expanding inside of me. Do you have a room with a better view? I am experiencing the X-ray of Civilization. The minimum speed required to break through the earth's gravitational pull is seven miles a second. Since economic conditions prevent us from gaining access to rockets or spaceships we would have to learn to run awful fast to achieve escape from where we are all heading . . ."*

/

My friend across the table says, "There are no more people in their thirties. We're all dying out. One of my four best friends just went into the hospital yesterday and he underwent a blood transfusion and is now suddenly blind in one eye. The doctors don't know what it is . . ." My eyes are still scanning the table; I know a hug or a pat on the shoulder won't answer the question mark in his voice. The AZT is kicking in with one of its little side effects: increased mental activity which in translation means I wake up these mornings with an intense claustrophobic feeling of fucking doom. It also means that one word too many can send me to the window kicking out panes of glass, or at least that's my impulse (the fact that winter is coming holds me in check). My eyes scan the surfaces of walls and tables to provide balance to the weight of words. A thirty-five millimeter camera containing the unprocessed images of red and blue and green faces in close-up profile screaming, a large postcard of a stuffed gorilla pounding its dusty chest in a museum diorama, a small bottle of hydrocortisone to keep my face from turning into a mass of peeling red and yellow flaking skin, an airline ticket to Normal, Illinois, to work on a print, a small plaster model of a generic Mexican pyramid looking like it was made in Aztec kindergarten, a tiny motorcar with a tiny Goofy driving at the wheel . . .

My friend across the table says, "The other three of my four friends are dead and I'm afraid that I won't see this friend again." My eyes settle on a six-inch-tall rubber model of Frankenstein

DAVID WOJNAROWICZ

/

from the Universal Pictures Tour gift shop, TM 1931: his hands are enormous and my head fills up with replaceable body parts; with seeing the guy in the hospital; seeing myself and my friend across the table in line for replaceable body parts; my wandering eyes aren't staving off the anxiety of his words; behind his words, so I say, "You know . . . he can still rally back . . . maybe . . . I mean people do come back from the edge of death . . ."

"Well," he says, "he lost thirty pounds in a few weeks . . ."

A boxed cassette of someone's interview with me in which I talk about diagnosis and how it simply underlined what I knew existed anyway. Not just the disease but the sense of death in the American landscape. How when I was out west this summer standing in the mountains of a small city in New Mexico I got a sudden and intense feeling of rage looking at those postcard-perfect slopes and clouds. For all I knew I was the only person for miles and all alone and I didn't trust that fucking mountain's serenity. I mean it was just bullshit. I couldn't buy the con of nature's beauty; all I could see was death. The rest of my life is being unwound and seen through a frame of death. And my anger is more about this culture's refusal to deal with mortality. My rage is really about the fact that WHEN I WAS TOLD THAT I'D CONTRACTED THIS VIRUS IT DIDN'T TAKE ME LONG TO REALIZE THAT I'D CONTRACTED A DISEASED SOCIETY AS WELL.

On the table is today's newspaper with a picture of cardinal O'Connor saying he'd like to take part in operation rescue's

POSTCARDS FROM AMERICA

/

blocking of abortion clinics but his lawyers are advising against it. This fat cannibal from that house of walking swastikas up on fifth avenue should lose his church tax-exempt status and pay taxes retroactively for the last couple of centuries. Shut down our clinics and we will shut down your "church." I believe in the death penalty for people in positions of power who commit crimes against humanity—i.e., fascism. This creep in black skirt has kept safer-sex information off the local television stations and mass transit spaces for the last eight years of the AIDS epidemic thereby helping thousands and thousands to their unnecessary deaths.

My friend across the table is talking again. "I just feel so fucking sick . . . I have never felt this bad in my whole life . . . I woke up this morning with such intense horror; sat upright in bed and pulled on my clothes and shoes and left the house and ran and ran and ran . . ." I'm thinking maybe he got up to the speed of no more than ten miles an hour. There are times I wish we could fly; knowing that this is impossible I wish I could get a selective lobotomy and rearrange my senses so that all I could see is the color blue; no images or forms, no sounds or sensations. There are times I wish this were so. There are times that I feel so tired, so exhausted. I may have been born centuries too late. A couple of centuries ago I might have been able to be a hermit but the psychic and physical landscape today is just so fucking crowded and bought up. Last night I was invited to dinner upstairs at a neighbor's house. We got together to figure out how to stop the landlord from illegally tearing the roofs off our apartments. The buildings department had already shut the construction crew down twice and yet they have started work again. The recent rains have been slowing destroying my western wall. This landlord some time ago allowed me to stay in my apartment without a lease only after signing an agreement that if there were a cure for AIDS I would have to leave within thirty days. A guy visiting the upstairs neighbor learned that I had this virus and said he believed that although the government probably introduced the virus in the homosexual community, that homosexuals were dying en masse as a reaction to centuries of society's hatred and repression of homosexuality. All I could think of when he said this was an image of hundreds of whales that beach themselves on the coastlines in supposed protest of the ocean's being polluted. He continued, "People don't die—they choose death. Homosexuals are dying of this disease because they have internalized society's hate ..." I felt like smacking him in the head but held off momentarily, saying, "As far as your theory of homosexuals dying of AIDS as a protest against society's hatred, what about the statistics that those people contracting the disease are intravenous drug users or heterosexually inclined, and that this seems to be increasingly the case. Just look at the statistics for this area of the lower east side." "Oh," he said, "They're hated too ..." "Look," I said, "after witnessing the deaths of dozens of friends and a handful of lovers, among them some of the most authentically spiritual people I have ever known, I simply can't accept mystical answers or excuses for why so many people are dying from this disease—really it's on the shoulders of a bunch of bigoted creeps who at this point in time are in the position of power that determine where and when and for whom government funds are spent for research and medical care."

I found that, after witnessing Peter Hujar's death on November 26, 1987, and after my recent diagnosis, I tend to dismantle and discard any and all kinds of spiritual and psychic and physical words or concepts designed to make sense of the external world or designed to give momentary comfort. It's like stripping the body of flesh in order to see the skeleton, the structure. I want to know what the structure of all this is in the way only I can know it. All my notions of the machinations of the world have been built throughout my life on odd cannibalizations of different lost cultures and on intuitive mythologies. I gained comfort from the idea that people could spontaneously self-combust and from surreal excursions into nightly dream landscapes. But all that is breaking down or being severely eroded by my own brain; it's like tipping a bottle over on its side and watching the liquid contents drain out in slow motion. I suddenly resist something I want to see clearly, something I want to witness in its raw state. And this need comes from my sense of mortality. There is a relief in having this sense of mortality. At least I won't arrive one day at my eightieth birthday and at the eve of my possible death and only then realize my whole life

DAVID WOJNAROWICZ

/

306

was supposed to be somewhat a preparation for the event of death and suddenly fill up with rage because instead of preparation all I had was a lifetime of adaptation to the preinvented world—do you understand what I'm saying here? I am busying myself with a process of distancing myself from you and others and my environment in order to know what I feel and what I can find. I'm trying to lift off the weight of the preinvented world so I can see what's underneath it all. I'm hungry and the preinvented world won't satisfy my hunger. I'm a prisoner of language that doesn't have a letter or a sign or gesture that approximates what I'm sensing. Rage may be one of the few things that binds or connects me to you, to our preinvented world.

*

My friend across the table says, "I don't know how much longer I can go on.... Maybe I should just kill myself." I looked up from the Frankenstein doll, stopped trying to twist its yellow head off and looked at him. He was looking out the window at a sexy Puerto Rican guy standing on the street below. I asked him, "If tomorrow you could take a pill that would let you die quickly and quietly, would you do it?"

"No," he said, "Not yet."

"There's too much work to do," I said.

"That's right," he said. "There's still a lot of work to do . . ."

*

POSTCARDS FROM AMERICA

/

I am a bundle of contradictions that shift constantly. This is a comfort to me because to contradict myself dismantles the mental/physical claims of the verbal code. I abstract the disease I have in the same way you abstract death. Sometimes I don't think about this disease for hours. This process lets me get work done, and work gives me life, or at least makes sense of living for short periods of time. Because I abstract this disease, it periodically knocks me on my ass with its relentlessness. With almost any other illness you take for granted that within a week or a month the illness will end and the wonderful part of the human body called the mind will go about its job erasing evidence of the pain and discomfort previously experienced. With AIDS or HIV infections one never gets that luxury and I find myself after a while responding to it for a fractured moment with my pre-AIDS thought processes: "All right this is enough already; it should just go away." But each day's dose of medicine, or the intermittent aerosol pentamidine treatments, or the sexy stranger nodding to you on the street corner or across the room at a party, reminds you in a clearer than clear way that at this point in history the virus' activity is forever. Outside my windows there are thousands of people without homes who are trying to deal with having AIDS. If I think my life at times has a nightmarish quality about it because of the society in which I live and that society's almost total inability to deal with this disease with anything other than a conservative agenda, think for a moment what it would be like to be facing winter winds and

DAVID WOJNAROWICZ

/

shit menus at the limited shelters, and the rampant T.B., and the rapes, muggings, stabbings in those shelters, and the over-whelmed clinics and sometimes clinic doctors, and the fact that drug trials are not open to people of color or the poor unless they have a private physician who can monitor the experimental drugs they would need to take, and they don't have those kinds of doctors in clinics because doctors in clinics are constantly ro-tated and intravenous drug users have to be clean of drugs for seven years before they'll be considered for experimental drug trials, and yet there are nine-month waiting periods just to get assigned to a treatment program. So picture yourself with a cou-ple of the three hundred and fifty opportunistic infections and unable to respond physiologically to the few drugs released by the foot-dragging deal-making FDA and having to maintain a junk habit; or even having to try and kick that habit without any clinical help while keeping yourself alive seven years to get a drug that you need immediately—thank you Ed Koch; thank you Stephen Joseph; thank you Frank Young; thank you AMA.

I scratch my head at the hysteria surrounding the actions of the repulsive senator from zombieland who has been trying to dismantle the NEA for supporting the work of Andres Serrano and Robert Mapplethorpe. Although the anger sparked within the art community is certainly justified and will hopefully grow stronger, the actions by Helms and D'Amato only follow stan-dards that have been formed and implemented by the "arts" community itself. The major museums in New York, not to mention museums around the country, are just as guilty of this kind of selective cultural support and denial. It is a standard practice to make invisible any kind of sexual imaging other than white straight male erotic fantasies. Sex in america long ago slid into a small set of generic symbols; mention the word "sex" and the general public appears to only imagine a couple of heterosexual positions on a bed—there are actual laws in parts of this country forbidding anything else even between consenting adults. So people have found it necessary to define their sexuality in images, in photographs and drawings and movies in order to not disappear. Collectors have for the most part failed to support work that defines a particular person's sexuality, except for a few examples such as Mapplethorpe, and thus have perpetuated the invisibility of the myriad possibilities of sexual activity. The collectors' influence on what the museum shows continues this process secretly with behind-the-scenes manipulations of curators and money. Jesse Helms, at the very least, makes public his attacks on freedom; the collectors and museums responsible for censorship make theirs at elegant private parties or from the confines of their self-created closets.

It doesn't stop at images—in a recent review of a novel in the new york times book review, a reviewer took outrage at the novelist's descriptions of promiscuity, saying, "In this age of AIDS, the writer should show more restraint . . ." Not only do we have to contend with bonehead newscasters and conservative members of the medical profession telling us to "just say no" to sex-

DAVID WOJNAROWICZ

/

uality itself rather than talk about safer sex possibilities, but we have people from the thought police spilling out from the ranks with admonitions that we shouldn't *think* about anything other than monogamous or safer sex. I'm beginning to believe that one of the last frontiers left for radical gesture is the imagination. At least in my ungoverned imagination I can fuck somebody without a rubber, or I can, in the privacy of my own skull, douse Helms with a bucket of gasoline and set his putrid ass on fire or throw congressman William Dannemeyer off the empire state building. These fantasies give me distance from my outrage for a few seconds. They give me momentary comfort. Sexuality defined in images gives me comfort in a hostile world. They give me strength. I have always loved my anonymity and therein lies a contradiction because I also find comfort in seeing representations of my private experiences in the public environment. They need not be representations of my experiences—they can be the experiences of and by others that merely come close to my own or else disrupt the generic representations that have come to be the norm in the various medias outside my door. I find that when I witness diverse representations of "Reality" on a gallery wall or in a book or a movie or in the spoken word or performance, that the larger the range of representations, the more I feel there is room in the environment for my existence, that not the entire environment is hostile.

To make the *private* into something *public* is an action that has terrific repercussions in the preinvented world. The govern-

POSTCARDS FROM AMERICA

/

ment has the job of maintaining the day-to-day illusion of the ONE-TRIBE NATION. Each public disclosure of a private reality becomes something of a magnet that can attract others with a similar frame of reference; thus each public disclosure of a fragment of private reality serves as a dismantling tool against the illusion of ONE-TRIBE NATION; it lifts the curtains for a brief peek and reveals the probable existence of literally millions of tribes. The term "general public" disintegrates. What happens next is the possibility of an X-ray of Civilization, an examination of its foundations. To turn our private grief for the loss of friends, family, lovers and strangers into something public would serve as another powerful dismantling tool. It would dispel the notion that this virus has a sexual orientation or a moral code. It would nullify the belief that the government and medical community has done very much to ease the spread or advancement of this disease.

One of the first steps in making the private grief public is the ritual of memorials. I have loved the way memorials take the absence of a human being and make them somehow physical with the use of sound. I have attended a number of memorials in the last five years and at the last one I attended I found myself suddenly experiencing something akin to rage. I realized halfway through the event that I had witnessed a good number of the same people participating in other previous memorials. What made me angry was realizing that the memorial had little reverberation outside the room it was held in. A tv commercial for handiwipes had a higher impact on the society at large. I got up and left because I didn't think I could control my urge to scream.

There is a tendency for people affected by this epidemic to police each other or prescribe what the most important gestures would be for dealing with this experience of loss. I resent that. At the same time, I worry that friends will slowly become professional pallbearers, waiting for each death, of their lovers, friends and neighbors, and polishing their funeral speeches; perfecting their rituals of death rather than a relatively simple ritual of life such as screaming in the streets. I worry because of the urgency of the situation, because of seeing death coming in from the edges of abstraction where those with the luxury of time have cast it. I imagine what it would be like if friends had a demonstration each time a lover or a friend or a stranger died of AIDS. I imagine what it would be like if, each time a lover, friend or stranger died of this disease, their friends, lovers or neighbors would take the dead body and drive with it in a car a hundred miles an hour to washington d.c. and blast through the gates of the white house and come to screeching halt before the entrance and dump their lifeless form on the front steps. It would be comforting to see those friends, neighbors, lovers and strangers mark time and place and history in such a public way.

But, bottom line, this is my own feeling of urgency and need; bottom line, emotionally, even a tiny charcoal scratching done as a gesture to mark a person's response to this epidemic means whole worlds to me if it is hung in public; bottom line, each and every gesture carries a reverberation that is meaningful in its diversity; bottom line, we have to find our own forms of gesture and communication. You can never depend on the mass media to reflect us or our needs or our states of mind; bottom line, with enough gestures we can deafen the satellites and lift the curtains surrounding the control room.

*

David Wojnarowicz (1954–92) channeled a vast accumulation of raw images, sounds, memories, and lived experiences into a powerful voice that was an undeniable presence in the New York City art scene of the 1970s, 1980s, and early 1990s. Through his several volumes of fiction, poetry, memoirs, painting, photography, installation, sculpture, film, and performance, Wojnarowicz left a legacy, affirming art's vivifying power in a society he viewed as alienating and corrosive. Wojnarowicz died of AIDS-related complications on July 22, 1992 at the age of thirty-seven. This essay, from 1989, is reprinted courtesy of the Estate of David Wojnarowicz and P · P · O · W, New York.

DAVID WOJNAROWICZ

/

NANSI CISNEROS, A SISTER WHOSE PAIN AND DEMAND FOR JUSTICE KNOWS NO BORDERS

NIDIA MELISSA BAUTISTA

As a journalist and activist raised in Los Angeles and now living in Mexico City, I feel compelled to share the story of a woman whose drive for justice is so strong, it transcends a grief separated by a national border. Unfortunately I'm all too familiar with the injustices that riddle Mexico in the realm of human rights, due to my Mexican parents. Nansi Cisneros, like me, was born in Los Angeles. Her brother was disappeared in their home state of Jalisco after he was forcibly removed from the United States and inserted in a volatile, militarized context. But it is Cisneros's resolve, her inextinguishable energy to search for him and others, despite suffering great pain as each day goes by without her brother, that demonstrates the power that victims of Mexico's crisis and their families have to turn sorrow into contestation. Her struggle inspires me to continue looking across the US-Mexico border in search of ways we can help bring justice to all those still connected by loss and, ultimately, the relentless search for justice. This is her story.

*

For Cisneros, an overnight flight to her family's hometown in central Mexico marked the beginning of a cross-border search for her missing brother. When she found out armed men had

/

taken her younger brother, Francisco Javier Cisneros Torres, from his home in Tala, Jalisco, she drove to the border to board the first flight out of Tijuana. She traveled fifteen hundred miles and arrived at her brother's house a few hours later, where shell casings and blood still soaked the living room floor.

Javi, a tattoo artist, grew up with his sister in Los Angeles, but was deported in 2007. Six years later, several men in bullet-proof vests brandishing shotguns arrived in a white car and entered his home, where he was hanging out with friends, and dragged him into their car. Distraught, his mother, who lives only six houses down, witnessed everything and tried to run after the car. Her son was forcibly disappeared on October 19, 2013. His family hasn't seen Javi since.

Desperate for help, the family approached local police, who brushed them off, saying they were overburdened with other investigations. The Jalisco State Prosecutor's Office was also unhelpful. Although it opened an investigation regarding Javi's disappearance, it took the office two years to share developments in the case. Last October, the State Prosecutor's Office informed the family that they had found a body that could be Javi and that testing would be done. The case stalled, however, and the family has yet to receive any updates.

When their pleas for help were met with cruel indifference, Cisneros took it on herself to find her brother. For over two years now she has traveled to Mexico to meet fellow activists, and has taught herself how to conduct DNA testing, better understand human right laws, and build relationships with families, activists, and civil society organizations that also seek justice for disappeared persons. In her desperate search for Javi, she has forged relationships with organizers on both sides of the border, and has become a staunch critic of corruption, state violence, and the US-funded war on drugs.

In summer 2015, Cisneros traveled to Mexico City to join the School of the Americas Watch, a US activist organization that monitors human rights and US foreign policy in Latin America. She shared her personal story with organizers from the United States and Mexico, and joined in conversations about how to support and extend the demand globally for justice for Mexico's disappeared.

She also participated in the #USTired2 protests organized in fifty-four US cities in 2014 that demanded an end to US security funding, known as the Merida Initiative, cited as responsible for financing military and human rights abuses like disappearances in Mexico.

In Los Angeles, where Cisneros was raised as well as born, she has built new initiatives to bring together other families that are searching, too. Cisneros linked up with local activists in 2015 to organize Bordamos Por La Paz, an art and activist gathering that began in Mexico City in 2011. Bordamos Por La Paz brings together dozens every second Sunday in Los Angeles's MacArthur Park, where families and friends embroider the names of their missing loved ones in fabric, share updates on cases, and honor the disappeared. Through this, Cisneros has met around fifteen families in Los Angeles that are also searching for missing loved ones.

The monthly gathering is just another iteration of the activist's commitment to raise awareness locally around human rights issues that effect Latinx communities in the United States. For Cisneros, the commitment to publicize and visibilize this shared grief is paramount.

"I will continue [this work] and seek to help more families, not just Mexican families but all who have someone disappeared or murdered in Mexico. There are lots of families in the United States, not just Los Angeles, that have been directly or indirectly affected by the War on Drugs. I will be working on this for the rest of my life. I am committed to finding my brother and facilitating the steps for others to do the same."

As one of the only US-based activists attempting to raise awareness around these issues, Cisneros has used her brother's story to mobilize consciousness and anger. She has catalyzed despair into transnational protest. "I am committed to seeking justice and mak[ing] sure the Mexican government and those responsible for these war crimes are judged. I know it may seem a lot of work, and I am sure it will [be], but I have plenty of strength," says Cisneros.

In a city where street food and music culture is often indistinguishable from Mexican metropolises like Juarez and Mexico City, families in Los Angeles are being affected by Mexico's violence as well. Conversations around missing relatives and violence ravaging small hometowns are examples of the far-reaching influence that the drug war and corruption has on communities in Los Angeles.

For Cisneros, organizing in Los Angeles is an important step in building cross-border momentum to demand an end to human rights abuses in Mexico. "I found out really quick that we were all victims, not just us, the direct victims of the drug war but everyone, including those who had never been directly affected," says Cisneros. "What I want from our Mexican compatriots and allies here in the United States is help to end this so-called War on Drugs that has only successfully disappeared and murdered thousands of our youths throughout Mexico."

According to Cisneros, justice also means putting an end to the US security package known as the Merida Initiative. Through the Merida Initiative, the United States has invested more than $2 billion since 2006 to militarize Mexico under the pretext of fighting drug cartels. It has thus funded the security forces largely responsible for human rights abuses. Instead of mitigating violence, it has heightened it to unbearable levels.

"We need to pressure our government to acknowledge that Mexican government officials, military, [and] police are participating in human rights violations every day all over the country, and that those who are questioning them are being murdered or imprisoned," Cisneros explains.

Her sharp critique of US foreign policy complements her resolve to continue organizing on the ground. In the coming year, she is planning to participate in protests in Los Angeles and Washington, DC, and continue collaborating with the School of the Americas Watch.

Her plans for travel to Mexico includes a trip to Mexico City with her family to join artist Alfredo Lopez Casanova's art show dedicated to Mexico's disappeared, titled Siguiendo Tus Huellas, or Following Your Steps. She also intends to travel to Jalisco to work with graffiti artists on an homage to disappeared persons and join families in physical searches for their loved ones.

When asked if she is ever afraid to travel to Mexico or organize for the safe return of her brother, Cisneros expresses courage and determination to keep searching. "I have to find Javi. I have no choice. My family comes first, and my love for him is more important than life itself."

*

Nidia Melissa Bautista is a journalist who reports on human rights, gender issues, youth protests, and culture through a feminist and social justice lens in Mexico, the United States, and the borderlands. She's currently a graduate student at New York University's Global Journalism program, and is increasingly committed to heralding the stories of women who manifest anger, violence, and injustice into social change. Inspired by dozens of women she's interviewed throughout the years, she believes la hermanidad *or the sisterhood is power. To read more of her work, see ellaestaporembarcar.com.*

WHAT IS POSSIBLE

HARMONY HAZARD

There is a picture of me that was taken almost a decade ago in Oaxaca, Mexico, where I am smiling in a splash of sunlight, in a moment that felt like the beginning of something. I am twenty-one years old when my sister invites me to leave New York and vacation with her for a month in the summer. "Of course I want to," I tell her. But I am a student whose walls are made of books about cultural and political matters, and soon after I say yes to my sister, I thumb Jamaica Kincaid's *A Small Place* and find, "A tourist is an ugly human being," and feel the stump of guilt.

Oaxaca is a city with buildings painted cobalt blue and coral orange, where children throw long balloons at the sky, mangy dogs roam the streets without acknowledging stop signs, and mangoes and avocados are sold in crowded markets by the bucket. A city meant for the magic hour—that time of day when the sun drips toward the horizon and even the dust starts to gleam, people stroll along the cobblestoned streets and laugh when the bus is late, shawls are swept over shoulders while dresses are pulled up to show the gold tint of knees, couples now ready to touch each other's hands. The whole city seems to exhale all at once, or maybe that was just what I did when I arrived.

*

/

A couple of weeks before visiting Oaxaca, I heard the news. Every year since 1981, teachers throughout Oaxaca strike for increased budgets by camping in the city's center square as a form of peaceful protest, but this year the governor sent in police and helicopters to evict the teachers. Rumors about protesters being killed or injured by police circulate, and a New York City demonstration is organized in solidarity with the teachers.

Although I wasn't able to properly pronounce the state a few months ago, now I am attending a protest in support of its teachers. I whoop along to the chants and bounce a handwritten sign in the air as I trudge in slow circles with the protesters. My friend Brad shows up, late as usual, with one eye already looking through a camera. He is older than me, in his mid-thirties, an anarchist with enthusiastic gesticulations, eyebrows that are often raised with a question or flirtation, and an anger at authority that is ancient in a way I don't yet understand. Months before, Brad and I sat in a hot warehouse full of dusty bicycles on West Thirty-Sixth Street in New York, picking at soggy, dumpstered fruit salad, making plans for a protest at Victoria's Secret, which was chopping down the boreal forest in Canada for its catalogs. A week later, Brad and I held a banner at the protest together, and soon after that the campaign won: Victoria's Secret agreed to use recycled paper. I am learning that winning is possible.

As we march in the small circle, I watch Brad with his camera. It appears so much more useful than the flimsy sign in my hand.

HARMONY HAZARD

/

Perhaps my vacation offers an opportunity: I can do more than just be an ugly tourist. I'll document the movement, I decide.

*

On our first day in Oaxaca, my sister and I walk to the center square, the Zócalo, which is being called a *plantón*, an encampment, as people have come from throughout the state to inhabit the already-bustling public area. The teachers' strike has grown to a social movement to oust the governor, Ulises Ruiz Ortiz. Banks and hotels in the plantón are closed, covered in graffiti, with recent cracks in their windows. Tents and tarps hang by a spiderweb of strings, and people sleep on cardboard. Business as usual has stopped, and in its place is a new kind of busyness. Vendors who once sold bootlegged videos of Mexican movies are now selling videos of the June 14, 2006 attack, playing it over and over on tiny televisions. I watch blurry footage of a helicopter spinning its propeller in the clouds, smoke erupting in the streets, people scattering, a woman's face opening in a scream. I don't buy the video but instead I pick up a sign that says in English, "Sorry tourist, we are busy making history. When Ulises is gone, we will welcome you back with open arms," and I bring it to the apartment that my sister has rented and tape it defiantly to the wall.

*

WHAT IS POSSIBLE

/

I have a friend whose high school history teacher was also a dancer, and so he explained *revolution* by breaking the word down to *revolve*, as in "orbit" or "turn," and demonstrated this by spinning slowly in front of the class, saying, "See? You end up where you began." I had been told this story about the dancing history teacher so many times that as I walked around the plantón, watching the teachers shake each other's hands, the indigenous women slicing the air with sassy laughs, the students opening their notebooks for one another, the idea of democracy swirling, surging like wind, I thought, *Yes, of course this is a kind of dance.* No wonder it is a called a movement.

*

The protesters have a radio station, Radio Plantón, which broadcasts day and night with updates, interviews, and analysis about the movement. We play it in the kitchen as we slice jicama and get mango slop on our hands, and through my sister's translations, I learn that an organization has been formed: the Popular Assembly of the People of Oaxaca, or APPO. During APPO meetings, representatives listen to each other, despite conflicting political perspectives, in an attempt at true democracy. In the afternoons when my sister isn't there, I still gorge on fruit and nod my head to the fervor of the voices on the radio, even when I don't fully understand the words.

Barricades surround the plantón, made of piles of bricks, rocks, and sheets of metal. One day, I walk past a desk that has been hauled into the middle of the street to block an intersection and think, *What a symbol: a desk being used for revolution.* I do not think about what the barricades are trying to keep out.

*

The summer before I visited Oaxaca, I drove across the United States and stopped at the Civil Rights Memorial in Montgomery, Alabama. The memorial is close to the church where Dr. Martin Luther King Jr. was pastor during the Montgomery bus boycott and the capitol steps where, in 1965, the voting rights march ended. For the exhausted marchers from Selma whose flags never ceased to wave, Montgomery was a destination. For me, it offered a place to pee, a respite from the road. Designed by Maya Lin to honor forty-one people who died—who were killed—in the civil rights movement, the memorial is a fountain where water trickles over King's engraved words: "[We will not be satisfied] until justice rolls down like water and righteousness like a mighty stream." My hands lingered on the cold granite of the fountain and traced the hollow of the names. Water flowed into the crevices, over my fingers, then gushed away. I closed my eyes to imagine that mighty stream.

*

Because the language barrier and my self-awareness as an outsider makes me uncomfortable photographing people, I begin to photograph the infrastructure of the movement: the makeshift

WHAT IS POSSIBLE

/

barricades, the tarps that match the sky, the tables of free literature, the runny stencils, the graffiti that says "rise up, campesino," the banner that says "occupy and liberate spaces." One day, men are painting over "Viva la Lucha Popular" with long strokes of white, hired by some landlord who is not in the business of revolution. The next morning, as if in response, there is fresh graffiti. When I photograph it, I flash my I'm-just-a-tourist smile. But soon after that, I pass some graffiti that says, "tourista, go home." I pause to take a picture and then stand there instead, reading it over and over. I snap a photo and walk away.

*

As I meander the streets one evening, I stumble on a documentary being projected onto a dirty sheet, while people sit on the ground, dappled in its light. *This is what can happen when you take over your city*, I think. *You can watch movies in the streets.* A man hiding under his hoodie approaches me shyly, asking, "*Cómo estás?*" and listens to me blunder in Spanish for a few minutes before he admits that he speaks English and is from the United States, white like me. I search his face, where he has a tattoo of a kind of spiral, and then below the shadow of his hoodie, I search his eyes. He tells me that he has been working with one of the local organizations for the past few months, tells me he uses the dirty sheet to sleep with at night if it gets cold. His voice is soft; maybe his lips are too. *This must be what revolution feels like*, I think, as I sense what is possible.

HARMONY HAZARD

/

330

I sign up for Spanish classes, and in class I learn that the word *esperar* means both "to wait for" and "to hope." *Espero*, I practice out loud, *espero*. I realize that this is what people in the social movement are doing: they are waiting, they are hoping.

*

One day, I come across a black-and-white copy of a photograph that's been wheat pasted on a wall. I squint at it and then realize that it's the protest in New York at the Mexican consulate— the one that Brad and I attended, stuck to this public wall as a kind of proof of solidarity. The image is gray and splotchy, and I can't find our faces in the crowd, since perhaps it was shot be- fore we had even arrived, but somehow I feel that we are in it. This is what photographs do: they hold memories that are much larger than what is contained within their frames. They commu- nicate despite borders, language, time. Then they stay the same even when everything changes.

*

Five years later, the Occupy movement will start near Wall Street, and I will hear about it from the farm where I'm living in Upstate New York—the farm I moved to because on a later trip I took to Oaxaca, a farmer, crouched in a bed of squash and corn, looked up at me, saying, "Why are you here? Why not return to the land you're from and plant seeds?" I was harvesting my carrots from under the snow when I heard about Occupy, and I wondered, *Are they learning from Oaxaca? Do they understand that what happened there was not an occupation but instead a reclamation? Do they know what is possible?*

*

I invite the man with the tattoo on his face to the little apartment where my sister and I are staying. We walk the cobblestoned streets, past men in shadows making bottle rockets, to the warm roof under the smear of stars, our bodies close and curious. On his shoulder is a tattoo of Ferdinand the bull from the children's book about the animal who wants to smell flowers instead of participating in bullfights. The book was banned during the Spanish Civil War and later became Mahatma Gandhi's favorite book. *Do revolutionaries make better lovers?* I wonder as I follow the tattoo with my fingers. I kiss him to find out.

*

The day before I leave Oaxaca, the women march. Old and young, indigenous or Mexican or some combination; women who have maybe never protested before; teachers, grandmothers, housewives, students; middle class in business casual or straw hats, and from the country; hundreds crowd the square, some wearing traditional aprons, except written on them is *fuera Ulises*, meaning kick out the governor. The women raise pots and pans in the air, clang and bang on them with metal spoons, stomping their feet, accessing a passion that seems five hundred years old. I take photos that are incomplete because they are silent. When it starts to rain, the banging just gets stronger, the stomping louder, the air thicker with love.

I later learn that the women went to the radio and television stations that day. They said, "We are taking over this station. We are going to tell our real stories." The security guards frowned. "We are the women," they said. "Let us through." The security guards dropped their eyes and guns, and moved aside. The women collected the microphones and went in front of the cameras. "We are the women," they began. "We are here to tell our stories." They are winning, I felt then. It is happening.

*

I return to my room of books in New York with photographs, footage, and nostalgia for a place that is not my home. I tell everyone about the revolution that is going on in southern Mexico. Nobody seems to care.

Weeks go by and then I receive a mass e-mail from Brad, my anarchist friend whose camera had inspired me to bring out my own. When I hear he's in Oaxaca, something inside of me leaps. Maybe he too will understand. I e-mail the man with the tattoo on his face. When he writes me back from Oaxaca with the subject "heartland," I'm not sure if he is referring to his heart or the Oaxacan land. The concepts feel inseparable to me now.

WHAT IS POSSIBLE

/

My sister, the tourist, leaves a couple of weeks after I do, but before she departs, she brings the protesters her bags of uneaten food: cans of beans, oil, and a bag of masa. In that simple act, she offered more support than anything I had thought to give.

*

One night in late October, I receive a phone call. "Did you hear what happened to Brad?" a friend asks. "No," I say, but the mention of his name allows me to conjure him in the streets of Oaxaca, and I wonder what time it is there, if the blur of stars is out or if the sun is still crossing the clear sky. There is a pause on the phone. "He was shot," my friend says. The night shakes; it becomes jolted, jarring, as if I'm holding a camera. I walk to Bluestockings, the bookstore where Brad's friends are gathered for an emergency meeting. Brad had been filming near a barricade in Oaxaca when he was shot by government paramilitaries. "He died?" someone asks. "He was killed," someone clarifies. My hand moves to cover my mouth. It stays there all night. The territory of what is possible expands. I'm swallowed up by it.

*

I met Brad on Halloween one year before at a sweaty dance party at the Times Up bike space on Houston Street, long before the space closed and disappeared into the folds of buildings lost to the gentrification of New York City. The music was too loud, the way it should be. He wore a police cap and the largest grin. A few days after his death, on the year anniversary of meeting him, skeletons and people covered in blood laugh past me on the street, and I walk as quickly as I can, not sure what is real anymore.

*

Some people mourn by dropping flowers at gravesites while others pour liquor, light candles, open their hands to the sky, or make art because that is all they can do. For Brad, we do what he would have done, what he lived his life for: we begin to organize. There is another protest at the Mexican consulate. We do not march in a circle or whoop; there isn't time to make signs. Someone locks herself to the door of the consulate, someone lies down in the street, someone else ties a banner to a lamppost—a fast choreography of anger. My hand is not covering my mouth anymore because I have started to scream. Everyone is screaming by now.

*

Photographs of Brad are suddenly everywhere: there he is, dancing at a party without his shirt on, his fingers and toes pointed in opposite directions, as if he wants to occupy all the space of the frame; there he is, in Oaxaca, transfixed with a scowl of thought, gesticulating in front of the corner where I first met the man with the tattoo; there he is, again in Oaxaca, but lying on the ground this time, a red bullet hole beating at the center of his chest. *This is revolution*, I learn. It is a thing that can destroy me. To the world, his death becomes a brief international headline; to his friends, his death is the world. The Mexican government blames his death on the protesters, and uses it as an excuse to send in the army to descend on the plantón and force out the protesters. It is the opposite of what Brad would have wanted.

*

In the wake of death, there is a strange adrenaline. In the following days and weeks, articles are written, banners are painted, protests are organized, and mostly, people talk. There are meetings about the US-funded militarization of Mexico, formal workshops about what solidarity looks like across borders, conversations tucked into the sidelines of a press conference about the colonialist behavior of white people preferring to get involved with the politics of a different country rather than taking a long bus to the other end of town. Busy days are followed by nights in which I stare at the ceiling as I picture the faces of Brad, the man with the tattoo, people I met in Oaxaca, but right before I fall asleep, as if a filter on a film, the faces turn red, saturated with blood.

*

For days at protests, when someone yells "Brad Will," we answer back "*presente!*" We yell the names of the other people who were killed in Oaxaca—"Emilio Alonso Fabian" and "Fidel Sanchez Garcia"—and for each of them, we yell " *presente! presente! presente!*" Some people are remembered at the dizzying pinnacle of a mountain or above moving water, but if Brad is alive anywhere, it is in the dirty streets of a surging movement. How can someone be present after death? It is community that does that work—the work of keeping someone not alive but at least memorized in the places they still belong.

*

That year, I attend the Day of the Dead celebration at St. Mark's Church, as I will for years to come, thinking of Brad and Oaxaca. The room flickers with candles, the air smothered with the smell of prayer, with a shrine of glossy photographs and paper flowers on display. There are tiny figurines of happy skeletons dancing, eating, and playing musical instruments; I imagine one holding a video camera. I'm here because I want to remember that there is another way to think of death: it can be laughed at, accepted, made useful. But when the Mexican writer Octavio Paz wrote, "The Mexican is familiar with death, jokes about it, caresses it, sleeps with it, celebrates it," he was not speaking about murder.

*

At a restorative justice training I did years later, the facilitator spoke about how conflict grows the way that mushrooms do.

WHAT IS POSSIBLE

/

Conflict between individuals, like the head of a mushroom, is the only visible part of a dense underground structure called mycelium, which is the community in which the conflict grows. Like conflict, every death is linked with the long, intertwined roots of community, and it's impossible to know how deep and how far the impact of a death reaches. For Brad's death, his mycorrhizal roots stretched across the world.

*

I e-mail the man with the tattoo on his face and ask if he met Brad. He writes back, saying he needs help. He has received death threats and believes that Brad had footage of the undercover police who threatened him. I offer him the contacts I have, close the laptop, and slump at my desk. I think of that other desk, the one at that futile barricade that I walked by, and wish I could return there to sit and draft letters: to the man with the tattoo on his face, to Brad, to Oaxaca. I could write about that stream that Dr. King believed in, how it can spread into a river, flow down those Mexican streets, or I could write about the cascading sound of pots and pans slapped by women's hands, or I could dream of sitting at that desk with my sharpened pencil, floating into the clouds, leaving all the bloodshed behind me, on the ground.

*

HARMONY HAZARD

/

338

The history teacher was wrong. I did not end up where I began. All loss is political in a way because it moves you, rattles you up, leaves you disoriented; but the process of mourning a political death forces an inconclusive question: How is one supposed to respond?

What is it that makes us political? Not political in a voting, political party way, but the kind of political that we become out of the rage of haunting need, the thing that beats further down in us than any theory, as committed as the ink on the face of the man I briefly loved, when revolution is not a vacation but the place we reside.

To the people of Oaxaca, the movement wasn't just the slather of stencils and graffiti on walls, movie screenings on dusty sheets, kisses on warm rooftops, the banging of pots and pans through falling rain. It wasn't just revolution in its romanticized form. It was what comes before revolution: injustice, impunity, oppression, and death. It was what the video of the June 14 attack was about, it was what the street art was about, it was what the barricades were meant to protect against yet what they failed to protect against because rocks and sheets of metal and desks will always fail to protect against death. I was surrounded by it the whole time but never did I realize that it could actually become real. By which I mean, real for me.

These days, I'm thinking of Black Lives Matter, this new movement that exists in response to death. Michael Brown,

Eric Garner, Freddie Gray, Walter Scott, and Sandra Bland are only names to me; they are not friends or the people I bump into sometimes on the streets. Their deaths remain abstractions.

Each day in Oaxaca, while my sister went to restaurants and museums, I went to the plantón, but in many ways, our motives were not that different. We were voyeurs. Oaxaca was not just a place I traveled to but an idea. I was a tourist of revolution. I think again of Kincaid and imagine replacing the word *native* with *revolutionary*: "Every native would like to find a way out, every native would like a rest, every native would like a tour. But some natives—most natives in the world—cannot go anywhere."

It was a privilege to be able to visit and then leave Oaxaca; it is a privilege to be able to visit the idea of Black Lives Matter and then leave. What would it mean to stay?

*

At the 2016 May Day march, people chant about workers, immigrants, police brutality, and the complicated intersections between these issues. Some carry signs that simply say "43," referring to the missing Mexican students from Ayotzinapa. They're called missing instead of killed. I'm taking pictures when I see him. He's back, raising his eyebrows behind his camera, moving fast, alive. He's been alive this whole time. *Brad*, I want to shout, but he disappears into the crowd. Then I remember he's gone.

HARMONY HAZARD

/

340

At least seventeen people, including Brad, were killed by the time the last tarp was ripped down in the 2006 movement. Oaxaca continues to face human rights violations, repression, and impunity. The man with the tattoo on his face and I haven't spoken in years. I hope he's OK, by which I mean, alive.

What I have are my photographs. There are many images of the barricades, a few of the tents standing bright against the gray clouds, one of the "tourista, go home" graffiti. There are some of the streets lit up at the magic hour. There is one of a woman with gray hair lifting a pot in the air, close to her wrinkled face, with a look that says she knows everything about the world, just go ahead and ask. I look back at the picture of myself, where it seems I was not quite sure if I was waiting for something or hoping for something, but I am smiling. I knew nothing about the world. What a beautiful, fleeting, moment in time.

*

Harmony Hazard hails from both Tucson and New York. She is completing her masters of fine arts in creative writing at Stony Brook. She edits the Participate column in make/shift *magazine, and has been published in* CALYX, Tiny Donkey, *and* Catapult. *Thanks to* Border Crossing *for publishing an earlier version of "What Is Possible"; Alison, Michael, Ellice, and Eric for their support and feedback; and Friends of Brad Will for calling attention to the injustices in Mexico. Rest in power Brad Will and the others killed in Oaxaca.* La lucha sigue.

WHAT IS POSSIBLE

/

"THEY COULD BE MY GRANDCHILDREN"

ANDALUSIA KNOLL SOLOFF

Our bus snaked through the rural roads along the Guerrero coast. My mind wandered between sleep and consciousness, with a Manu Chao song wafting in one ear and the distant chants of "*Ayotzinapa Vive Vive*" (Long Live Ayotzinapa) entering the other. Manu Chao's *Clandestino* album, a classic in lefty Latin American circles, remixes voices of resistance in Mexico with music. The forty-three students from the Ayotzinapa Rural Teachers' College were disappeared over a decade after this record was released.

The chants didn't come from my headphones. They emanated from families that had blockaded the highway, wanting to show their support for the Julio César Ramírez Nava caravan that was traversing this southern Mexican state to lift up the voices of a group of parents searching for their sons, who had been kidnapped by Mexican police six weeks earlier, on September 26, 2014.

We were in the Costa Chica region of Guerrero, and a crowd of people had gathered. Their brown, sun-weathered faces expressed deep anguish. They had prepared sandwiches and converted the front porch of a municipal building into a stage, allowing a student spokesperson from Ayotzinapa and some of the parents to share words about their search. Students from the Ayotzinapa school spoke about the repression they have faced

/

for decades because of their fight to ensure not only that poor rural farmers and indigenous youths have access to free higher education but also that marginalized communities have teachers and schools.

Each parent tightly clenched a banner emblazoned with their son's face and name. Just as the Say Her Name campaign in the United States publicly names the black women who have been murdered by police violence, the parents of Ayotzinapa engage daily in acts of resistance by making visible those who have been disappeared. The Mexico government disappears people and then disappears their story.

The parents are mostly from humble, campesino backgrounds; many were former undocumented immigrants who worked in the United States. They survive off the food donated to their struggle since all had to leave their fields to join the search for their sons. Back on the caravan in Guerrero, an intergenerational group blockades the road to give out *chilate*, a regional chilled cacao drink. A women, her decades-old face bearing an intense grief, holds a sign reading, "The disappeared could be my grandchildren. We the grandmothers of this town stand with you in your struggle for justice. We want them alive!"

As we traveled from town to town, I asked housewives, students, teachers, activists, and street vendors why they had come out to support the families and students of Ayotzinapa. Everyone responded with the same phrase, "*Fue la gota que derramó el vaso.*" Ayotzinapa was "the straw that broke the camel's back."

ANDALUSIA KNOLL SOLOFF

/

346

When Ayotzinapa happened, tens of thousands of people had already been assassinated in Mexico, and thousands more had disappeared as a result of the inappropriately named "war on drugs" and other failed security strategies. What is it about Ayotzinapa that brought people out into the streets when all the other murders had caused them to further retreat into their own homes? How much violence can a population tolerate until it explodes?

Enforced disappearances have the explicit goal of invoking terror among the general population. To understand what an enforced disappearance is it's crucial to understand that it is something that someone actively does to you. It generally starts with an armed kidnapping, and ends with family members never knowing whether or not their loved one is alive or dead.

To speak about the disappeared is to use the language of a purgatory between past and present tense. To successfully disappear someone, the kidnapping must never be investigated, the cell phone never traced, the surveillance camera footage tampered with, and fear invoked in the family and any possible witnesses so that they won't denounce the crime. At best, the name of the person will enter into a database with twenty-seven-thousand-and-counting other disappeared people.

The families of Ayotzinapa refused to be intimidated, and quickly realized their collectivity is what gave them strength and helped them combat despair. When I finally broke down into tears one day after hearing so many stories about the disappeared students, a fellow reporter said, "This is nothing; just imagine the sadness when their families are just at home waiting for them to return and they never go out."

Guerrero, known for constant social and political conflict, has a large indigenous population and one of the highest poverty rates in the country. In the 1970s, small guerrilla armies challenged wealthy landowners and corrupt politicians. The state clenched its fist, killing all the major guerrilla leaders, and kidnapping and disappearing thousands of people who were believed to have some kind of connection to the rebel armies. Two of these martyred leaders, Lucio Cabañas and Genaro Vasquez, were former students at Ayotzinapa. Their legacy is omnipresent. Sometimes their faces appear on shirts, and at other times people proudly claim their bloodlines related to the Cabañas or Vasquez family. There is nostalgia for a time when armed groups struggled for what they believed was a common good, instead of the dark times now, when armed groups merely engage in power disputes.

These disputes are what have converted Guerrero into the powder keg that it is, with splinter groups of larger organized crime entities battling for control of drug trafficking routes to the United States and the sale of opium paste, which is increasingly being produced in the state. Often, the local as well as the national press writes about how organized crime now has more power than the government, but that is inaccurate. In many counties in Guerrero, criminal elements and the government are one.

According to the Mexican government, the corrupt local police of the city of Iguala detained the Ayotzinapa students and handed them over to some local members of the organized crime group, Guerreros Unidos, because they thought they were members of Los Rojos, a rival drug gang. Then, according to an alleged member of Guerreros Unidos detained by the government and allegedly tortured, the students were incinerated and reduced to ashes in a garbage dump. There is no proof that this is actually what happened, and numerous witnesses have said that both the federal police and army were present at the various crime scenes.

During the search for the students, dozens of clandestine graves were uncovered in Guerrero's lush hillsides. None contained the students; instead they were filled with hundreds of other corpses. For years people knew that bodies were being dumped but feared reporting them. The security forces are directly linked with those responsible for these disappearances, and reporting them can lead to you literally digging your own grave. In the 1970s, the ocean was converted into a cemetery when the army implemented "flights of death" to toss subversives into the ocean to drown and disintegrate.

The Ayotzinapa parents called the government's bluff, saying that there wasn't even actual scientific proof that their sons had been killed this way. Society at large stood behind them. Students and teachers in Guerrero set government institutions on fire in protest, and hundreds of thousands of people took to the streets all over the country and world to decry the government's necropolitics. A survey found that 66 percent of the people in Mexico didn't believe the government's version of the attack, and 75 percent doubted that justice ever would be served. Repeatedly people told me at marches that they had never taken to the streets before to express their outrage, but that Ayotzinapa warranted it. A student from the school explained to me that before people would criticize their marches, but now lined up to hand out water during their protests in Chilpancingo, the state's capital.

The image of the parents of Ayotzinapa marching throughout Mexico clutching banners with their sons' faces on them filled the front page of mainstream Mexican media outlets, and became synonymous with courage, dignity, and defiance of a status quo that has permitted so much violence. Violent state regimes' best friend has always been short-term memory, yet the constant repetition of forty-three portraits of young boys reduced *el olvido*, "people's ability to forget."

The faces of the forty-three multiplied and morphed. The disappeared students acquired hundreds of thousands of new family members as people accepted them as their own. A graphic campaign was launched, Artists with Ayotzinapa, where each participant produced a portrait of a specific disappeared student in whatever medium they desired, stating that they were looking for that missing student. "I, Patricia Barron, want to know where Jorge Aníbal Cruz Mendoza is," for instance, with a hand-drawn portrait of Jorge on top of a map of Mexico with numbers representing the thousands of disappeared people across Mexico. These portraits breathed life into the boring black-and-white school portraits that were previously the only visual reference that existed for the missing students. They went viral and were also printed on banners to be hung in the students' communities of origin across southern Mexico.

Public plazas, schools, and malls filled with people doing performance art, chanting the names of the disappeared students, doing die-ins and other forms of creative resistance to remind the society that the forty-three students still hadn't been found. At Mexico's main film art center, the Cineteca, filmmakers launched a monthly event to project videos about the forty-three students. Poets united to release poetry books, and journalists created the blog Periodistas con Ayotzinapa (Journalists with Ayotzinapa) to step beyond the facade of objectivity, and compile their own reports and photos about Ayotzinapa. Horrified by the discovery of clandestine graves that they witnessed, the journalists said with this project that they hoped to "transform the horror" as well as "discover the seams of humanity and the crack where the light comes through."

The Ayotzinapa parents also traveled in caravans to northern Mexico, where the scars run deep from all the death and disappearances that were a result of Mexico's former president Felipe Calderón's deeply flawed security strategy. Once again, their courage helped those who had previously remained silent emerge from the shadows to denounce the terror that had been inflicted on their communities and name those who were disappeared.

On November 20, 2014, the anniversary of the Mexican Revolution, hundreds of thousands of people took to the streets of Mexico City to receive the caravans of parents that had traversed the country. A profound sadness expressed in rage and solidarity could be felt among all protesters. At the end of the march, an enormous effigy of president Enrique Peña Nieto was burned in the Zócalo, and shortly after, police arbitrarily detained eleven people, threatened to disappear them, and sent them to two different maximum-security prisons. The government transmitted a simple message to the thousands who had gathered publicly for the first time: criticizing the government can land you in jail—or worse. The numbers at demonstrations immediately dropped.

How long can people sustain collective grief? In the beginning it was easier for common folks to imagine that one of these forty-three students was their own son or grandchild. The Ayotzinapa parents had brought their forty-three sons into the consciousness and homes of thousands, as names and faces,

ANDALUSIA KNOLL SOLOFF

/

still embodied, still vital, still here. As time went by, though, this presence faded, and the Ayotzinapa forty-three have gone missing, figuratively, again. The government, with the aid of the media outlets that act as its mouthpiece, successfully convinced a large percentage of the population that the students are indeed dead, and that the parents should just *superarlo*, "get over it" and move on.

Yet the parents keep looking for their children, more than two years later, driven by the complete lack of evidence that they are dead. The case is still open. More clandestine graves have been discovered all over the country, forced disappearances still happen daily, and other families now have to personally know the same pain felt by the Ayotzinapa parents.

What has changed is not the parents' loss, or their fight for a justice that may never come. The shift is that despite the government's efforts to disappear resistance, more collectives have been emboldened, composed of family members of other disappeared. They, too, comb the hillsides looking for their loved ones, and act as networks of support for people when someone else is disappeared.

Guerrero is full of lush, green hills that are so beautiful, it makes it hard to imagine that such cruelty lies hidden within. The violence that ravages the state, touched on Ayotzinapa's door again when alleged robbers attacked the collective van two of them were traveling in and killed them. This occurred just one week after the two-year anniversary of the students' disappearance yet was just a blip in the press. When death becomes so normalized and a school's name becomes so stained with blood, people often stop paying attention.

As I travel the state in the collective transit, I often speak with fellow riders about Ayotzinapa. As they prod to try and figure out why someone like me is journeying to small, isolated towns by myself, I let on that I am going to interview parents or students of Ayotzinapa. When they recognize the names of the families, they typically say something like "oh yes, they killed their sons, no?" In the least offensive way possible, I usually remind them that there is no proof that the boys were killed, and that if it was their son, they would be surely still be searching for them. Alive they took them, and alive we want them back.

> Can't you hear me mama call
> Can't you hear me crawling
> Can't you hear me mama call
> Can't you hear me trying
> Can't you hear me when I call
>
> I'm a long way from sight
> Tonight tonight
> It's a long long night
>
> —MANU CHAO, *Clandestino*

*

ANDALUSIA KNOLL SOLOFF

/

Andalusia Knoll Soloff is a freelance multimedia journalist from New York City who lives in Mexico City, but her heart resides in Guerrero. She has reported on the disappearance of the Ayotzinapa students since the tragic event occurred and is currently producing the graphic novel Alive You Took Them *about the parents' search for them. Andalusia is a regular correspondent for AJ+, Democracy Now! and VICE News.*

"THEY COULD BE MY GRANDCHILDREN"

/

FIGHTING TO BURY THEIR CHILDREN

/

ON THE NECROPOLITICS OF OCCUPATION

BUDOUR HASSAN

The Israeli obsession with controlling Palestinians and keeping them under surveillance is not limited to the living but also includes the dead. This is epitomized by the practice of withholding Palestinian bodies, a form of posthumous revenge perpetrated on rebellious Palestinians.

Withholding the bodies of slain Palestinian resistance fighters is not just about punishing them and their families. It strives to reassert control over Palestinian bodies and space, including Palestinian corpses and burial sites.

Withholding bodies is an emergency tactic employed by Israel when its perceived sense of sovereignty over Palestinian lives comes under threat. As a result, its use intensifies during periods of turmoil when Palestinians challenge Israel's apparatus of control and surveillance, and shake the oppressive status quo that slowly suffocates and grinds them down.

Since the youth uprising that began in October 2015, Israeli forces have withheld the bodies of about ninety Palestinians in total, the highest rate in fifteen years. While most bodies were eventually released and handed over to their families for burial, though with strict conditions, this was only possible after popular Palestinian pressure.

Funerals of martyrs in Jerusalem are among the rare occa-

/

sions where Palestinians can reclaim the streets of their city, and transform mourning into anger and protest. They transcend personal sadness and politicize grief, transmuting it into a revolutionary and collective act. The power of this collective grief constitutes a threat to Israel's false sense of hegemony, and as such, it has to be contained and suppressed. The symbolic power that the martyr espouses carries the capacity to mobilize people without the need for any call to action and regardless of political affiliation.

Thus, withholding the bodies of martyrs and adding conditions, such as only allowing a few family members to take part in the funerals, aim to contain the symbolic power of the martyr, on the one hand, and privatize grief and eradicate its revolutionary force, on the other.

The restriction sends a message to subversive Palestinians that even after their death, Israel can sentence them to a post-mortem detention that will only end according to Israel's own conditions.

The problem for Israel, however, lies in the fact that Palestinians often refuse to follow the script carefully written by their oppressor. Tactics used to crush Palestinians' resolve often end up empowering them. The funeral of Alaa Abu Jamal serves as a case in point.

On May 23, 2016, Israeli police finally agreed to release the body of Alaa, slain in October after killing an Israeli settler.

The compromise came after Israel's High Court ordered the

police to release the withheld bodies of Palestinian Jerusalem-ites before the beginning of the holy Muslim month of Rama-dan, pending severe restrictions.

The body of Alaa, a native of the Jerusalem village of Jabal al-Mukabber, was to be buried late Monday night. Only forty peo-ple were allowed to attend his funeral.

Desperate to bury their son after eight months of excruciat-ing delay, Alaa's family agreed to the repressive conditions. The residents of Jabal al-Mukabber did not.

In an act of civil disobedience, hundreds of Palestinians turned up to the funeral, chanting Alaa's name and vowing to resist the Israeli occupation. While heavy military presence prevented them from entering the cemetery where Alaa was buried, their mere presence represented a blow to Israel's sense of control. Not only did they challenge the ban and defy police orders, they reiterated that grief is a powerful form of public dissent that extends far beyond the martyr's own family.

Unsurprisingly, Palestinians were punished for disobeying the master's orders. Hours following Alaa's funeral, Israeli pub-lic security minister Gilad Erdan ordered a halt on the return of the remaining withheld bodies, describing the funeral as outra-geous. Making matters worse, Israel's newly appointed defense minister, Avigdor Lieberman, issued an order on June 9, 2016, freezing the return of all Palestinian bodies killed during sus-pected attacks against Israelis. The decision was announced fol-lowing a shooting attack in Tel Aviv that left four Israelis dead.

FIGHTING TO BURY THEIR CHILDREN

/

The decision means that the bodies of eight Palestinian martyrs are still languishing in Israeli morgues in terrible conditions.

They are Thaer Abu Ghazaleh, Bahaa Alayan, Abdel-Mohsen Hassouna, Muhammad Abu Khalaf, Abdel-Malik Abu Kharroub, Muhammad al-Kalouti, Abdel-Hamid Surour, and Ansar Harsha. Their families are stripped of the right to bury them in peace and dignity; their people are prevented from honoring their sacrifices; and their bodies are treated as pawns and tools of revenge.

For the families of Thaer and Bahaa, who were both killed in October, the plight has been ongoing for eight months, as of this writing in mid-June 2016, with no closure in sight. Below is a window into the world of Muhammad Alayan, Bahaa's father, when he was only some three months into his fight for his son's body.

*

In her 1969 book *On Death and Dying*, Swiss psychiatrist Elisabeth Kübler-Ross outlined five major emotional stages that people tend to go through while coping with the death or loss of a loved one: denial, anger, bargaining, depression, and acceptance.

Over three months have passed since the killing of his son Bahaa, but Muhammad has not been able to experience any of them. The sixty-year-old lawyer has been too immersed in the struggle to recover the body of his slain son to actually contemplate his loss.

"More than a hundred days have gone, and I couldn't sit with my wife and three (remaining) children at one table together and realize that there is an empty chair no longer occupied by Bahaa," Muhammad told me. "We have had no time to discuss his absence because our entire lives have revolved around getting him back."

Parents whose children's bodies or remains are detained by Israel, either in morgues or the infamous "cemeteries of numbers" (where the remains of at least 268 Palestinian combatants have been buried for decades in closed military zones) wait to receive their bodies as if they were waiting to welcome living people after their release from their prisons.

Muhammad completely identifies with this sentiment. Waiting to warm his son's body with his own palms gives him the sense that Bahaa, needing a hug, might knock at the door at any moment.

"While people around the world wait for midnight to light up fireworks, we are waiting to warm the bodies of our children," Muhammad wrote on his Facebook page on New Year's Eve.

For Muhammad, the battle to release the corpse of his twenty-three-year-old son from Israeli morgues and cover him with the warm soil of his country, the country he has sacrificed his life for, has left no room for grief. Private grief, Muhammad feels, is a privilege he cannot afford right now. In fact, he hasn't been able to shed a single tear over the loss of Bahaa, who was his best friend, since his killing on October 13, 2015. As the driving force behind the popular campaign to retrieve martyrs' bodies in Jerusalem, Muhammad is encumbered with the onerous obligation of appearing strong, and sheltering his vulnerability and pain.

On October 13, the day of Bahaa's killing, the Israeli security cabinet resumed the decades-long policy, officially halted in 2004, of withholding Palestinian martyrs' corpses. The stated purpose of the policy, included among a package of punitive measures such as the demolition of suspected attackers' homes and declared at the outset of the latest Palestinian revolt, was to "deter" potential attacks against Israel and prevent their funeral processions from turning into mass protests.

The detention of corpses in Israeli morgues, and concerns that they were being held in poor conditions, sparked a major outcry, particularly in Hebron, where thousands of Palestinians protested on multiple occasions, demanding Israel turn over the bodies. Far from dispiriting or intimidating Palestinians, Israel's retaliatory measure of withholding the bodies of alleged Palestinian attackers has propelled Palestinians into direct action. Not trusting the Palestinian Authority to act on the matter, the families of Palestinians whose bodies are detained by Israel looked to the streets for support. Support came, pouring in. The case of detained corpses did not just relate to the families but became a national cause, too.

BUDOUR HASSAN

/

Israel began releasing the bodies gradually, and in patches. On January 2, 2016, tens of thousands in Hebron south of the occupied West Bank participated in the funeral of seventeen martyrs whose bodies had been released in the previous day despite bad weather. But ten bodies of Palestinians (including Bahaa) killed since October, all residents of Jerusalem, remained in detention in Israeli morgues.

So on January 21, 2016, the families staged a symbolic funeral for their children, carrying empty coffins in a march that reached the UN headquarters in Ramallah in the occupied West Bank. "Empty coffins are too heavy," remarked Muhammad after the march.

*

The battle of Jerusalem's families to reclaim, mourn, and bury their slain children is part of the struggle against Israel's system of surveillance over public space and bodies. Israel's efforts to impose control over a city and people in rebellion is not limited to the living bodies and living spaces but extends to the dead as well. Even in their death, Palestinians are perceived to possess the sort of power that shakes Israel's illusory sovereignty over Jerusalem to its core. Even in their death, Palestinians have the capacity to mobilize thousands to attend their funerals and reclaim, if only temporarily, their urban space.

This symbolic power carried by dead bodies poses a challenge to Israel's control and surveillance over its colonial subjects, and buttresses its obsession with security and order. Israel's fear of dead Palestinian bodies, which leads to their treatment as a security threat, manifests itself in the conditions laid out to release the bodies. The conditions stipulate burying the martyrs in areas located outside the boundaries of Israel's wall, restricting the number of participants in the funerals, only allowing burial at night, and demanding a bail to guarantee that those conditions are fulfilled.

This policy of taking the dead hostage, imposing conditions on their release, and the psychological torture and blackmailing of their families constitute layers of Israel's necropolitical regime of dispossession. In this regime, Palestinians are punished and persecuted even posthumously, and Israel controls Palestinian sites of burial, the freedom of Palestinians to mourn, and the right to honor their dead publicly and properly.

This apparatus of surveillance, control, and punishment has been backed by Israel's judicial system. This explains why Palestinian families have opted not to take the case of detained corpses to the Israeli Supreme Court, known—in true Orwellian fashion—as the High Court of Justice. Their reluctance stems from Palestinians' confidence that Israel's top court will uphold the position of the government. And their conviction is fully justified in a state where security trumps justice, and where even the so-called liberal High Court, as it is hailed in the West, has approved and legitimized flagrantly arbitrary policies such as punitive home demolitions, to name but one.

BUDOUR HASSAN

/

Meanwhile, Muhammad reiterates that only after laying the body of Bahaa to rest will he find some privacy and time to reflect on his death. Only then will grief turn from an unattainable luxury to a long-overdue right.

*

A scout leader, community organizer, and self-taught graphic designer, Bahaa was a widely admired grassroots activist in Jerusalem. In 2013, he helped found the first public library in Jabal al-Mukabber, a village southeast of Jerusalem. Striving to offer an alternative space for Palestinian children, youths, and kids with disability, he helped establish an independent Palestinian community center in his village one year earlier.

He also founded the first all-female scout group in Jabal al-Mukabber, training the guides while encouraging them to challenge social taboos and conservativism. So inspiring was Bahaa for those young women and girls that they have pledged to build on his work with the local community, and keep the scouts alive and growing, as Bahaa had always dreamed.

In March 2014, Bahaa and his friends organized a human chain of readers around the walls of Jerusalem's Old City, mobilizing thousands of Palestinians to carry their books and reclaim the streets of their city.

Bahaa was aware of the intersection of political, social, and economic struggles that Palestinians in Jerusalem had to undertake. While he believed in the importance of culture and education, he also rejected Israel's efforts to depoliticize and co-opt culture and education for the objective of internalizing the occupation.

Living under occupation in Jerusalem is a struggle for survival. For the vast majority of Palestinians there, they live below the poverty line and can hardly make ends meet. It is convenient, perhaps even logical, for people to be preoccupied by their everyday problems, such as high taxes, fines, lack of services, poor infrastructure, and scarcity of classrooms. Living in Jabal al-Mukabber, one of the poorest neighborhoods in Jerusalem, Bahaa was no stranger to those problems. But he also believed that they are the fruit of the political reality created by Israel.

Important as it is to foster a vibrant, educated community in Jerusalem, it is equally crucial, Bahaa argued, for this community to be self-sufficient and politically conscious. Born in this contentious climate, cultural activities in Jerusalem have to strengthen Palestinian identity and foster political consciousness rather than domesticate it; they should seek to lay a solid ground for full liberation and decolonization rather than incite assimilation within the Israeli state and society. Despite his faith that knowledge and culture are potent weapons for people under occupation, Bahaa recognized their limitation in the murky reality Palestinians are forced to navigate.

*

BUDOUR HASSAN

/

On October 13, 2015, along with Bilal Ghanem, Bahaa launched a knife and gun attack on an Israeli bus in the Jewish-only settlement of Armon HaNatziv, a colony constructed and expanded on lands confiscated from Jabal al-Mukabber following the 1967 occupation of East Jerusalem.

The attacks left three Israelis dead and several others injured. Israeli police eventually executed Bahaa, while Bilal was injured and arrested. On November 9, 2015, Bilal was indicted on charges of murdering three Israelis and the attempted murder of seven others.

The dual bus attack by Bahaa and Bilal occurred at the height of the Palestinian youth uprising against Israeli occupation, which marked the largest wave of extended unrest in Jerusalem and the West Bank since the second Intifada. The escalation prompted many analysts to wonder whether this could be regarded as the "third Intifada," with some calling it the "Intifada of knives," as individual stabbing attacks have been the underlying tactic adopted by young Palestinians.

Beyond the shock and disbelief that overcame Muhammad at Bahaa's involvement in planning and executing the bus attack, he had to be clear in his position.

Bahaa was a bright young man who helped amplify the voices of those around him. He was the son of a generation abandoned by the political and intellectual elite, and left to chew on the charade of peace talks and the so-called political process.

FIGHTING TO BURY THEIR CHILDREN

/

Muhammad himself spent ten years in Israeli occupation jails for his affiliation with the Palestinian Liberation Organization before his release in a prisoner exchange deal in 1985. But he believes that the actions of Bahaa and many others are a damning indictment of the failure of the old guard and his own generation. Muhammad doesn't believe that he had passed the torch of resistance to his son. Rather, he blames his generation for creating the political vacuum that deprived his son's generation of hope.

Bahaa's involvement in the bus attack led Israeli occupation forces to demolish the Alayan family's house on January 4, 2016. They have been living in a tent next the rubble of their demolished home ever since.

The involvement of Muhammad's generation in paving the way for the Oslo Accords, which hijacked the first Intifada, and transmuted it from an unprecedented popular uprising to a mere quest for power and statehood, led Israeli occupation forces to demolish the future of the entire next generation.

In the face of increasing Israeli colonization, land theft, restrictions, and assaults, Bahaa used the knife or gun to articulate his people's grievances. This passionate reader resorted to violence not only because he had nothing to lose but also because he thought this was the way to reclaim agency and change the status quo.

Muhammad respects his son's decision, and so do Bahaa's

BUDOUR HASSAN

/

students with the scouts and his colleagues at the community center. Bahaa's killing not only made Muhammad rediscover his son but made him rethink his political experience and rediscover his fighting spirit, too.

There is still fire in the old man's belly. In an uprising led by teenagers and youths in their early twenties, Muhammad has fast become a role model for many. "Even my sons, especially Bahaa, never treated me as a father figure, and we never had that paternal hierarchy at our home," Muhammad recalls. "But people are so disillusioned with their current leadership that they are looking for reference points and leading figures to occupy that void, leading many to regard me as a father figure or example."

This makes the already-heavy weight on Muhammad's shoulders even more burdensome, with so many counting on him for inspiration and support.

He found himself marching in protests, speaking at the funerals of other martyrs, being beaten up by Israeli soldiers, and sleeping in a tent after Israeli bulldozers razed his home to the ground. He had to put up with all the fake promises as well as outright lies of the Palestinian Authority and its agents, who left Palestinians alone in their fight and only reappeared to pose in front of the cameras.

But those trying months have also provided him with warmth along with overwhelming love and popular solidarity. They have offered an example of mutual aid among Palestinian families, as the shared cause of reclaiming their children's corpses increased their solidarity and reinforced social cohesion, keeping alive the memory of their slain loved ones in the process.

*

Collective memory is a strategic battlefield between Zionists and Palestinians. Since its creation in 1948, Israel has systemically and institutionally worked to erase the Palestinian narrative, redefining the uprooting of hundreds of thousands of natives as "independence," calling ethnically cleansed villages "abandoned," and fragmenting Palestinian society.

Refusing to return corpses of Palestinian martyrs is part of this war on Palestinian memory, as Israel seeks to turn the dead into numbers and prevent Palestinians from celebrating them as heroes. The policy, however, has completely backfired: withholding the bodies has created a strong bond among martyrs' families and has only increased people's respect for the martyrs' sacrifices.

Thus, instead of throwing the stories of those martyrs into oblivion, Israel's policy of withholding Palestinian bodies led the entire society to share the martyrs' stories, and remember and honor them as people.

"When I receive Bahaa's body, I will turn my attention to those buried in the cemeteries of numbers," said Muhammad, referring to those Palestinians buried anonymously in grave-yards designed by Israel as military zones.

Even though withholding bodies weighs mightily on the hearts of those waiting to bid loved ones farewell, it has brought them together and urged them to organize without waiting for instructions from above. And their individual battles to retrieve the bodies of their children have morphed into a collective struggle against oblivion.

*

Editor's addendum: On September 1, 2016, after 325 days, Israel returned Bahaa's body to his family. According to a report in Mondoweiss, "His body was buried at the al-Mujahidin cemetery near the Old City of Jerusalem, in accordance with stipulations from Israeli police, which has allowed the release of bodies of slain Palestinians from East Jerusalem accused of 'terrorism' on the condition that they no longer have funerals in their neighborhoods or villages, but would instead be buried in cemeteries chosen by the police. The stipulation comes amid a wider set of preconditions for the release, as only 25 people were allowed to attend [Bahaa's] funeral, and his family was made to pay a 20,000 shekel ($5,292) 'insurance fee' to make sure they abided by the rules. Israeli forces were heavily deployed in the area ahead of the funeral, as attendees were searched three times at checkpoints and saw their phones confiscated during the burial.... Israeli police also reportedly photographed people inside the cemetery.... [His father said, 'Bahaa's] eyes sunk inside his skull as if he did not have any, [his] muscles [had] atrophied and his skin peeled off easily. It was difficult to identify him; except that I am his father and I know him well.' ... [T]here were three bullet marks on Bahaa's body, including one in the chest, near the heart."

*

Budour Hassan is a Palestinian law graduate and writer based in occupied Jerusalem. She is a frequent contributor to the Electronic Intifada, blogs at budourhassan.wordpress.com, and tweets at @Budour48. This piece weaves together portions of two separate articles, which originally appeared online at telesur and ROAR magazine.

BUDOUR HASSAN

/

GHOST STORIES

/

ROCK, PAPER, ASHES

CINDY MILSTEIN

As the crow flies, it's a short distance from the spot on Bernal Hill where police murdered Alex Nieto to the sidewalk on Folsom Street where police murdered Amilcar Perez-Lopez. Eleven months separate their deaths, yet the geography of class war in San Francisco's Mission District forever binds them.

When disappearance becomes daily, even hourly, linearity disappears. One is made dizzy in this neighborhood, dancing with all the ghosts.

So there's no telling if their killings were before or after the arsons and lockouts, landlords as thugs and 24/7 police presence. No knowing where they fall on the timeline of white supremacist erasures of culture and myriad evictions by any means necessary. If they were slaughtered before or after blocks of luxury housing rose up overnight like mushrooms following a rainstorm, like pioneer wagons enclosing land, like gray cold-steel tombstones.

But those who desired to stay put in their community did know a simple truth. When state-sanctioned guns felled Alex and then Amilcar, neighbors instantly pointed to the culprit: gentrification.

It's common knowledge here that cops and condos go hand in glove in fist.

*

/

As the bullet flies, it's split seconds for people within earshot between life and execution, between being in one's own home and pouring out into the street to converge with others.

On the night of February 26, 2015, the police went door-to-door, admonishing those living on both sides of Folsom, between 24th and 25th Streets, to keep indoors. The cops tried to tidy up their mess. A brown person shot in the back, now dead on the concrete, between two parked cars, outside his rented apartment. A person with a name, with friends and girlfriend here, with parents and siblings left behind in a small village in Guatemala.

Yet from behind curtains, people had heard and seen. They not only watched but also documented. They hung, suspended in disbelief, on the details of loss from within their houses. Then, after the police had shoved off, they scurried outdoors and hung onto each other.

Word spread. Photos too. Soon, across the Mission, others heard and saw.

Candles, flowers, crosses, sympathy cards, and other pallbearers of mourning were gathered. Images of Amilcar, coupled with words like *Justicia* and *Yo Soy Amilcar*, were color copied or screen printed. Adorned with such offerings, fused by tears and the heat of stunned silence, the sidewalk, the crime scene, became altar.

I've no memory of whether it was that night or the next, but this bit of pavement held us. From around our embattled neighborhood, we huddled together, in what was part wake, part witnessing, part rage and fear, wholly grief.

I remember being there with a friend who'd come here over a decade ago from Oaxaca. Her eyes stayed damp with "not again?" We hugged for a long time. She leaned her head against me, so close I could feel her breath, and looked over at her son, standing nearby. He, ten years old, was the exact same height as Amilcar, now forever frozen in his early twenties. He, her son, another brown person, could have been "mistaken" by police for another mother's son, Amilcar.

I remember all the other eyes, shell-shocked embers in the candlelight. I remember Alex Nieto's parents joining in this vigil, along other parents, sisters, and uncles of those who lives were stolen—people thrown together as now forever-bonded family, not out of choice, but from police-inflicted wounds only they could fully understand. I recall, too, Amilcar's friends and housemates, struggling to speak, in Spanish, with others struggling to translate their words, into English—because no words could make sense of this in any language.

Someone figured out how to call the one community phone in Amilcar's hometown. Someone told his family. What got translated to us was that his mother collapsed on hearing the news. It hadn't been long since Amilcar had sent toys home to his younger siblings and money so that his parents could buy a tractor for their subsistence farming.

A mere block or so away, not long after Amilcar's callous

GHOST STORIES

/

end, other immigrants found themselves in the bull's-eye. Their corner store and apartment above were ravaged by fire. Two were killed, father and child. The mother and her two surviving kids were left homeless. Their belongings, charred black and with the acrid smell of death, were heaped on the sidewalk, left for days, as if warning—by landlord, city, or police?—to spark further fear among the marginalized and precarious.

Such a sign was hardly necessary. Similar conflagrations were becoming regular occurrences in our neighborhood. Funny, people in the Mission observed, how a sprawling three-story building at Mission and 22nd Streets was consumed by flames, killing one and permanently evicting dozens of low-income and mostly Latino residents, but the extremely expensive new Vida—Spanish for "life"—apartment complex right next door received not a smudge. Here on 24th Street, where a haphazard array of bedraggled flowers clung desperately to the padlocked security gate pulled tight across the front of the burned-out corner store, neighbors with worn-out eyes greeted each other with, "Another arson." Chalked words on the storefront's pavement, done by a friend with solemn respect and raw pain, punctuated this point: "My neighbors keep getting killed and displaced by fires, gentrification, and police."

That fire, Amilar's death, were only two of so many losses that one can't even keep them to memory, because minds only have so much room for pain. Mine is no exception. I was deep in grieving both my biological parents' deaths, mere months apart, after over a year of caretaking them. My beloved collective house at 16th and Mission, and one of the few remaining autonomous political spaces in San Francisco, was in the midst of our own anticipatory grief. While we boldly proclaimed "RESISTING OUR EVICTION" from painted fabric hung outside our building and went on an equally bold offensive against our landlords, the anxiety was already tearing our home apart. And almost daily it seemed, I was going to yet another in a string of direct actions organized by Eviction Free San Francisco in often-vain hope of saving others from displacement. More than a few times, once ousted from their homes, longtime residents died within a week or month. Thousands of others were living on cardboard beds laid on patches of concrete—a city within a city.

Quickly we learned that Amilcar's entire building, crowded with some two-dozen immigrant men seeking a better life, had for some time been targeted for eviction. The landlord probably leaned on police to be the "stick" to get the tenants to leave. The carrot was reserved for the landlord: the promise of tripled or quadrupled rent in a housing market out of control. That likely explained why undercover cops were lurking outside Amilcar's home that February night, and why housemates, fearing for their own lives, "self-evicted" shortly afterward.

The banner "EVICTION = DEATH" seemed to be unfurled frequently, not slogan but cruel reality.

*

GHOST STORIES

/

As the mosquito flies, it's mere hours between my mom's terminal cancer coming out of its dormancy and my dad going into a coma from West Nile virus. One minute they're lying together in bed, my mother sick from restarting chemo treatments that day. The next, my father topples onto the floor, into ambulance, into intensive care, ultimately onto the "life support" that made him captive to nonlife. That, in turn, compels my mom onto a walker, into a studio apartment in an independent living facility, among other women whose husbands are no longer.

Dust bunnies suddenly become the only inhabitants of my parents' once-lively Midwest home, until a year later it too will no longer be part of my family.

Death didn't do them part after decades. Their union was torn asunder by forces so much larger than themselves. My mom's cancer was a rare type, eating away at her bones. A virus had incapacitated my dad. But my dad's long years laboring for the State of Michigan had allowed retirement with fantastic health insurance, so they had only the finest "care" money could buy. They believed in that, and that it would cure them.

Through my "anarchist glasses," to borrow from anthropologist James C. Scott, it looked altogether different. I saw not their symptoms but pathologies like capitalism. I saw cancer as the ubiquitous by-product of commodification, churning out toxins while making consumer goods, or making consumer goods that are themselves toxic. I saw a tiny insect, newly

/

382

weaponized and relocated by military-industrial climate catastrophe. And I saw clearly a health insurance complex that views ill bodies as growth industry.

One minute I'm in a vibrant metropole, surrounded by social movement and anarchists, community and possibility. The next, sleepless, I'm in an airport. I'm on my own, waiting for a connecting flight to a tired Rust Belt town. CNN plays on the television by my gate. "West Nile epidemic in Michigan" flashes across the big screen; four or five deaths reported across the state. I recall thinking how it wasn't an epidemic at all. How relative to population, so few people had perished. How mainstream media sensationalizes. Then I didn't give it another thought. I boarded a plane to end up in a hospital.

A week later, the diagnosis came in. It surprised us all, even though one health worker after another suggested testing for the virus. "They watch too much television," I mumbled to myself. I now imagined CNN adding one more miniscule number to its rolling-repeat story on the Michigan epidemic.

None of the medical staff knew what to do. The disease was rare, and they had little knowledge about it and no experience. I dived into research, becoming as expert as I could through the fog of two parents simultaneously facing death and my life irrevocably altered. I advised numerous doctors-who-didn't-listen-well. The head one said I needed to give permission to insert a tracheotomy into my comatose dad, who couldn't breath on his own. The temporary tube ensured oxygen, but air and time were running out. Meanwhile, feeding, hydrating, and excrement tubes snaked around his paralyzed body. As reply to my direct question, this particular doctor-who-didn't-listen-well declared, "There are no downsides. It's a simple procedure." I signed the form.

During the overnight shift, a chatty nurse pulled me aside, an enormous crucifix hanging across her chest. She said she'd pray for me. As I would come to find, there were a lot of crosses among the workers. There were a lot of offers of prayers and "God bless you." My being godless Jew seemed incomprehensible, and so went unremarked. "Here's what the doctors didn't tell you," she confided. An hour later, I knew the downside: suspended life, suspended death; that is, until ugly death in ugly institution making bank from stockpiling zombie-like beings. I knew I should have said no. "Hospice," she said, without a hint of discomfort. "Bring everyone together. Surround yourselves with what has meaning and say good-bye while he's still here. Let him die well."

I often think back to that nurse. She became my temporary breathing aid—that nurse who did the right thing when she didn't have to. Who cared more about people than she did the bureaucracy of hospitals, mounds of paperwork, and hierarchy of doctors. Who, like so many other lower-rung care workers I would encounter in sociable Michigan, was a lowercase christian, practicing not preaching.

CINDY MILSTEIN

/

I knew well that both my parents had long ago signed living wills, spelling out "do not resuscitate," no life without quality. I also knew that it was my decision to make, as their anointed power of attorney. As eldest kid who, almost from my birth, had always been their single parent. As anarchist suddenly on their own, adrift in an endless series of bad choices without the compass of what I thought was my community, my "faith." As person striving toward some common good among all family members, but having to finally, after too long, bypass consensus in order to fulfill my parents' wishes.

I would sign many forms over the next thirteen months that felt like thirteen years that felt like the unlooked-for bad luck of a Friday the thirteenth. I'd think hard before doing so, often seeking counsel from nurses, after that tracheotomy mistake. But the only forms that felt like comforters—not cold, hard paper—bore the word *hospice*.

*

As the airplane flies, it's only hours between a continent where anti-blackness has long been one key criterion of who is considered human and who is not, and another continent where anti-Semitism has for centuries served as a key yardstick for this same question. Historical specificities and philosophical underpinnings separate their unfolding, yet they willingly share a metrics of hatred, an efficiency of eradication. On both landmasses, for blacks and Jews, for indigenous and Roma, among

GHOST STORIES

/

others, eugenicists have measured skulls to calculate who is worthy of life.

Yet such virulent forms of racialization, for all their genocidal logics, see through distinctive lenses, shaping society and selves. So in the lands called North America, I am usually read as white. In the place called Europe, I'm typically read as Jewish. It's as if the metal detector at the airport, coming and going, somehow transports me into another realm, altering my body.

I am not exempt. I, too, peer through different lenses in these different worlds. Each time I've journeyed to the world some of my family escaped—those who made it out of eastern Europe, without papers, across waters, into Chicago ghetto, speaking in Yiddish not English—I see almost nothing but vast graveyard. I feel as if I've lived there before. That I should be there, shouldn't be there, should have been turned into ash, smoke, nothingness.

I see ghosts there. I see ghosts here, too, but not as such constant companions. In Europe, my ancestors visit me at every moment. When I do laps at a pool in the middle of Berlin, something besides the water chills me; I learn later that in 1935–36, it's the first place Jews were banned from swimming. When I take a local train to visit a remote concentration camp in Poland, now museum, panic grips me; I find out afterward these were the same tracks used to ship humans to gas chambers. I sip coffee in a charming café in Vienna and feel sick to my stomach, discovering hours later that it was where Adolf Hitler, as young

CINDY MILSTEIN

/

artist, hung out. Buildings and streets; forests, fields, and ponds —all house spirits not at rest, reaching out to me.

I myself become part of this army of phantoms. I'm routinely identified as Jew, questioned about my name or eating habits by those who think they've seen an apparition. Some are eager to tell me stories of deportation or extermination, family or town history, complicity or purported resistance. Yet the tales nearly always involve some Freudian slip, as if they've forgotten they're talking to an actual, still-living Jew. In the eyes of others, usually wizened-old Europeans, I'm mirrored back as ghost, as one who got away.

I grow confused, mixing up decades, blurring centuries. By my side, burned witch-ghosts and charred peasant-ghosts; family-ghosts that my dad told me about, burned alive in a synagogue; incinerated Jew-ghosts, anarchist-ghosts, and gender-queer-ghosts, merging in flames; refugee-ghosts, lost in the fires of wars still raging today. I become obsessed, seeing continuity at every turn. Smelling death, as if bloodhound. Feeling flesh tear at the bark of every German Shepherd.

This translates into compulsion to pay homage to all those murdered. And so with each visit to this continent-cemetery, I've traipsed to more mass sites of slaughter than I can count— many now quiet fields or lush, deep woods. At each, silently, I place a small stone. Something solid as small offering to counter all that melted into air. Something rock hard, as resistance against disappearance.

GHOST STORIES

/

387

On one trip to yet another concentration-camp-as-museum, I glanced down at the jigsaw-puzzle pebbles beneath my feet. Tuffs of weeds sprung up between rocks on this desolate country path that led to sections of the camp. Was it my imagination? Here and there, shapes on stones. Bits of what almost seemed human-made, peeking out from the overgrown brush. I kneeled down for a closer look, and fragments of Yiddish letters came into view. Broken and repurposed gravestones, transported from faraway European cities to this remote killing factory, cobbled together into walkway.

Some years back, in Warsaw, at the edge of the infamous ghetto, I wandered through what from one angle looked like an enormous forest and from another an enormous cemetery. It was one and the same. Trees grew out of remnants of tombstones, brutalized by weapons strong enough to smash them to bits. Or was it tombstones trying to rebirth themselves out of the trees, as ongoing gesture of defiance against fascism, itself being resurrected globally in 2017?

Tens of thousands of stones in Warsaw were barely recognizable. All the written records of who was laid to rest there were destroyed during the Nazi time. Tens of thousands of ghosts unsettled, demanding not to be lost lives, lost people. Demanding that National Socialism's project of resolving the "Jewish question" by complete erasure of all traces of life, including death, not be allowed to succeed. Stones not merely as mourning but also as battleground.

CINDY MILSTEIN

/

At the front of this forest-graveyard sat a man who'd voluntarily taken up his now-deceased father's work: to re-create the record of each and every name—each and every person—buried in this place. From the lines on his face, it looked doubtful that he, any more than his father, would finish this task before the grim reaper visited him. Yet he diligently did his public work of grief, unpaid bookkeeper for the dead, sharing memory of lives lived and resistance fighters.

In other death sites across the cemetery that is Europe, one can see much evidence of ghosts who, too, strived to do the work of grief. Ghosts like me, still doing the labor. When I toured Buchenwald, thousands of little bits of proof that people had lived and loved were on display in a glass tabletop-like case, stretching many feet across the museum. It tenderly held what seemed tens of thousands of buttons, hairpins, beads, and trinkets, all secreted away in the death camp's barracks and found after "liberation." Those slated for crematoriums kept mementos of those already gone—reminders that people still hadn't been extinguished as human.

At Auschwitz, some of those who collectively sabotaged the ovens had buried photographs and letters with their names on them in the camp's ground, witnessing loss for the future, mourning themselves in advance of dying on their own terms.

And in Prague's Pinkas Synagogue, emptied out of its Jews in the Shoah, the walls are now covered with the names of some seventy-eight thousand Czech and Moravian Jews who perished under the Nazis—hand-scripted dignity against disappearance, penned over some ten years in this synagogue-turned-museum.

When I fly back across ocean, little does airport security know that my backpack is overfull with stowaway ancestor-ghosts. Or maybe I'm the stowaway, never at home in this world —a world where, for now, again, barbarism trumps humanism. Maybe I'm a diasporic already-ancestor-ghost carrying a heart overfull with the suffering of ages.

When murderous social conditions corner us, when loss is almost inevitable, witnessing becomes rebellious. Meaning is bestowed to what and who are being made to appear meaningless.

*

Hospice. From the Latin *hospitium*, "hospitality"; from *hospes*, "host," "stranger," "guest." From medieval times, referencing places of rest for the weary, shelter from storms, gifted from one stranger to another.

Centuries later, in the mid-1800s, women picked up the concept, creating homes for the dying. But it was in the late 1940s, after Nazism and Bolshevism soaked Europe's soil with blood and ashes, that hospice found its ground, cultivated by Cicely Saunders, a nurse in England. After death itself had been made mass and anonymous, mechanized and dehumanized, hospice aspired to give it worth again.

"Life-support systems were intended as bridges, if there's

quality of life visible on the other side," said the physician assistant who shepherded the eight-bedroom residential hospice
I'd stumbled on, just a hop, skip, and jump from my parents'
now-former home and where I'd grown up. "It was never intended for how it's used now, when there's no hope. Sure, doctors *can* keep people alive longer. But the question in each case
is, *Should* they?"

I glanced from her eyes to the window while she spoke.
Outside, to the unfolding of spring on these twenty-two acres,
tucked away in an abandoned quarry. At blossoming and fading,
commingling in this gentle setting. At the shock of the new that
is forsythia, tulips, cherry and crabapple trees, bleeding hearts,
all opening to the sun until their flowers curl up and drop, the
makings of the next cycle.

After nearly nine months of countless medical professionals
dispassionately asserting "we can" when I knew "we shouldn't,"
her words were balm. Verification, contra to all those who'd
made me feel crazy or cruel. And completely alone. So alone in
the necessity of choosing death for my dad over "life." Especially given the sadness trapped in his eyes in his prison-like
nursing home, a warehouse for lifeless bodies tethered to machines—one of only a handful of such facilities in Michigan that
took those forever chained to trachs.

From my earliest memories, his eyes had always harbored
sorrow—pupils held hostage to accumulated ancestral trauma.
Now that they were the only nuanced communication left him,

GHOST STORIES

/

a lifelong talker, their pain knew almost no end. The only time those eyes of his lightened, gave temporary refuge to joy, was when birds came to the feeder outside the tiny window in his room-cell. And so for his six months of nonlife here, in a nondescript cinderblock building an hour from where my mom now lived, I obsessively brought birdseed. I obsessively filled the feeder. Obsessively watched for birds and then the flight in his eyes. I did this instead of signing the form that would free him, as free as the occasional birds that showed up. Even they didn't want to be near this place—neither a place of nursing nor a home.

The physician assistant sat me down on a comfy couch within minutes of my walk-in visit to the hospice, though it was plain I was interrupting her day. She asked if she could hug me. She embraced me with warmth, and spoke with neither artifice nor sugarcoating, but always empathy. I felt as if she could read my mind, give voice to what in "normal" society one wasn't supposed to think or say. "You want your father to die, right? Not if things were different. But they aren't. He's already gone. In a better world, he would have already been allowed to die naturally, in his home and community, the way it was for most of history."

She conversed amicably about hospice. To strive, in egalitarian ways, to accentuate quality of life in every moment for everyone on this journey, while aiming to alleviate suffering for all. Treating all bodies with inherent worth and dignity, not as commodity. She spoke not of logistics and paperwork but rather aspirations, not as mere words but instead as everyday, collective practice. A commons where the seasons of life and death are given permission—with consent, with transparency and honesty—to unfold, mirroring the ephemeral beauty of the springtime enveloping us, and its interdependent ecosystem.

This world is not ours to fix, she made clear, this woman who was now fast family. It is a process of which we're only one, humble part.

With a few steps through this door, I went from loss of support system and cold immersion in the Kafkaesque world of hospitals and nursing homes, into a caring community of "care workers" who kept saying that this wasn't a job. Hospice, they matter-of-factly explained, was a "calling," "an honor," "something we do with and for each other."

During that time, far from my big-city home, and what I thought was my political and chosen family, I felt abandoned by my anarchist friends, my anarchist world. Too often I heard, "Come back when you're done," as if death were some solitary chore with distinct end. As if experiences were outside our circle, disconnected from our culture. I felt that my labors of care over the years, through others' impactful losses, were neither reciprocated nor made visible. I felt exiled.

Even as I was convinced I'd lost all belief in anarchists, I found myself born again into something that lived out the ethics of anarchism. Because it's true what us anarchists contend, though too rarely actualize: when people create a new culture together, they in turn become better people, in an upward spiral that births anew society and us.

Here, among these midwives of death—largely apolitical, at times offhandedly prejudiced or heteronormative—there was no need for political label, much less countercultural trappings, to compel care. These people, flaws and all, were able to educe the best parts of themselves because they were embedded in the culture of hospice. Perhaps it was also because they were mostly female, already used to inhabiting bodies that aren't valued when doing care labor for others, or when they themselves are aging, sick, or dying, seen neither as sexual, reproductive, nor productive.

Here, within a homey circle revolving around mutualism, it was never clear who was taking care of whom. Everyone was looking out for each other and doing whatever needed to be done together. People made do with what life threw at them, drawing out quality of days or even seconds, precisely because we humans will always know loss and heartbreak. It wasn't that people were perfect, or all even nice. It was that they allowed themselves to be vulnerable with each other. They didn't walk away from all the messiness of life and death and emotions. They stepped closer, with an authenticity that shouldn't be reserved for moments when we're face-to-face with our own mortality.

So when I told the physician assistant that my dad's one wish after nine months of hell was to sleep next to my mom again, she did something she'd never yet done: allow the breathing machinery to follow him into hospice for twenty-four hours before she would slowly turn it off and let his body takes its own course. Commitment to quality of life, for all involved in this most intimate of experiences, translated into breaking rules when the rules didn't make sense.

It may sound strange to those who haven't sat with and gotten to know death, who haven't had the honor of helping someone die well, but I think those twenty-four hours counted as one of the best days of my dad's life.

The hospice folks pitched in to rearrange his spacious room into part honeymoon suite, part family room, part community space. Two single beds were made into a double, covered in handmade quilts. Everything in the room faced outward, to a wall of windows opening onto unobstructed view—trees, pond, hills, and sky—and soft breezes. The hospice staff let me borrow bird feeders from around the grounds, relocating them within my dad's view. Within minutes, around the clock, the feeders were traffic jam of birds, acrobatic squirrels, wild turkeys, and ducks. At dusk, a deer stood silently outside the glass and stared in at us.

My dad's toenails were clipped—something he continually wanted done in the nursing home, to no avail, unless we did it. He was dressed in street clothes, his hair trimmed and washed, despite that fact that he couldn't move and wasn't going anywhere ever again. Friends came to visit. Relatives from around the continent called to say how much he'd meant to them, as my sister held the phone to my dad's ear. Photos, cards, and kids' drawings, all made for him, papered the walls. We read aloud a letter from the one person, an occupational/physical therapist, who'd been good to him in the nursing home—a good-bye that was a thank you for all he'd given to her as a friend.

He was showered with dignity and love that last day—in a way that most of his life he hadn't been shown love, including by me and my sisters, friends, kin, coworkers, and neighbors. That lifelong sorrow in my dad's eyes reflected his inability to express and receive love in a way that brought him mutual dignity and affection in return, much as he tried. Only my mom got him, and he got her, love at first sight, unbroken. But those twenty-four hours transformed his gaze. His eyes shone, mirroring back what was finally reciprocal, just when one could say it mattered the least. As hospice taught, minutes are what we make of them together.

We stayed with him the whole of those twenty-four hours, except for a few. My mom changed into a beautiful nightgown; my dad was changed into pajamas. His one semi-good hand reached out slightly to pat a spot next to him, and my mom crawled in. They smiled mischievously up at us. I felt privy to a joy they shared alone many decades ago, as newlyweds. We left them there, hand in hand for a last night that felt like a first night.

When the physician assistant turned his ventilator off at the end of those twenty-four hours, we could hear birds chirping in the flowering red tree outside my dad's open glass door, no longer muffled by the mechanical whir of the machines. In that moment, it was all of us who held our breath—not him. My dad kept going. Because of that one day of abundant life, he wasn't ready to die. So for nearly eight more days, he slept peacefully as his breath slowed. I was sure he could hear, though. Hear and savor, as we turned his room into slumber-party space and neighborhood. As we shared things with him, from crying and laughing, to the smells of his favorite food or sounds of his favorite radio show, the Thistle and the Shamrock.

In that week of deathwatch, the lines blurred between biological family and the chosen family of this hospice. One day I was listening ear for a hospice staffer whose parent had just died. She became mine soon after. Through her own weeping, she apologized at first for burdening me when my parent was dying nearby. Then we both recognized that our lives and our parents' deaths were part of the same cycle, not stopping when one clocked into work or checked into a hospice.

So when my father's breath ultimately came to a still, the lines became fuzzy again in terms of who grieved, who honored him with washing his body, changing his clothes, wrapping him in yet another quilt as send-off. My family, biological and hospice, stood with watery eyes, watching my dad respectfully placed into an ambulance, driven to the anatomy program he'd donated his body to, where my mom's body would join him less

GHOST STORIES

/

than four months later—side by side for some two years in the same classroom, then side by side as ashes. And two times within less than four months, after bearing witness to two parents' last breaths, I'd place stones on rocks by ponds, near to where each died in their own hospice rooms with a view.

As good a death as one could hope for. As good a life, too, in this place called hospice.

At my dad's transition between the thin line of life and death, my mom and I were stroking his arm and forehead, repeating like incantation "We love you." When his breath quieted, and chest failed to rise, my mom looked up at me. "This," she said, pointing from herself to him to me. "This is all we have. People. Each other."

*

There is a wooded area in Lithuania, quiet and restful, outside a small village seemingly untouched from peasant times. I walked to those woods many years ago, after debarking from a local train resembling those in Holocaust era photos, past townsfolk staring *suspiciously* at me. I stood in the forest, listening to birds chirp, a tender breeze caressing my face. I looked at gently rounded mounds that a historic marker told me had been large dugouts. Nazi death squads and their Lithuania collaborators rounded up the town's Jews and marched them along the same road I'd just walked, had them stand in small groups with their faces toward the pits, and then shot them in the back. Bodies fell, by the hundreds, one on top of the others, into the holes, until all were full. Soil was tossed on the heaps. Today, trees and weeds grow out of composted humans.

Those woods looked almost identical to the ones outside my dad's hospice room; those bullets that struck Amilcar's back, sent by modern-day willing executioners, are so like those that erased whole villages of Jews. Ghosts seem to dart between the foliage and firearms, caught in the cross hairs of life and death. Ancestors in our DNA make kin of us still-living human beings, across skin tones and languages, beyond borders. We become willing accomplices with each other.

And so on that street in February 2015, when Amilcar's life was taken, we poured out our collective sorrow. All that we have lost, are losing, and will lose in this war-zone neighborhood called the Mission, itself a moniker for colonial massacres in the past. Grief converged in this public space. Emotions, unchecked and shared, as varied as the colors of melted candles, flower petals, and hand-lettered messages of condolence.

One speaker at the first vigil raised a hand up toward Bernal Hill and then brought it slowly back to the now-hallowed sidewalk. Our eyes followed the path. We felt the sweep of Alex to Amilcar, as if they are coming to meet each other. But unlike the first nights after Alex's murder, when his family and friends still trusted the legal system, Amilcar's neighbors immediately sought justice not from the structures that assassinate so nonchalantly, with impunity. This time, harsh lessons learned and

GHOST STORIES

/

passed along, justice was sought proactively, within community, for community. To further solidify our social relations and the opening this creates for giving pain meaning. Or to quote Ann Finkbeiner from an essay on the death of her husband, "The pain doesn't go away; but somehow or other, empathy gives the pain meaning, and pain-with-meaning is bearable. I don't actually know how to say what the effect of empathy is, I can only say what it's like. Like magic."

Like the magic that transformed our outdoor wake into hub of grassroots organizing, and shape-shifted that hub into wake again. Like the magic that made it impossible to untangle the communalized work of grief, social struggle, and mutual caretaking. We turned toward each other and had all that we needed when we combined efforts—from resources and know-how, from lawyers, artists, cooks, and teachers, to tradespeople, writers, herbalists, and nurses. We set about doing-it-ourselves, as neighborhood self-defense. People stayed one step, and often many, ahead of the police and their fabricated stories. People went on the offensive.

In those first few days and weeks, those on the street set about documenting what had occurred. With a thoroughness that would be the envy of any detective's office, people gathered eyewitness and other evidence. Community members pulled together a press conference, outpacing the police in detailing what had really happened, so that in contrast, the police lies were pointedly apparent. Funds were collected to con-

CINDY MILSTEIN

/

400

duct an independent autopsy, which showed six shots to the back, contradicting the SF Police Department's official version. Money was also raised so that once the autopsy was done, Amilcar's body could be returned home to his family in Guatemala.

When the police held a community meeting soon after murdering Amilcar, people crowded into the hall. The officials were barely able to get a word in edgewise. All the pain and rage and heartbreak of this neighborhood were hurled at the cops, sitting smugly at a table in the front of the room. One of the first to speak was the usually shy ten-year-old son of the friend who'd stood next to me at that first vigil—the boy who was the same height as Amilcar. His family lived a mere block away from the police's crime scene. He'd heard the shots. With uncharacteristic fierceness, he leaped onto a table, launching into an oration of his anger and fear, gesturing with his arms for punctuation. It could have been him; it could have been his friends. It was Alex, Amilcar, and others. "Stop it, stop it," he implored. "Stop it."

City and state, police and courts, haven't stopped. They still delay and deny justice. Still constitute, by definition, the injustice system. More die, on these hills and streets and across other stolen lands. Yellow caution tape separates hard lives from bad deaths, grief from cover-ups, and tries to divide us from each other.

People in this neighborhood haven't stopped. There will be no official justice for evictions, for murder by cop. Yet Alex and Amilcar have been gifted in death the dignity that white su-

GHOST STORIES

/

401

premacy didn't want to grant them in life. Hundreds of vigils, memorials, and affirmations of their lives have been organized. Birth and murder anniversaries are scrupulously celebrated. Something about those two deaths, wrapped in the shroud of sorrow that tries to bury this neighborhood, touched the frayed nerves of people barely hanging on themselves.

Looking into each other's eyes, shiny-wet flames in the light of our self-organized shrines on a sidewalk cleaned of Amilcar's blood but not his presence, let us see deep into common pain, and for a time at least, we found common cause and common humanity. Their deaths illuminated the shared indignities perpetuated by landlords, techies, the nonprofit-industrial complex, cops, and their many allies, all in league to steal what remains of San Francisco's heart. The monsters in the Mission suddenly had to contend with a populace that knew which side it was on. That still does.

Only because we fight—against losses that shouldn't happen, and for spaces to grieve together in cities that increasingly isolate us and care for nothing. We fight not only for quality of life. We struggle for quality of death, for lives and deaths of our own making and mourning. We battle for a return to natural loss, such as change of seasons and the seasons of life.

Maybe dignity, out of the ashes we're handed too frequently, is the only justice we can hope for in this life.

As the heart continues to break, dignity.

*

CINDY MILSTEIN

/

Cindy Milstein is the author of Anarchism and Its Aspirations, *coauthor with Erik Ruin of* Paths toward Utopia: Graphic Explorations of Everyday Anarchism, *and editor of the anthology* Taking Sides: Revolutionary Solidarity and the Poverty of Liberalism. *Long engaged in anarchistic organizing, contemporary social movements, and collective spaces, Cindy has recently been part of solidarity projects countering displacement, gentrification, prisons, and police. Cindy was death doula for three (biological and chosen) parents over the past four years, while also grappling with eviction and losing their home. For more writing, see cbmilstein.wordpress.com.*

GHOST STORIES

/

403

SEEDS BENEATH
THE SNOW
/
ANARCHISTS
MOURN OUR DEAD

PATRICK O'DONOGHUE

On Saturday night, December 17, 2016, the snow-swept statue of the revolutionary Emiliano Zapata on Lake Street in Minneapolis was cast in the light of emergency flares and surrounded by a black-clad crew, as anarchists held a memorial observation for our comrades fallen in recent weeks.

We gathered to mourn three tragedies—the death of Michael Israel and other freedom fighters in Rojava, the murder of Guilherme Irish by his nationalist father in Brazil, and the dozens of dead friends lost in Oakland's Ghost Ship fire.

Michael, from California, was an anarchist and revolutionary unionist. A cofounder of the Sacramento Industrial Workers of the World, he went to Rojava in northern Syria to join the People's Protection Units (Yekîneyên Parastina Gel, or YPG), and defend the autonomous cantons from Daesh (Islamic State of Iraq and Syria, or ISIS) and state repression. Michael's unit was advancing on Daesh's capital in Raqqa as part of the Syrian Democratic Forces' offensive to take the city, via Operation Euphrates Wrath. Although the Erdoğan regime in Turkey claims to be part of the coalition against Daesh, it has continued to attack the Syrian Democratic Forces—a strategy to weaken and destroy the revolution in Rojava, which the Turkish state views as a threat to its own occupation of Kurdish-majority lands. On

/

the night of November 29, Turkish jets bombed a small village that the YPG had liberated from Daesh, killing Michael and many other revolutionary fighters.

Guilherme was a Brazilian anarchist student of mathematics at the Universidade Federal de Goiás. He was actively involved in student occupations of schools in Goiânia. This past summer, the Workers' Party administration in Brazil was impeached in a putsch organized by the country's wealthiest families, and the new Temer government launched a series of attacks to limit political freedom for students, reform high school curriculum, and dramatically freeze social spending. Since the beginning of November, students have occupied over a thousand high schools and nearly a hundred universities in protest. Guilherme's father did not accept his son's involvement in the movement, and had threatened to hand him over to the police or kill him. He had gone armed to demonstrations against school privatization to threaten his son and other militants. On November 15, Guilherme left his home for the Occupation of Campus 2 at the university. His father ambushed him with a pistol and shot him to death. Guilherme was twenty years old.

Ghost Ship was a do-it-yourself (DIY) space in the Bay Area and home to the Satya Yuga artist collective. It was inside a warehouse in the Fruitvale neighborhood, one of many arts and living spaces that turned to unsafe, low-cost buildings in the midst of the city's housing crisis. For black, brown, and queer artists especially excluded by the music scene, the warehouse parties in Oakland, California, provide a platform even in the United States' most expensive metro, where tech industry gentrification has pummeled working-class neighborhoods of color. On December 2, at 11:20 at night, a fire broke out in Ghost Ship during a concert, spreading quickly through the crowded building. Those inside struggled and aided one another in escaping the fire, but for too many it was impossible. Thirty-six people died. In the aftermath, alt-right fascists have made a project online of harassing DIY spaces by reporting them to fire marshals, hoping to use the tragedy as a way to bring state repression on the DIY movement.

At the Zapata statue, anarchists gave eulogies to our fallen comrades, read passages in commemoration, and poured out whiskey in celebration of their lives. Wobblies in attendance recited the poem "Red November, Black November":

> Red November, black November,
> Bleak November, black and red;
> Hallowed month of labor's martyrs,
> Labor's heroes, labor's dead.
>
> Labor's wrath and hope and sorrow—
> Red the promise, black the threat;
> Who are we not to remember?
> Who are we to dare forget?

SEEDS BENEATH THE SNOW

/

Black and red the colors blended,
Black and red the pledge we made;
Red until the fight is ended,
Black until the debt is paid.

As anarchists, we do not make a fetish out of death, especially not in the way that fascists, armies, and nations do. We do not prefer our comrades, friends, and lovers to be cold and stern memorials, or rose-colored memories revived in the haze of sentimental poetry. We prefer them beside us, creating with us the spaces and struggles of our liberation, and fighting alongside us in defense of our lives. We do not ask for martyrs.

We do, however, know that is inevitable that those of us who struggle, who revolt against the crushing daily violence of the state, capital, and all existing hierarchies, will be put in the cross hairs of repression. We know that those of us who seek to build new worlds in the cracks and unstable edges and boundaries of the old will face all the dangers of the current world's collapse along with threats from those who try to cement it together again in blood and terror. We are born in the history of the Haymarket martyrs hanged for resisting the industrialists' police, Suga Kanno strangled by the empire of Japan, and Carlo Giuliani shot down by the Italian cops. We inherit a flag stained black in the remembrance of our dead, the negation of their killers, and the promise to never surrender.

PATRICK O'DONOGHUE

/

The tragedies ended our comrades' lives, but not the visions they lived for. The revolution in Rojava carries on the fight for autonomy as the Syrian regime batters its opposition, the Erdoğan regime attacks Kurds on both sides of the border, and foreign powers, confident in the YPG's defeats of Daesh, prepare for their inevitable betrayal of the revolutionary cantons. The rightist coup in Brazil will be opposed every inch of the way, and the popular movement against it will not be leashed and captured by the ineffectual Workers' Party whose capitulation to neoliberalism paved the way for the rise of the reactionaries. DIY spaces and projects of reclamation will continue to seize the structures left gutted and abandoned by globalization and deindustrialization, and fill them with those displaced by gentrification. We will improve the security of these spaces, both from accidental fires and collapses, and Far Right and state attacks. Every day we wake and draw breath, we strive to undermine and attack the systems that murdered our comrades and friends.

In memory of Michael and Guilherme along with Denalda, Feral, and all the other victims of the Ghost Ship fire, we remember the verses of the Greek poet Dinos Christianopoulos, echoed in the Mexican counterculture: "They tried to bury us; they did not know we were seeds."

*

SEEDS BENEATH THE SNOW

/

411

Patrick O'Donoghue is an anarchist worker and writer in the upper Midwest. Involved in labor struggles and community self-defense work, his writing typically focuses on rural issues, industrial conflict, and antifascism. The ceremony in Minneapolis was the work of anarchists affiliated with Conflict MN as well as members of General Defense Committee Local 14.

PATRICK O'DONOGHUE

/

412

AK Press is small, in terms of staff and resources, but we also manage to be one of the world's most productive anarchist publishing houses. We publish close to twenty books every year, and distribute thousands of other titles published by like-minded independent presses and projects from around the globe. We're entirely worker run and democratically managed. We operate without a corporate structure—no boss, no managers, no bullshit.

The Friends of AK program is a way you can directly contribute to the continued existence of AK Press, and ensure that we're able to keep publishing books like this one! Friends pay $25 a month directly into our publishing account ($30 for Canada, $35 for international), and receive a copy of every book AK Press publishes for the duration of their membership! Friends also receive a discount on anything they order from our website or buy at a table: 50 percent on AK titles, and 20 percent on everything else. We have a Friends of AK e-book program as well: $15 a month gets you an electronic copy of every book we publish for the duration of your membership. You can even sponsor a deeply discounted membership for someone in prison.

E-mail friendsofak@akpress.org for more info, or visit the Friends of AK Press website: akpress.org/friends.html.

There are always great book projects in the works—so sign up now to become a Friend of AK Press, and let the presses roll!